EVERYDAY LIFE
IN BABYLON
AND ASSYRIA

EVERYDAY LIFE
IN BABYLON
AND ASSYRIA

By

GEORGES CONTENAU

The Norton Library

W · W · NORTON & COMPANY · INC ·

NEW YORK

FIRST PUBLISHED IN THE NORTON LIBRARY
1966 BY ARRANGEMENT WITH ST. MARTIN'S PRESS

Books That Live
The Norton imprint on a book means that in the publisher's
estimation it is a book not for a single season but for the years.
W. W. Norton & Company, Inc.

τῆς δὲ Ἀσσυρίης ἐστὶ τὰ μέν κου καὶ ἄλλα πολίσματα
μεγάλα πολλά, τὸ δὲ ὀνομαστότατον καὶ ἰσχυρότατον
. . . ἦν Βαβυλών . . . ἐκεκόσμητο δὲ ὡς οὐδὲν ἄλλο πόλισμα
τῶν ἡμεῖς ἴδμεν.

Herodotus I. 178

TRANSLATORS' FOREWORD

THE field covered by this book is one in which both the results of excavation and the translation of more tablets are continually expanding our knowledge. The steady accretion of fresh evidence necessarily means that there may not always be complete agreement on all points of its interpretation. Our aim in translating has been to follow the French text as closely as possible, adding our own notes only where they seemed strictly necessary. These appear as asterisked footnotes; the author's own references to authorities are gathered together at the end, as they were in the French edition, and are indicated in the text by superior numbers. We have added a number of English sources to the original bibliography.

We have chosen illustrations in order, as far as possible, to illustrate particular points in the text, and have, where we could, relied upon English sources, as these are more easily accessible to English readers.

We wish to thank most warmly the many friends who have generously helped us, and especially Professor Sidney Smith, F.B.A., for his help on the mathematical sections, and Mr. C. J. Gadd, F.B.A., and Mr. R. D. Barnett of the Department of Egyptian and Assyrian Antiquities of the British Museum.

Institute of Archaeology,
Regent's Park,
London, N.W.

CONTENTS

CHAPTER IV

RELIGIOUS LIFE 241

ILLUSTRATIONS

(*Note.*—The titles of Layard's and Botta's works, referred to below, are misleading. Both purport to refer to Nineveh, but Botta's excavations were at Khorsabad and many of Layard's were at Nimrud. The site of the ancient Nineveh was in fact the modern Kuyunjik.)

Plates between 136 *and* 137

Drawings in the Text

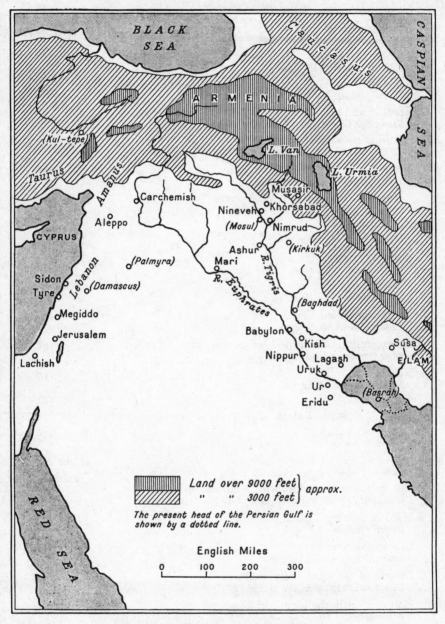

Map of Mesopotamia and surrounding lands

AUTHOR'S INTRODUCTION

FROM its earliest beginnings in about 2900 B.C. until the invasion of Alexander the Great in 330 B.C., the civilization of Mesopotamia endured for some twenty-six centuries. A phrase like 'everyday life', applied to so vast a period, is meaningless, and, though imperfect knowledge may lead us into certain involuntary inaccuracies and anachronisms, we are bound to confine ourselves to some comparatively limited phase within the wider span. But which are we to choose?

Two factors must govern our choice, for not only must the period be truly representative of Mesopotamian civilization but, within that category, it must be that about which we know most. These two considerations guide us to the years between 700 and 530 B.C. During these years, events on a scale not previously experienced in history were unfolding themselves in Western Asia. First, the power of Assyria reached its zenith and extended over the whole of the Near East, including, for a time, even Egypt. Then Babylon, Assyria's vassal, aided by the Medes from the Iranian highlands, cast off her yoke and, in 612 B.C., destroyed Nineveh. This was the opening of a period of Babylonian prosperity, echoes of which still reach us from the pages of the ancient authors, and which is generally linked with the name of Nebuchadrezzar. Finally, Babylon herself fell a victim to Persia. The Near East bowed to a fresh master and for two centuries her destinies were in the hands of the Achaemenid monarchs.

For this period, so pregnant with events which changed the face of the ancient world, we have many sources of information at our disposal. Pride of place must go to the original clay tablets from Babylonia and Assyria, those imperishable documents from which we know more of the trivial details of everyday family life under the Sargonid* dynasty of Assyria than we know, for example, of that of the Norman peasant. The political history

* The term Sargonid is used in this book alternatively with 'late-Assyrian' and refers to the period covered by the reigns of the Kings Sargon II, 722–705 B.C.: Sennacherib, 705–681 B.C.: Esarhaddon, 680–669 B.C.: and Ashurbanipal, 668–626 B.C. [Translator's note.]

of the period is covered by the royal Annals: the religious life by the rituals and the hymns: we possess not only the private contracts, but also the correspondence of high officials with the palace and the letters which passed between private individuals: while the official library of Nineveh, assembled by King Ashurbanipal in the seventh century B.C., represents the learning of the age. We cannot in reason expect more from the tablets.

We have another, and an important, source in the shape of the written accounts, the first of which date from slightly after our period, derived from the earliest systematic contacts within our knowledge between Greece and the Near East, the ancestors of the line of traveller-historians. And finally we possess the evidence of the monuments, excavated successively at Khorsabad and Nineveh, at Nimrud and Ashur, and, at Babylon itself, subjected to a critical and detailed examination.

The book ends at the point when the Achaemenid dynasty was about to build its vast palaces in Susa and Persepolis, its imperial capitals.

CHAPTER I

GENERAL INFORMATION

The Country

ASSYRIA in the north and Babylonia in the south together comprise Mesopotamia, the land between 'the two great rivers', Tigris and Euphrates, which are the source of the fertility which has aroused the admiration of travellers throughout history. But whereas Egypt, a country which, like Mesopotamia, is entirely dependent upon irrigation, could be described as 'a gift of the Nile', whose retreating waters confer their annual benison on the country in the shape of a deposit of mud, in Mesopotamia by contrast the vast inundations of the Tigris and Euphrates might, on account of the nature of the soil through which the rivers flow, easily be disastrous unless kept under strict control. The two rivers rise in the Armenian highlands. Both flow with torrential force, scouring out their channels through the mountains, and churning and polishing the fragments of rock which they dislodge in their violent passage. When the snow melts, and the rivers are in spate, the waters flood over the plain, laying waste everything in their path.

From the earliest times the inhabitants of Mesopotamia have controlled this yearly threat by the natural method of regulating the flow of water by a network of canals, which at the same time both irrigate the soil and also form navigable waterways which can carry as much freight as the caravan routes. By this means the huge head of water built up by the two rivers is reduced and so does less damage, while the river beds continue to follow broadly the same channels. Without some measures of this kind the physical contours of the country might change unpredictably each year. This is all the more important because once the mountains are left behind the soil, which consists partly of mud deposited by the floods, is comparatively loose and liable to shift under the pressure of the water. Nearer the Persian Gulf the soil is wholly alluvial. There are extensive marshes and each year the delta encroaches slightly upon the Gulf.

At the period with which this book deals the Persian Gulf extended farther north than it now does.* The Shatt-al-Arab had not yet been formed and the Tigris and Euphrates each entered the sea by separate mouths.

Owing to its great extent and to the fact that while the mountains in the north are high the south is absolutely flat, the two parts of Mesopotamia differ greatly. The heat of the climate in the north is tempered by the mountains and gives rise in Upper Assyria to a flora generally like that of Western Europe. In the plains, however, although the summer heat is scorching, although the spring is short-lived, and the absence of rain and the sun shrivel all vegetation, yet the alluvial character of the soil ensures its fertility and life is co-extensive with irrigation. The extreme south consists largely of marshes covered with tall reeds. Gradually, towards the south, the tree species of the temperate zone vanish and after Baghdad, which lies north of the ancient Babylon, the banks of the rivers are lined with palm trees.

Southern Mesopotamia was the earliest home of cereal crops, whose yield was a constant source of wonder to antiquity. Other passages in Herodotus may strain our credulity, but Mesopotamia has justly won the title of one of the granaries of the ancient world.

In early epochs the animal life included certain species which had become extinct by the period of this book, such as the bison and the long-maned ram with spreading horns, but sheep and goats still flourished in large numbers. The cattle belonged to the species *bos primigenius*, while the Asia Minor buffalo and the Indian hump-backed ox had become acclimatized. Pigs were not extensively bred, but herds of wild boars roamed the reed beds in the marshes. The ordinary domestic fowls were goose, ducks and chicken, and a common game bird was the francolin.† Many kinds of fish abounded in the canals and fishing was carried on in the shallow waters of the Persian Gulf. Dangerous animals included lions, less impressive in appearance than those of North Africa, panthers, jackals, hyenas, snakes and poisonous insects

* This opinion is now challenged in the light of recent research (See Bibliography). [Translator's note.]

† A kind of partridge, resembling a pheasant. [Translator's note.]

such as scorpions. The marshes of the delta were infested with mosquitoes.

The subsoil of Lower Mesopotamia is poor, and because of its alluvial character it contains no stone; but both stone and minerals are found in the hills of Assyria. This is balanced by rich oil deposits in Central Assyria, especially round Kirkuk, while deposits of bitumen are concentrated in the south.

These are the main features of the country with which we are principally concerned, but the Assyrian Empire, as a result both of its conquests and of the incessant wars which it waged in the seventh and sixth centuries B.C., extended as far as the frontiers of modern Persia to the south-east, and on the west to the shores of the Mediterranean, to the very frontiers indeed of Egypt. Thus it was in a position to command by trade or tribute all the resources of the ancient world.

The Inhabitants

The Babylonians and Assyrians are members of the Semitic racial group, but they contain certain foreign elements originally represented by the people whom we now know as 'Asianic',[1] who, if not actually indigenous, were at least among the earliest recognizable inhabitants of Asia Minor, and form a group distinguishable alike by language, religious practice and physical type. The most individual feature of their languages, of which there were many varieties among the 'Asianic' tongues, was a verbal root which remains unaltered both in conjugation and the formation of nouns. Their religion was based upon the great forces of nature, with special emphasis on fertility and fecundity. The measurements of such skulls as have been recovered during excavation are in fact inconsistent with the features reproduced by their sculptors, but if we may accept the evidence of their monuments, their physical appearance was distinguished by a boldly hooked nose, a low forehead, a deep and slanting cranial vault and a flat occiput. These features are all typical of the modern Armenian group. It is thus clear that these 'Asianic' peoples differ from both Semites and Indo-Europeans, though some archaeologists have been inclined to suggest that pre-Indo-Europeans could be recognized among certain of them.

The earliest examples of this group are represented by the

Sumerians (properly regarded as the civilizing element in Meso-potamia), the proto-Hittites* in Asia Minor, the Hurrians north and east of Assyria, and the races stretching along the Zagros from the Caucasus to Elam. The Babylonians and the Assyrians originally comprised a single group, the Akkadians. They belonged to Semitic stock whose archetypal characteristics are an aquiline nose and a high domed skull. In the Semitic language, as in French, the verbal roots can be modified by internal inflec-tions. The cult of astral divinities is an important feature of Semitic religion. By the beginning of the historical period in Mesopotamia, Semites and Sumerians had already long been intermingled, with the majority of the former established to the west of Upper Syria from which quarter they mounted their invasions against Middle and Lower Mesopotamia, which at that period formed the country of Sumer. Later, and indeed precisely in our period, new waves of Semites, known as Arameans, who had been nomads from time immemorial, made their way into Mesopotamia in such numbers as to form an important element in its population.

The Semites first borrowed the elements of Mesopotamian civilization and then adapted them to suit their own genius. A respect for an earlier stage of civilization was always notice-able among the Akkadians, who often could make but small improvements on what they had borrowed from Sumer. The spirit which they displayed was one of admiration and imitation, and this left its mark on every aspect of thought and applied skill.

The third distinguishable element in Western Asia is the Indo-European. This seems to have exerted its influence not through its intrinsic size but through its rôle as leader of the recurrent 'Asianic' invasions from the east throughout the historical period. The Indo-Europeans were the directing or commanding element in these invasions and left their mark on the countries which they conquered, like the Indo-European Hittites in relation to the 'Asianic' proto-Hittites, the Hurrians in North Assyria, the Kassites in Babylonia and the Persians in Iran.

Undoubtedly many of the profound differences between the characters of the less advanced Assyrians and the more highly

---

* For a further discussion of this term, see O. Gurney, *The Hittites*, London, Pelican Books, 1952, ch. 1. [Translator's note.]

civilized Babylonians derive from the nature of the indigenous population which they encountered in the countries which they occupied, and with which they became fused, or from the differing proportions of the three main racial elements described in the preceding paragraphs. But in saying this it would be a mistake to under-estimate the influence exerted by the widely differing climates of Assyria and Babylonia in forming the character of their inhabitants.

The Language

Akkadian is the name of the language which was spoken in both Assyria and Babylonia. The two forms of the language are practically identical in grammar and vocabulary, and probably differed most markedly in their method of pronunciation; where, on the evidence of the language in its written form, the Babylonians seem to have tended to harden certain sounds. An analogy can be found in modern Italy where the normal Neapolitan pronunciation of 'Cristo' is 'Gristo'. But by the late Assyrian and neo-Babylonian period Akkadian itself was obsolescent, and Aramaic, which was spoken by the peoples surrounding Mesopotamia, had spread to all parts of the country. It had two advantages over Akkadian. Not only was it more flexible, but it was also written in an alphabetic script and not in cuneiform, which was too difficult a medium for the dissemination of ideas and could in any event be mastered only by the class of the scribes, who formed but a tiny fraction of the population.

From that time onwards the two languages were in simultaneous use. Few traces of Aramaic, by reason of its simplicity the more commonly employed, have survived, because it could be written in ink on impermanent materials which have disintegrated, but Akkadian remained in use as the traditional language, used only for official documents and inscribed on clay tablets which, when fully baked, were virtually indestructible. From the time of the Sargonid dynasty onwards, but especially under the Babylonians and the Persians, Akkadian, written in cuneiform characters, occupied a position analogous to that of Latin in Western Europe during the Middle Ages. Aramaic had taken the place of Akkadian as the language of everyday speech precisely as Akkadian had taken the place of Sumerian.

Mesopotamian History, 700–500 B.C.

Before embarking upon a description of daily life in Babylon between the years of approximately 700–530 B.C., we must briefly recapitulate the events of the period within their historical setting.

Throughout the second millennium B.C., Babylonia and Assyria were engaged in a bitter struggle for supremacy,[2] but from about 1000 B.C. fortune favoured Assyria and by 700 B.C. her ascendancy was undisputed. King Sargon II (722–705 B.C.), who had recently died, had emulated his predecessors by leaving, some 10½ miles north-east of Nineveh,* a palace whose magnificence is attested by the fact that the sculptured bas-reliefs which it contains, placed end to end, would stretch for rather over a mile. The Assyrian Empire was near its zenith, and Sargon's successor, Sennacherib (705–681 B.C.) was himself extending its boundaries, not, however, without first being forced to put down the rebellions which in the ancient East traditionally accompanied a new King's accession (see Pl. II). Thus, after defeating a pretender to the throne whose claims were backed by Elam and repelling the Aramaeans, a nomadic race whose envy was always excited by the wealth of more settled peoples, Sennacherib put down rebellions in Phoenicia and Judaea, both supported by Egypt, and installed a nominee of his own on the throne of Babylonia, which had decided once again to try its fortune at the instigation of its deposed monarch Merodach-baladan. Sennacherib with his fleet pursued him to the region of the Persian Gulf, where he had fled, but Elam, lying in the south-western area of modern Iran, came to the support of the rebels and the campaign ended inconclusively. Sennacherib was therefore forced to postpone his punitive measures, since he was faced with the necessity not only to repress the Arabs in the south-west of the Empire, but also to retrace his steps to Palestine where rebellion had again broken out. Finally, returning again to Babylon, he sacked it in 689 B.C. and established one of his sons as Governor: but rebellion broke out in Assyria itself and Sennacherib himself was assassinated.

The following reigns, at least in so far as they were concerned with rebellions and palace intrigues, need not long detain us. Sennacherib's successor, Esarhaddon (680–669 B.C.), devoted most of his strength to attacking Egypt, Assyria's traditional opponent

---

* At Khorsabad. [Translator's note.]

in her rôle of supporter of the nations of the West who were anxious to free themselves from the Assyrian yoke.

Esarhaddon conquered the delta; next, rebellion in Phoenicia received severe punishment. The King of Sidon was captured and beheaded; the city itself was razed to the ground and replaced by a new town on an adjacent site, which remains unidentified, from which it appears likely either that it was soon abandoned or that it never attained great importance. Meanwhile the East was menaced by the Medes, established in the north-west of Persia, and by the Scythians, a nomadic race of Indo-European stock who were trying to penetrate into Assyria by way of Armenia. Despite all these anxieties, King Esarhaddon found time to plan a new palace at Nineveh; but he was not destined to enjoy any respite, for Egypt was once again rising in opposition and the King met his death on the way to a campaign against her.

Esarhaddon was succeeded by his younger son, Ashurbanipal (668–626 B.C.), whose elder brother inherited the throne of Babylon. He took as his first task the restoration of Assyrian power in Egypt, and Assyrian forces moved from Memphis to Thebes, which was sacked. It was almost inevitable that Ashurbanipal's elder brother, the rightful heir to the throne of Assyria, should have chosen this moment to revolt against him, and once again Assyria was forced to tread the road to Babylon. The city was captured, and the rebel brother met his death in his burning palace (an event which gave rise to the legend of Sardanapalus), and the same fate overtook the city of Susa, the capital of Elam, which became an Assyrian province. This marked the zenith of the Empire, which was destined to dwindle in size under Ashurbanipal's successors.

Cyaxares, King of Media, and Nabopolassar, the Governor of Babylon, acting in alliance, made a joint expedition against Nineveh and captured the city in 612 B.C. The efforts of the last King* to regroup his forces in North Syria were unavailing, and the whole Assyrian Empire was partitioned between the two victors. Henceforth the whole of the north, from Media in the east to Asia Minor in the west, was to form part of the Median Empire. Babylonia, Assyria and the coastal region were to be united under the sway of Nabopolassar, while Babylon emerged as the head of a new Empire, commonly known as the neo-

* Sin-shar-ishkun (621–12 B.C.) [Translator's note.]

Babylonian. Nabopolassar, who ruled as its first king for several years, was succeeded by Nebuchadrezzar (605–563 B.C.). During his long reign he was able to restore the beauty of Babylon, after its sack by Ashurbanipal, and to embellish it with monuments to which both his own inscriptions and the writings of the Greek historians testify, and whose remains were brought to light by the excavations of the German expedition under Koldewey during the years 1899–1917.

The former adversaries of Assyria were soon once again united in opposition to the kingdom of Babylonia. Nebuchadrezzar made himself master of Jerusalem in two Palestinian campaigns, in 597 B.C. and again in 587 B.C. On the second occasion he showed no mercy. Many of the inhabitants were killed, while King Zedekiah together with the princes of his house, the nobility and the skilled craftsmen, were carried off to Babylonia. This was the beginning of what is known to Jewry as the Great Captivity, which was destined to last until the time of the Persian Empire. The city of Tyre was taken after a long siege (no less than thirteen years according to the historian Menander) and Nebuchadrezzar at least planned an expedition to Egypt (568 B.C.) from the natural base afforded by the coast, though there is no record of whether he ever undertook this campaign or, if he did, with what degree of success.

There is little to record during the reigns of succeeding kings beyond the usual disturbances, but the stage was being set for events of greater moment. The Persians, who were settled in southern Iran, rose in revolt against the Medes and reduced their former masters to a state of vassalage. Cyrus (546–529 B.C.) came to the Persian throne during the reign in Babylonia of Nabonidus (555–539 B.C.), who was more concerned to restore the religious monuments than to preserve the interests of his Empire. However, his plan of gathering in his capital the statues of the most sacred gods from the outlying temples aroused the opposition of the priesthood, and Cyrus, who had in the interval advanced his frontiers as far as the Ionian coast, met only slight resistance when in 539 B.C. he made a direct attack. His policy was one of unprecedented moderation. He returned the gods to the cities from which they had been removed, permitted the Jews to return to Jerusalem and showed his respect for Babylonian custom and tradition. An entirely new spirit was indeed to be discerned with the arrival of the Persians: the severity of the Babylonians and the cruelty of the Assyrians yielded place to breadth of understanding and, despite occasional outbreaks of violence, to a tolerance to which the East had hitherto been a stranger.

We have sketched in outline the history of two centuries and it is time to ask what kind of life the ordinary Mesopotamian of the period lived. It must indeed have been unsettled and punctuated with moments of tragedy for the inhabitants of the capital cities of Nineveh or Babylon which were destroyed during those years: more tranquil, no doubt, for those who dwelt in the countryside. But what is beyond doubt is that it was unremittingly busy. We need look for proof no further than the documents which prove the wealth and renown of the civilization under the last of the Assyrian kings and the neo-Babylonian monarchy.

Chronology

Before proceeding further, we should be quite clear how the historical events of the preceding section can be assigned to particular dates.[3] To the modern world the dating of events is a relatively simple matter. Our use of the Christian era means that the years follow in sequence from a fixed starting point and, after making due allowance for various corrections which have been introduced into the calendar during the centuries, our system of chronology covers this long period with complete reliability. We have also projected this method backwards in time and in calculating the passage of years B.C. we apply the same convention, again starting from the beginning of the Christian era. But the ancient world naturally could not foresee the event which has fixed the starting point for our system of chronology, and so had to pursue a different method. Its attempts, though persistent, were bound to fail, lacking as they did any fixed point. We will see how it tried to make good this deficiency.

The Mesopotamians, like other peoples, took the day as their unit for the measurement of time. According to their reckoning, however, it began at sunset, and was divided not into twenty-four hours but into twelve periods of two hours, which gave their name* to the distance which could be covered in that space of time.

* *bēru* in Akkadian. [Translator's note.]

Their next unit was the month. Refinements introduced into the calendar of Western Europe have led to the adoption of one month of twenty-eight days and the remainder of thirty or thirty-one, so that the year consists of 365 days. This corresponds within about six hours to the length of the solar year, and the variation is made good by adding, every fourth year, one day to the month of February which normally has only twenty-eight.

The Mesopotamians, by contrast, had adopted the lunar month of thirty days. This system results in an annual shortage of slightly over five days, so that after six years the time lag amounts to a month. At that point the Mesopotamians inserted into their calendar what they called an intercalary month of the normal length, thus catching up again with the true year.

Possessing as they did this unit of measurement, the Babylonians employed two different methods for dating years, which, like Western Europe until the Renaissance, they regarded as beginning in the spring. According to the first method they named each year after its outstanding event, such as 'the year when such and such a king built such and such a temple' or 'the year in which a particular king defeated a certain enemy', resulting in lists which form a catalogue of events. Alternatively, they counted up the number of years in each reign. This method would be thoroughly reliable had all the documents only been preserved in their proper order: but unfortunately they have not.

But, just as we do, the Babylonians have left us lists of their different dynasties in which each king is shown in strict order of succession together with the number of years of his reign, while usually at the end of each dynasty the scribe gives the total both of the kings and of the aggregate years of their reigns. This method too would be entirely satisfactory but for errors and omissions on the part of the scribes. There is yet another kind of document which ought to relieve us of all uncertainty. Frequently, when a king records an important feature in his reign, he refers back to some past event and specifies the intervening period of time.

It is therefore somewhat surprising to realize that only a limited reliance must be placed upon these written records. As long as only comparatively few of these texts had come to light, it was possible to accept the accuracy of the system of chronology as reconstructed on this basis, but with the growing volume of excavation and the more frequent discovery of dating evidence, the conclusion became inescapable that two series of documents, Assyrian and Babylonian, coexist in Mesopotamia. Further, within each series there are discrepancies between different texts, both in the actual numbers of the kings and the years of their reigns.

The method employed by the scribes in drawing up their chronological tables affords yet another ground for uncertainty. Whereas the modern practice, in compiling similar lists, would be to put kings, princes or events which were contemporary with each other in parallel columns, the Babylonians listed them one after the other. They were in no doubt about the correct interpretation, thanks to the oral tradition which played so large a part in their system of education. We on the other hand are in the dark until some fortunate accident happens to disclose that two events previously believed to have been separated by a period of time were in fact contemporary. In recent years, for example, it has been established that Hammurabi, a king belonging to the first dynasty of Babylon, was a contemporary of a certain Shamshi-Adad of Assyria. It had been believed that the latter lived more than two generations after Hammurabi, and the truth was realized only as a result of the discovery of the correspondence between the two monarchs: incontrovertible evidence, not to be gainsaid by the official lists, no matter how carefully they may appear to have been compiled.

Astronomy has been invoked to help in finding a way out of this uncertainty. It is not only possible to calculate the future dates of the successive appearances of phenomena such as an eclipse, or the heliacal rising or the occultation of a planet or a star, but also the dates of their past appearances. In fact the Mesopotamians, who were interested in both astronomy and astrology, often recorded events of this kind in their histories of their kings. Thus we happen to possess a complete record of astronomical observations over a known period of the reign of a certain King Ammi-zaduga, who belonged to the first dynasty of Babylon, and, as explained above, we can calculate the date at which these phenomena must have occurred.

The German astronomer Kugler, after lengthy calculations, specified the precise date to which this reign must be assigned, and so, by implication, the dates of the other kings belonging to the dynasty. The English astronomer Fotheringham, however, working on the same problem independently, reached a different result, while Kugler himself, in recent years, has repeated his earlier calculations and has reached a different conclusion from the one which he published previously. The obvious elements of uncertainty inherent in this method are attributable in the main to the fact that a choice lies between a number of alternative dates. In practice the particular astronomical phenomena which are being studied recur, sometimes with such frequency as to render two or three successive dates possible. This is the cause of the differences of opinion among Assyriologists who compare these results with the surviving Mesopotamian documents.

Despite these various difficulties it is true to say that all the different interpretations of evidence broadly point to a shortening of the general chronology. The earliest date proposed for the beginning of the historical period, which was formerly placed beyond 4000 B.C., has now been brought down only to the opening centuries of the third millennium B.C. As we approach the Christian era the uncertainties proportionately decrease to the point of disappearance, and they are virtually negligible for the period covered by this book. For several centuries before this date the Assyrians had described individual years by the name of an eponymous magistrate called the *limmu**, and we have lists of these officials. Further, the scribes of this period composed a simultaneous history of events in Assyria, Babylonia and neighbouring countries, and this has been preserved. Finally, Ptolemy the Egyptian established for the preceding centuries a 'canon' of events which can be used for purposes of comparison. So when this book speaks of dates between 700 B.C. and 500 B.C. they can be taken as accurate to within a few months.

THE STRUCTURE OF SOCIETY

The Family. The House

Although the daily life of a member of the upper classes in Mesopotamia differed strikingly from that of the ordinary man,

* In Assyrian and Babylonian names the letter 'u' is pronounced as in 'shoot'. The letter 'e' is never silent.

they had none the less certain features in common; but by contrast there was no resemblance whatsoever between the life of a king of Babylon or Assyria and that of any of his subjects. Our immediate concern is with the ordinary man in the street. The kings will occupy a separate section of this book.

In its earliest stages Mesopotamian society recognized a three-fold division among its members. Between the free man and the slave there was an intermediate class worth, in the literal sense of the term, less than the former and more than the latter. There is, however, so little direct evidence of its existence that it is probably fair to conclude that, from the time of Hammurabi onwards (about the eighteenth century B.C.) this class was of only minor importance. In brief, it was the class of the *mushkinu* (the Arabic word for 'poor') from which the French word 'mesquin' is derived: the class of men worth only a little, but distinct from the slave who was worth nothing.

Free Man and Marriage

At the top of the social scale stood the free man: 'man' in the true sense. He was no other man's property. Admittedly he was subject to the law, but alike in the courts and in the penalties to which he might be exposed he was accepted as being of greater value than the slave, whose legal status, which was the precise opposite of that of the free man, will be described later.

The foundation of the family was marriage. In theory monogamy was the rule, but in practice what might be called 'secondary wives', drawn from among the slaves, were also tolerated. Until the time of her marriage a girl remained under the protection of her father, who was free to settle her in marriage exactly as he thought fit. Even if the girl happened to be in the service of some third party, for example as security for a debt of her father's, she was none the less dependent on her father for getting married, or on her brothers, should her father have died. The creditor was free to dispose of her as he liked only if she had neither father nor brothers.

Marriage was preceded by the ceremony of betrothal, during which the girl's future husband poured perfume on her head and brought her presents and provisions. Thereafter the girl was so fully a member of her future husband's family that, if he died, she would marry one of his brothers, or, if he had no brothers, one of his near relatives. It would be unusual to find no one in an Oriental family who fulfilled these conditions: but if this were the case, her father resumed all his rights over her, and gave back all the presents which she had received except any which might have been consumed. Conversely, if the girl died and her intended husband did not want to marry one of her sisters, he would take back all the presents which he had given her except those consisting of food.

The actual marriage, as we know from a text, took the form of a delivery of the wife to her husband, while if both belonged to the class of free citizens, the husband veiled his bride in the presence of witnesses and solemnly declared 'She is my wife'. Assyrian law defines the significance of the veil, which has been the subject of much research, and lays it down that it was the distinguishing mark of a free woman, and that anyone who met a slave or a courtesan wearing a veil had the duty of denouncing her. The veil cannot in fact always have been worn lowered over the face, for there are many neo-Hittite monuments which portray women wearing a veil which covers their hair and hangs on either side of the face. In this case it was only necessary to draw it together (and to this day many Oriental women keep it closed by holding it in their teeth), or, if it was gathered on the top of the head, to let it fall loose. This way of wearing it can be seen in sculptures from Palmyra and paintings from Dura Europos, a town on the Euphrates near Der ez-Zor. Thus, though its significance has changed, the veil worn by Moslem women reaches far back into history. Custom has since widely extended its use, but it was already accepted in parts of the East as early as the second half of the second millennium B.C.

Although under the late Assyrians and the neo-Babylonians wives were not, at least in theory, bought and sold, none the less there are certain texts which make it clear that purchase in a disguised form did in fact take place. One such text records, for example, that for the price of sixteen shekels of silver, a lady called Nihtesharu acquired a certain Ninlilhatsina and had actually taken physical possession of her in order to marry her to Nihtesharu's son. The document states specifically that the purchase price has been paid in full and indemnifies the purchaser against all claims. The ceremony was accompanied by a proper

marriage contract, which helped to give the woman the title of
wife. If this formality were omitted, cohabitation over a period of
two years, at least in the case of a widow, was regarded as the
equivalent of a contract. Married life might involve either the
wife's staying in her father's house or her going with her husband
to his. In the former case, the husband gave the wife a sum called
the *dumâki* towards the maintenance of the house, and if the
husband died this contribution remained the widow's property
only if the deceased had left neither sons nor brothers. The
dumâki might, of course, have been wholly or partly expended.
In Assyrian law the onus of establishing his case rested on the
plaintiff and thus the sons or brothers would have had to prove
that the *dumâki* had not been wholly spent. This frequently
resulted in the calling of witnesses; if no agreement could be
reached, proof was established by means of an oath or by ordeal.
But in cases concerning the *dumâki* the plaintiffs were exempted
from these two methods of proof, and no doubt the evidence of
witnesses was sufficient.

If, on the other hand, the young couple went to live in the
husband's house, the wife brought with her a *shirqu* ('sheriqtu' at
the period of Hammurabi), or dowry, and often a trousseau
as well. The *shirqu*, together with the presents which the bride
had received, remained the inalienable property of her children,
and her husband's brothers had no claim upon it.

Besides these presents the bride might receive a marriage
jointure (*nudunnu*), by accepting which she would become jointly
and severally liable for her husband's debts, a special gift (*tirhatu*)
made to her on the occasion of her betrothal, which remained her
own property even if she were divorced by her husband, and
finally a present 'of gold, silver or lead' or simply of food called
the *zubullû* which was no doubt eaten at the wedding feast.

The difference between these various types of offering was that
while the *tirhatu* remained the wife's inalienable property, the
dumâki and the *nudunnu* could on certain conditions be revoked,
as could the *zubullû* provided that it was still intact.

The husband might, however, keep not only his wife but also
an *esirtu*, or concubine, entitled to wear the veil only on the
occasions when she accompanied the legal wife out of doors. This
right, which the Code of Hammurabi had granted to the Babylonians, remained in force in the first half of the first millennium

B.C. But the husband was not allowed to have two 'wives': this title belonged to the legal wife from the moment that he placed the veil upon her, and by comparison with the latter the concubine would always occupy a slightly inferior position. She was originally chosen from among the slaves and had to perform the duties of her station with proper respect for the legal wife, carrying her chair when she went to the temple and assisting her in her toilet.

There were scarcely any limits to a father's rights over his children. He could, for example, deposit them with a creditor as security for the repayment of a debt. In certain legal documents he was even described as 'master' or 'owner' of his child, a conception entirely alien to the modern idea of a father.

As we have already seen, a father had equally complete authority in the matter of a daughter's marriage, though no reference is made to any rights possessed by the mother. It is noteworthy that Assyrian law makes no mention of a number of legal rights which the mother of a family possessed in the much earlier epoch of Hammurabi.

If the husband died before the wife, and intestate, the widow was expected to continue to live in his house, and to be supported by his children, but if she had children by an earlier husband, the children of the second marriage could send her back to them as their responsibility. The natural misfortune of childlessness seems to be made doubly bitter by the disapproval implicit in the Assyrian law's dismissal of the childless widow. It says curtly 'She may go where she will', and leaves it at that.

Whether or not a family contained children by the legal wife or by the *esirtu*, who might be a member of it, it always had the right to adopt other children, who thereby acquired the same rights of inheritance as the other male children provided that this was not to the detriment of the sons born in wedlock. The ceremony of adoption took place in the presence of witnesses, and, in return for his newly acquired rights, the adopted child gave a small present to his new father. Some centuries earlier this practice had resulted in an ingenious means of circumventing the law, which prohibited the sale of property held in fief on a grant from the king, but allowed it to be passed on by inheritance. We actually find a wealthy merchant trader of the fifteenth century B.C., from near Kirkuk, adopting rich and poor alike wholesale and quite indiscriminately, while they in return gave their adoptive father 'presents', consisting of sums of money or estates equal in value to what they would themselves later inherit as a result of their adoption (see p. 85).

By the act of adoption, the father acquired very extensive rights. Thus he could end it at his pleasure and send back the adopted child, while the latter, if he renounced his adoptive family, would be simply expelled* and returned to his home.

After these glimpses at the family of an Assyrian freeman (*amêlu*) in the time of the Sargonid dynasty, it is time to turn and examine the legal status of the slaves, whose numbers made them an important element in society.

The Slave

A man might be born a slave if he were the son of one, or might become one from a number of causes, which were sufficiently numerous to account for a perpetual tendency for the number of slaves to increase. The first cause was war. One of the principal objects of the incessant campaigns conducted by the Assyrian kings was to ensure a labour force large enough to execute their various designs. Assyrian bas-reliefs depict lines of prisoners being led to the capital by the victorious armies, the men with bound hands driven like cattle by blows from the soldiers, and followed by the women carrying their children and their scanty possessions or, sometimes, mounted on the carts laden with grain which had been seized as plunder along with the population. The royal Annals give detailed accounts both of the booty and the prisoners, some of whom would be assigned to work as building labourers, on the upkeep of the canals, and in the service of the temples, while others would be sold in the markets.

A father of a family might also be driven by destitution to sell as slaves his wife or children or even himself if he were entirely unable to repay a debt which he had contracted. Finally the law provided that, if an adopted child disgraced himself, for example by renouncing his adoptive family, he might be sold as a slave. Although in strict theory the person sold into slavery as security

* Under law 186 of the Code of Hammurabi. Under law 192 of this Code the son of a woman with a vow, or devotee, who repudiated his foster parents, had his tongue cut out. [Translator's note.]

for a debt had the right to his liberty once the debt was discharged, in practice he was often unreasonably kept in slavery, and Assyrian law was at considerable pains to ensure that no one was kept in servitude without good cause after he was entitled to receive his freedom.

A slave had no human personality. He was merely an item of real property, and in legal documents he was referred to merely as 'slave unit' or, if his name was mentioned, that of his father was omitted. If he was injured, it was his master and not he himself who was entitled to compensation, while, since by definition he represented a certain monetary value to his owner, the law did not envisage the possibility of the latter's deliberately killing him.

We know that a slave was marked in some way like an animal, but despite the frequent references to the practice we do not know precisely what it represented. The expression commonly used 'He will be shaven' or 'He will be marked' is somewhat obscure, for though in Western Europe the shaving of a man's head in prison or in confinement stigmatises him among free men, this was not certainly true of Mesopotamia, since in the East the head is often shaved for reasons of hygiene. The mark must, in all probability, have been some symbol of ownership branded with a red-hot iron directly on the slave's skin. Indeed the Code of Hammurabi, more than a thousand years before our period, specifically provides against the cutting or burning away of the mark on a slave, by which it must mean the scar left by the branding. This act was liable to severe punishment. Anyone convicted of it was to have his hands cut off, or, if he had acted in ignorance at the instigation of a third party, then this latter was to be put to death. It is reasonably certain that the branded mark itself was either some symbol of identification, or sometimes the name of the owner. We learn from a contract of sale that a woman called Belit-silim was sold to a certain Nabu-shum-lishir, who stamped his own name on her hand. Besides this, a slave wore round his neck a small clay tablet bearing his name as well as that of his owner, which thus served as an identity disc. Several of these tablets are now in the collections in the Louvre.

A runaway slave was an object of pursuit not only by his owner but also by the public authorities. The Code of Hammurabi actually devotes no less than six sections to this subject, which proves how often it must have happened. The giving of help to a runaway slave, or his concealment, were severely punishable offences, and in contracts of sale the seller had to guarantee that the slave was not a fugitive and to pay a heavy indemnity if he turned out to be one. Similarly a debtor who gave a slave as security for a debt had to undertake to indemnify the new owner if his 'security' ran away.

The Sale of a Slave

The legal aspects of the sale of a slave were identical with those for other goods. A guarantee was given, as it was for an animal, that he was the absolute property of the seller and that he was not suffering from any incurable disease. Most such diseases would have been immediately obvious, so that those represented by the words *bennu* and *sibtu* by which they are described, cannot have been. The suggested translations of 'epilepsy' and 'leprosy' are plausible, but must remain conjectural. The period for which the guarantee held good varied according to the conditions stipulated: thus for epilepsy or leprosy it was one hundred days, but there was no limit in respect of claims by a third party. The clause dealing with disease, which had been universal in the time of the first dynasty of Babylon, had fallen out of use by the neo-Babylonian period, by which time the main emphasis was laid upon the fact that the slave was not royal property and that he was not 'the son of an ancestor' (*mar banutu*), or, in other words, free, whether by birth or by adoption.

A contract of sale from the reign of Nebuchadrezzar gives an exact idea of the kind of document used:—

'The children of Zakir, son of X . . ., have of their free will sold to the son of Y . . . their slave Nana-dirat and the child which she is suckling, at the agreed price of 19 shekels of silver. The sellers will guarantee the purchaser against her flight or a counter claim, or if she is found to be royal property or free.'

A female slave was under obligation to give her purchaser not only her labour but also herself, without any counter-obligation on his part. He could indeed actually give her over to prostitution. Even when she became her purchaser's concubine, and she had children by him, none the less she still remained a slave, as liable to be sold as before: but after her owner's death both she and her children received their liberty. If a female slave had been bought by a married woman both as her servant and as her husband's concubine (in order, if the wife was childless, to avoid the husband's taking another concubine), the slave remained the sole property of the wife, at least up to the time when she had children.

Since it was to the interest of the slave owners to increase the number of their slaves, they encouraged them to marry, and with this end in view they bought male or female slaves according to the sex of those whom they already possessed. The children of these marriages became the property of the owner, who was at liberty to sell them separately if he so chose. It was however quite common not to separate the members of a single family. A slave could, with his master's consent, marry a freewoman, and if she brought no dowry with her, she herself and her children would remain free. But if she did bring a dowry and invested it jointly with her husband in some undertaking, then, if the husband died or absconded the widow recovered her dowry but received only half of the profits of the concern, her husband's master receiving the other half.

Temple Slaves

Temple slaves were a special class, mostly drawn from prisoners of war, a certain number of whom would be dedicated to the gods by the king after a successful campaign, though many were presented to the temple by generous private benefactors. A mere recital of the various commercial activities in which the temples engaged is proof of their need for a large staff. These slaves, known as *shirku*, were under the orders of an official appointed by the temple authorities to ensure their employment in the best interests of the shrine. Their employment was however not confined to the temple itself, and they not only supplied forced labour for work in the towns at public expense but they could also be hired out to work for private employers. Their legal status was harsher than that of ordinary slaves, since they had no hope of adoption, while their children, even if their mother was a free woman, automatically became the property of the god. We should however realize that the *shirku* included not only slaves but, if we are correct in our interpretation of certain documents, some free Babylonians.

The most singular feature of slavery as practised by the Babylonians and Assyrians was that, despite their complete subservience to their masters, slaves were able to own businesses, to own slaves on their own account, and to save money. This was particularly the case during the period of this book, during which not only did an important part of the country's trade pass through their hands, but we see them working as craftsmen, besides owning cattle or banking, while they were at liberty to trade not only with each other but also with free men. We find, for example, a slave renting a house from a free woman for four years at an annual rent of a dozen meals a year and half a shekel of silver.

In the Persian period a slave called Ribat offered to rent the fishponds of one of the sons of Murashu (the great banker of Jewish descent) in return for half a talent of silver and a supply of fish for his table.

Further, a master who realized that his slave had a gift for commerce had no hesitation in entrusting him with important transactions and with large sums of money; we find a merchant lending 889 shekels of silver at 20 per cent per annum. Nevertheless, the equivocal status of a slave, at once the owner of property and the possession of his master, was a constant source of difficulty.

Redemption

There was one factor in a slave's legal status which could always keep alive his hope of regaining freedom, and we should remind ourselves of the conditions under which this was possible.

Firstly, women and children deposited as security with a creditor could not be kept for more than four years. Secondly, the children of a marriage between a free woman and a slave were free, while a slave concubine and her children regained their freedom after the death of her master: and finally there was a legal provision automatically conferring his freedom on a Babylonian slave who, after being sold in a foreign market, was brought back to Babylon. Besides this, a slave's ability to own and to save money offered him the chance of buying back his liberty, and if he did so he acquired it absolutely after undergoing a symbolical ceremony of purification.

On balance the chances of being reduced to slavery were clearly more numerous than those of escaping from it, and slaves who could claim their freedom on one of the grounds just cited were fewer than those who became slaves, a progressive increase in whose numbers was in fact assured by the law relating to birth and by military expeditions. It is perfectly clear that the immense wealth of the Assyrian and Babylonian Empires, to name no more, was largely dependent upon the institution of slavery. At this period, when, in the absence of all machinery, production depended entirely upon manual labour, and could be increased only by a corresponding increase in the labour force, the legal status of a slave was an absolute bar to his enforcing his claims by violence, as it was to strikes to slow up production or the payment of wages disproportionate to the value of what he produced. These were the means by which Babylonia and many other countries in the ancient world were enabled to become prosperous. Their political economy was founded upon what they produced and upon the accumulation of reserves of wealth, the alternative being merely a process of spending with a duration limited to the time required to exhaust the resources of the country.

The problems presented by slavery have resulted in some peculiar theories. For example, Major Lefebvre de Noëttes, a retired French cavalry officer, as a result of an historical study of horses' harness, realised that a horse, regarded as a draught animal, had never been used with complete efficiency until provided with a rigid collar resting on its shoulders. Before that time, as early illustrations prove, as it pulled its load its neck was constricted by the surrounding collar. Since its windpipe lies near the surface of the skin, each effort which the animal made throttled it and made it more liable to choke. From this the Major deduces that slaves were found preferable for employment on account of the poor performance of the horse, and its consequent abandonment. This goes too far, though it may contain an element of truth. The real reason for the general persistence of slavery lies without doubt in the ease with which this source of labour could be replenished and in the connivance of the public authorities of the time in this degrading practice, which is never far distant when the rights of the individual are subordinated to those of the State.

The overriding necessity for a large supply of labour in primitive societies finds expression in the frequent occurrence of large families. These enhanced the importance of the head of the family, who was for all practical purposes the ruler of a community, while the principle of adoption, in the sense in which it was then understood, can be traced to the same cause. The net result was that the family was able to grow in size more rapidly than it could have done by natural means.

Homes

Although no house dating from so early a period has been preserved in entirety, the appearance of towns in the East to-day must none the less be very similar to what it always was, and the poorer quarters of great cities like Baghdad would certainly closely resemble a Mesopotamian city of the first millennium B.C.

Firstly, archaeological excavation has demonstrated that for a variety of reasons the ground plan of a house in the East has hardly changed throughout history. Both ideas and their physical expression are much more conservative in the East than in the West, while the climate, with its small variations of temperature, affords but little stimulus to research and modification in house design. The most striking feature of the weather in Mesopotamia is the heat, and once the colonnade had been invented there was clearly little room for advance in that direction. In Europe, by contrast, the pattern of life changed more sharply and more rapidly and this in its turn affected both the design and the layout of houses. Indeed the climate of Western Europe, where summer and winter temperatures may well vary by as much as 70° F., has led to a variety of experiments designed alternatively to counteract the heat and the cold. These have considerably affected the planning of town houses, while the design of houses in the country has altered remarkably little.

The House

The primitive type of dwelling, which is still to be found unchanged in the Mesopotamian countryside, was the hut of intertwined branches, covered with thatch and cemented with mud which, when dried, holds the framework together.[4] The strata

representing the earliest human occupation contain still recognizable remains of these huts. At that date they were circular,
as we can see from designs on vases which, though much later
in date, reproduce the primitive type. This suggests that there
was a central post like that of a tent, to which the framework of
the outer wall was bent over and fastened, thus forming a kind of
vaulting. The walls were covered
with matting. There may perhaps
have been windows, and the door
hung on a pivot post firmly secured
to the wall. But architectural development relegated this type of
construction to the countryside,

Vase in the form of a circular hut

where it was employed principally for stables and sheepfolds. It is
still employed in the area under the name of *zorife*. The method of
construction consists of tying in bundles the stems of tall reeds and
fixing them in the earth at regular intervals and in a straight line.
Parallel to and on either side of this central line two more lines
of reeds are then firmly fixed in the ground, their tops being bent
over to form a kind of tunnel, and fastened to the central line,
along which a pole has been tied, to form the roof of the edifice.
The result is a shelter with a barrel-vaulted roof. It can be
extended as far as may be wanted, but its width is limited by the
height to which the reeds grow in the district. The walls may be
made from branches, from dried mud, from matting or possibly
even from thatch (like the Turkmen *yurt*).

The first sign of true architecture is associated with the appearance of quadrangular or rectangular buildings. These represented not only a genuine social advance but almost luxury by
comparison with the buildings of circular design, which enclosed
the smallest possible area of ground in proportion to the labour
and materials expended. But the quadrangular house demanded
the acceptance of new methods. The earliest houses of the type
of which any remains survive are constructed of lumps of diluted
clay, arranged in a kind of herringbone pattern like undressed
stones in a wall.

The Use of Clay

This pattern is quoted as evidence by the school of thought
which suggests that civilization was introduced into Mesopotamia

not by the indigenous inhabitants, but by a people coming from an area where the use of stone for building was already known. Be that as it may, by the late Assyrian and neo-Babylonian periods the inhabitants of Mesopotamia had long employed a method of building based upon the use of clay, which had remained virtually unaltered throughout the centuries. They had indeed carried the use of this natural material to a degree of perfection which could scarcely be bettered. As our survey of the natural resources of Mesopotamia made clear, while the inhabitants used clay because of the lack of building stone, it is in fact the material which gives the best results in the climatic conditions of the country.

The clay could be used in its natural state for manufacturing bricks, but centuries of experience of its use showed methods of treatment whereby its life could be prolonged. Modern builders pour cement round a core of metal reinforcing rods in order to prevent concrete from cracking: the Mesopotamians mixed their clay with finely chopped straw in order to reinforce its strength. Every nation which built in clay knew of this method. We are reminded in the Bible of what happened in the Nile delta when, after expelling the conquering Hyksos or shepherd kings who came of Semitic stock, the Pharaohs forced the Israelites, who were settled in the country, to undertake their arduous labours and how, as we can read in Exodus, Rameses set them to work on making the bricks for the buildings which he was erecting in the Delta; their task being deliberately made heavier by their being forced to collect the necessary straw from the fields without having their daily quota of bricks in any way abated.

When the clay and the chopped straw had been thoroughly mixed together, the compound was packed into plain wooden moulds. After the bricks were removed they were then left to dry in the open air, which they did more quickly in the hot summer weather than in winter, so that the first summer month, called Siwan, was also known as 'the month of bricks'. But although dried clay becomes extremely hard, its useful life is far shorter than that of baked bricks. It shrivels beneath the pitiless heat of the Eastern sun and it tends to disintegrate when exposed to floods, a disadvantage referred to in the magical texts which speak of certain demons as resembling the river which walls cannot keep out. But bricks cannot be baked without fuel, and this commodity was so scarce that the brick baked in the modern fashion was used only for buildings of particular opulence or for those in which a special degree of resistance was required.

Although the process of brick manufacture was sufficiently simple to be within anyone's capacity, it was in practice an expert occupation. Bricks of different sizes were required according to the particular kind of building which was planned, varying from bricks as large as great tiles for a palace or its terrace to others hardly larger than those used to-day for a cottage. The plan of a house may show some variations but has in essence remained unaltered in the East from the earliest times to the present day, since it satisfies the demands both of the climate and of social life. A typical plan consists of a central courtyard which lights a number of rooms leading off it, in one of which, so narrow as to be little more than a passage, is the door opening on to the street. Some of the rooms may communicate with each other and others may not, but generally speaking the door affords the only entry for light and air from the outside world. The main door referred to above is the only way out of the house, and no daylight enters through the external walls. The house is, in short, simply a box built without foundations upon levelled and beaten earth. Bricks are used when they are three-quarters dry, and are bonded with mortar made of diluted clay which, when it dries, makes a wall of uniform strength. The floor of the rooms, like those of the courtyard, will normally be made of beaten earth, though if the owners are well to do, some sections of it may be paved with flagstones or with floor tiles of baked brick laid sloping slightly towards the centre so that rain-water or waste can run away easily, while a drainage system with terra-cotta conduits leads to underground cesspools. Very often there is no separate kitchen, and a cooking range made of earth stands against the courtyard wall, while if a special room is devoted to this purpose it has no chimney and the smoke is left to find its own way out of the door or an extra hole cut in the wall. The domestic offices follow the 'Turkish' pattern, i.e., consist of flagstones with a hole in the centre, and, as is not unknown in some parts of Western Europe, are emptied only when the need for it can no longer be disregarded. The water required for domestic use is kept in huge half-sunk jars in the courtyard. Nevertheless both Assyrians and Babylonians, doubtless with an eye to food storage, saw the need for more vents in the walls in order to improve the circulation of air. These air vents took the form of channels through the wall, blocked halfway through with terra-cotta tiles pierced with a number of holes, large enough to let in a little air and a glimmer of daylight but too small to afford passage to any rats or mice which might be attracted by the grain.

The Roof and the Upper Storey

This type of house is roofed by first laying planks of palm-tree wood on the top of the walls so as to span the rooms, then covering them with reeds and palm leaves, and finally adding a layer of earth, packed down tight with a stone roller not unlike those used for tennis courts. In modern Syria every house has its roller on the terrace ready to carry out the unending repairs to the roof which are necessitated by the lightest shower of rain.

The terrace, which is used for enjoying the cool of the evening or for sleeping in summer, is reached either by an outside stair-case of wood leading from the courtyard, or, if the house is comparatively large, by an inside staircase in one of the corners. In the latter case it is generally made of baked bricks and cut in the thickness of the wall, with high and narrow treads.

Generally speaking the roof took the form of a terrace, but there are some Assyrian bas-reliefs which depict the kind of rectangular houses we have just described, set in a thickly wooded countryside, but either surmounted with a cupola or with a roof in the shape of a beehive.[5] A certain number of fairly large houses were in fact roofed in this manner. The cupola might cover either one of the rooms or, if the house stood in a garden and was already sufficiently airy, the courtyard itself, provided that it was not too large. In this case it formed a central room off which the other rooms opened. This particular plan necessitated the use of baked bricks and the employment of corbelling. Projections in each corner afforded a circular foundation for the roof, which was built up of successive courses of brick firmly cemented with either lime or bitumen, and each projecting slightly inwards over the course below. When the roof was completed it only remained, inside and out, to conceal the irregular outline of the overlapping courses of brick: and the result was a cupola.

Rectangular houses with beehive roofs

But this method could only be used on comparatively small surfaces.

The beehive pattern was a variant upon the foregoing, in which the successive courses of brick only overlapped fractionally, so that the roof rose to a point. Roofs of this shape were unusual in Mesopotamia, and were more common in Syria, where at the present day whole villages built on this pattern can be seen in the Hama district. It has the double advantage of being both easier to build and of allowing the use of somewhat inferior materials such as broken brick, more reliance being placed on the mortar to bind the structure together than on the actual thrust of the building itself, as in the cupola roofs.

Most of the houses in the ancient East had a garden adjoining and were only one storey in height. Villages in present-day Arabia commonly have houses of several stories: and this was certainly so in Nineveh, Babylon, and the provincial centres. The upper storey, built in exactly the same way as the ground floor, was erected on the foundation of a wall of extra thickness, in order to give more strength. The rooms on the upper floor were reached by a wooden balcony supported on beams and extending the whole way round the inner courtyard. This had the additional advantage of sheltering the entrance of the rooms which opened off the courtyard from the sun and from bad weather.

The doors of the house were made of palm-tree wood, but since this wood becomes fibrous when the tree attains any great age or size, doors could not be the solid affairs to which we are accustomed. They had to be specially constructed of panels of wood set in a framework, as they are in the East to-day.

Decoration

It is fairly certain that the poorer kind of house in Babylon was undecorated except perhaps for a coat of whitewash to conceal the roughness of the surface and the drabness of the clay wall. The outside walls, too, must have been whitewashed, as they are to-day, for the Mesopotamians cannot have failed to realize that a white surface absorbs the rays of the sun less than a black one, and that the greyish walls speckled with fragments of straw were thoroughly unsightly. In the houses of the better to do, if there were not actually panels painted with various subjects, the plinths were painted half way up with some dark colour, generally black, derived from diluted bitumen, with a band of some other colour above. Sometimes, too, the door frames were painted red, but it would probably be a mistake to regard this as representing deliberate aesthetic choice, for red, as we know from rituals and exorcisms, was regarded as a colour which frightened and kept away devils and thus barred the doorway against all evil influences. The red colour was iron sesqui-oxide, a scarlet pigment soluble in water. It is not surprising that every kind of creature seeking to escape from the intolerable glare of the sun made straight for these houses, little ventilated as they were as a protection against the heat. The walls were covered not only with spots of damp but also with variously coloured species of ants and cockroaches. In the eyes of the Babylonians everything had some supernatural significance, and we have a number of omen texts showing the significance to be attached to the animals which might be met both inside the house and on its walls—reptiles, lizards, scorpions, cockroaches, beetles and the other unwelcome visitors encountered in hot countries.

Furniture

The furniture in these houses was scanty, like that in common use in the same area to-day. The middle-class Babylonian slept

on mats, rugs, or mattresses, while the better off slept on rather
high beds, somewhat like a table with one end built up to form a
kind of bolster. Beds of this sort are to be seen on sculptured
panels depicting the exorcism of illnesses, or the huts belonging,
no doubt, to the officers, though not to the rank and file, of a
campaigning army. (See Pl. XXI.) The Babylonians sat either
on stools made of palm wood or more commonly on a kind of
armchair with a deeply curved back made of plaited reeds, very
much like those in use at the present day. The remainder of the
furniture consisted of a few chests. Pottery played a very important part in the furnishing of a house, including jars of varying
sizes for drink or food, and pots of an extremely ancient pattern
with little pierced lugs through which a string could be passed
to hang them out of reach of rats and mice. The crockery in daily
use consisted of bowls of different depths and platters, and we
possess some long terra-cotta dippers with curved ends for
scooping up liquids, very similar to the ladles used in dairies
to-day. Low tables were little more than trays standing on feet,
but the Babylonians had dining tables of an entirely different
pattern which stood quite high off the ground, about which we
shall have more to say later. (Pp. 132–3.)

Lighting and Heating

The Babylonian system of lighting can be briefly described as
the use of primitive lamps, originally shaped like a shallow saucer
with a pinched spout through which the wick passed, and, in our
period, like a pointed shoe with a hole for the wick. A lamp of this
shape is the ordinary symbol for Nusku, the god of fire. But the
Mesopotamians were fully acquainted with the use of crude oil,
which they called 'stone-oil', as an ordinary fuel. Although they
certainly did not know how to refine it, none the less it must
have given them a better light than the oil which was mainly
derived from sesame seed. If they wanted a blaze of light they
would use torches; soldiers are often shown carrying them on the
bas-reliefs of military expeditions.

Despite the normal mildness of the climate, there are occasional
days during the winter cold enough to require some form of
heating. A brazier, containing the glowing embers of the fire used
for cooking, inside a terra-cotta bowl, would normally give
plenty of heat.

The Town. Its Layout

In the centre of the town, as in the East to-day, the houses huddled closely together. The layout of the narrow streets was confused and the surface of the ground uneven, partly because

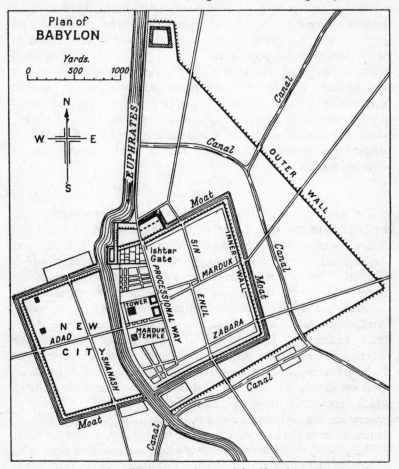

Plan of Babylon, *c.* 600 B.C. (after Unger)
(*Esagila* was the area covering the Tower and the Temple of Marduk)

houses were repeatedly rebuilt without any fresh foundations upon the roughly levelled debris of earlier ones, partly because the household rubbish was thrown into the streets, where what was not eaten by dogs and scavenging animals was burnt dry by the sun and trodden underfoot. Furthermore, with successive rebuildings the level of the houses gradually rose. The houses were jumbled together as they commonly are in Oriental towns of the present day, and it was only towards the outskirts that a certain number of houses with gardens were to be found. Thus, though the town might extend over a considerable area, the density of the houses at any given point was not necessarily proportionate to the density of the population.

But although the most thickly populated quarters were not built to any plan, the Mesopotamians did none the less observe certain principles in planning their large cities, and the chess-board layout with blocks of houses intersecting at right angles, which has been observed in towns dating from the Alexandrian period, was already the general rule in Mesopotamia several centuries earlier.

Babylon

The excavations at Babylon enable us to reconstruct the appearance of the city in the middle of the reign of Nebuchadrezzar, which covers the middle of our period. The city was divided into a number of rectangles by wide thoroughfares which afforded access for travellers, processions and goods both to the centre of the city and to the various blocks where the merchandise was unloaded and stored in warehouses. These roads, like the city gates, were called after the great gods of the Babylonian pantheon. Thus on the left bank of the Euphrates the streets of Marduk and Zababa were intersected almost at right angles by those of Sin, the moon god, and Enlil, lord of the earth, while on the right bank, from east to west, ran the street of Adad which crossed the street of Shamash, the sun god.

Between the ordinary houses in which the lower classes lived, which we have already described, and the royal palace or the great public offices, there were many houses of intermediate size. The owner of a large estate would live in a bigger house, built upon the same plan, but simply enlarged by the repetition of the original unit of a courtyard and rooms leading off it. In this case one of the rooms would be replaced by a passage leading to another courtyard which gave access to the further rooms required. The remains of a large building have been found in Babylon in the quarter known as the *Merkes*, which must have formed the centre of the business area. This strongly suggests that even if the policy of the municipality was to build the city to a regular plan the inhabitants cared less about it than their rulers. In certain instances it has been possible to verify this. When the Botta expedition excavated the palace of King Sargon II at Khorsabad, near Nineveh, the plan of the palace was recovered, but, in accordance with normal mid-nineteenth century practice, the lines were assumed to intersect at right angles, rather as geographical maps are drawn, either on an extended planisphere or rectified. In consequence the palace appeared to be entirely symmetrical, like a seventeenth-century building in France. This was however in fact quite inaccurate. When the American expedition which continued the excavations in about 1927 checked Botta's plans, it became quite clear that the palace was slightly trapezoidal in shape and was not symmetrical as it had been assumed to be, while this was also true of the adjacent palaces which Botta had not cleared, and of the palace of Nebuchadrezzar at Babylon, the plan of which was meticulously recovered by the German expedition which explored the town. The inhabitants of Mesopotamia in fact had none of the passion for uncompromising symmetry and for balanced features after which succeeding centuries have striven in their great architectural creations.

The Great Buildings. The Merkes

An examination of the great building in Babylon called the *Merkes* shows that it is built on a trapezoidal plan and that three of its fronts, each some forty or fifty yards long, are regularly indented like the teeth of a saw. No doubt this design resulted from a desire to break the monotony of long flat surfaces by the creation of alternating planes of light and shade, changing as the day wore on and adding a decorative element. Apart from this feature the plan is similar to that previously described, in having a series of courtyards linked with each other by rooms opening on to them, the only difference being that instead of the rooms of the normal house we find much larger and less numerous halls, no doubt a more convenient arrangement for a building primarily used for commercial purposes.

Towns in Mesopotamia had one other distinguishing feature, namely the little chapels or altars dedicated to various divinities which were set in the recesses of the walls, and which recall the *turbés* (tombs) of the sultans or high dignitaries which suddenly break the line of the streets in Istanbul. But the main difference between a city such as Babylon and a town in Western Europe is that in the former the streets resembled residential streets in the Near East to-day, with a blank wall on either side. They derived their life and animation solely from the passers-by.

The Euphrates and its Bridge

A walk across Babylon would lead to the Euphrates. By our period the river was flanked with wharves and with drainage canals to save the city from flooding, and it was crossed by a permanent bridge resting on five piers. This was a perpetual source of wonder to travellers, and not without reason: Baghdad, for example, until very recently had nothing but a bridge of boats. The piers, which were tapered in order to offer the least possible resistance to the pressure of the water on the bridge, were made of stones and covered with a broad wooden superstructure. The river bed has altered during the centuries and to-day the remains of the bridge can still be seen in the midst of the surrounding ruins.

Then, as now, the business life of the town centred on the wharves, while the importance of the waterborne traffic in a country where a canal system was the principal means of communication between different towns, inevitably led to the setting up of offices along the river banks which controlled the conduct of business. They were something like modern Chambers of Commerce: rates of exchange were regulated there and, where modern Europe speaks of the Exchange, the Mesopotamians called the place where these offices were established, *kârum* (wharf). The exact site of the market of Babylon is unknown, though it was presumably in the *Merkes*, the business quarter. In other respects it must have resembled modern bazaars in cities of the East—Istanbul, Aleppo, Teheran or Ispahan: a district with its own character, whose gates were closed at night, with narrow alleys, shaded by awnings, their walls containing countless stalls and housing every kind of trade, but grouped as they were in medieval Europe, with their legacy of street names like The Shambles or Bread Street. The flimsiness of the modern bazaars clearly shows the impossibility of fixing the site of those in the ancient cities of the East.

The city had neither pavements nor sewers, and indeed even capitals and important cities in the East had none until the present day, but the Assyrians were familiar with the idea of street paving. When Sargon II built his palace of Khorsabad during the last years of his reign, he planned a town which was intended to go with it and actually built the surrounding wall. The gates which gave access to the town were carefully paved with large blocks, while it is still possible to see that the road which led outside the town was also paved for a short distance. It soon degenerates into a track and then disappears altogether.

Water Supply

The concern which the rulers felt for ensuring a supply of drinking water is shown by the remains of the aqueduct built by King Sennacherib from Jerwan, a village several miles from Nineveh, to supply his capital with water. This aqueduct anticipated later design in every detail. The water ran along a strengthened conduit with a floor of hardened earth, waterproofed with bitumen and lined with stone flags. The aqueduct spanned the valleys on arches and was fed by a number of small streams so as to ensure a proper supply to the town.

Disregarding for a moment the huge spaces where the temples were built, the *ziggurat** of the great temple, and the royal palaces whose famous 'hanging gardens' could be seen from afar, and which will be described later in the sections dealing with the life of the king and the court, it is time to turn to the walls of Babylon, which antiquity classed with the hanging gardens as one of the wonders of the world.

The Walls

The walls of Babylon, strengthened by successive monarchs and notably by Nebuchadrezzar, together formed a virtually impregnable defensive system, and historians are agreed in thinking that on the occasion of the capture of the city by the Persians (539 B.C.) its fall was the result of surprise and owed

---

* The *ziggurat* or temple tower built in stages or stories of diminishing size towards its summit is described on pp. 276–9. The best known was that of Babylon, the Biblical 'Tower of Babel'. [Translator's note.]

more to the complicity of the governor Gubaru (the Greek 'Gobryas') than to military operations.

There was in fact a double row of walls a little distance apart and so designed that, if the outer were breached at any point, the attackers found themselves trapped between the two walls and overwhelmed by the defenders.

At regular intervals each wall was reinforced with towers, offering an advanced position from which the defenders could repel any enemy troops which might have advanced as far as its foot in an attempt to undermine it or scale it with ladders. The ancient historians lay great stress upon its width, which allowed two chariots to be driven abreast on the road which ran along the top and completely surrounded the city, along which a large number of men could be quickly rushed to any point that was seriously threatened. Beyond the outer wall there was a moat filled with water diverted from various canals in order to increase the difficulty of the assault, while the raw clay of the walls was strengthened with facings of baked brick. The written accounts differ in their estimates of the size of these walls, but all of them overstate the actual dimensions as revealed by excavation. Herodotus calculated the height of the towers as 300 feet and their width, including the thickness of the walls, as 150 feet: but excavation has proved that the width of the towers was about twenty-seven feet, which suggests that they can hardly have been more than about ninety feet high. Equally there were nothing like the hundred gates which the town was believed to possess. Ctesias' figure of about fifty-five miles for the circumference of the town is obviously wildly inaccurate, and excavation has proved that in fact the figure should be about ten miles. This shows the necessity for great caution in accepting any figures which cannot be checked by the results of excavation.

The Gates

The most unusual feature of the walls was the gates leading into the town, which were built on the same principle in both Assyria and Babylonia. The gates of all towns and buildings in antiquity were always especially strengthened since they represented a weak point in the defensive system. It was the method by which this was effected in Mesopotamia that gave them

The Ishtar Gate at Babylon: a reconstruction by Koldewey
(*By permission of The Town Planning Review*)

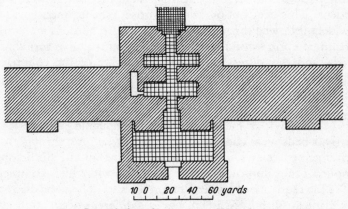

Ground plan of a gateway at Khorsabad

their distinctive character, and it was evidently largely conceived in terms of the unbaked clay of which they were built, whose defensive usefulness depended upon its mass. Each gate was heavily reinforced, on both inside and outside, with a curtain wall of mud bricks, pierced by an opening. Through the whole ran a passage, open at intervals to the sky. These openings could be commanded by archers posted on top of the walls in case attackers, after succeeding in forcing the outer gate, penetrated into the thickness of the walls. This method of defence can still be found in the gates of towns or palaces in present-day Morocco. The *Puerta del Sol* at Toledo in Spain derives from the same origin, though it is on a smaller scale as stone was employed there.

Apart, therefore, from the temple and palace areas, this account gives a glimpse of what a great Mesopotamian city, as exemplified by Babylon, was really like. Not only was Babylon one of the most important cities in the whole of the Tigris and Euphrates valleys, but we can compare the highly coloured descriptions with the remains of the city as it really was.

The Countryside. The Canals

A traveller passing the city gates and making his way into the countryside would have found that there the houses were set in gardens. This need not occasion surprise, for the practice was and is widely followed throughout the East. But gardens are entirely dependent upon a good system of irrigation which in turn implies canals, and this necessary feature of the life of the countryside calls for a brief description. From the earliest known periods the inhabitants of Mesopotamia had endeavoured to protect themselves against the catastrophic floods of the Euphrates and Tigris: an obvious menace since, on debouching on the plain, the river beds were comparatively shallow and ran through loose and shifting soil. During his excavations at Ur, Sir Leonard Woolley came upon a layer of river deposit which completely broke the sequence of civilization on the site. The same discovery was made at Kish by Watelin, but at a different occupation level. This pointed to two different floods, and it was repeated cataclysms of this nature which gave rise to the tale of the 'Babylonian flood' which takes up one whole section of the Gilgamesh epic.

The answer to this menace was the digging of a system of canals, some designed to run parallel with the river beds and prevent flooding, others to link already existing canals and others again to reach areas previously waterless. The result was threefold: a large increase in the number of navigable waterways, a system of communications connecting the different towns and an increase in the area of cultivable land.

The canals were constructed on a very simple principle. When the walls of a town were being built, a ditch was first dug which provided ready to hand the raw material of the bricks for the walls: by the same token during the digging of a canal the excavated earth was thrown up on each side to form embankments which ensured protection against flooding in case the water level should rise. The actual flow of water was regulated by a system of large sluices, while the distribution of the water into the small trenches which led off the canals and watered the gardens was effectively controlled by a drainage channel cut in the embankment which could be equally quickly blocked or opened. There is practically no rain in Mesopotamia, and agriculture is impossible without irrigation, but, if the ground is sufficiently moistened, areas of virtual desert are covered with vegetation and are amazingly fertile.

The Fertility due to Irrigation

A truer impression of the appearance of Mesopotamia in antiquity can be derived from Egypt than from the country's present aspect. In Egypt, vegetation along the banks of the Nile is coextensive with irrigation, and the same thing can be seen in the oasis of Palmyra since the war of 1914–18. During the course of history the cultivable area had been reduced to negligible proportions but has been doubled quickly since, under the French mandate, a judicious use of its springs has been introduced.

What might be described as this 'artificial' prosperity always naturally caught the imagination of travellers in antiquity. Some like Herodotus[6] actually preferred, in their own words, not to quote the statistics they had been given; others, less sceptical, repeated what they had been told about the size of the barley crop. Strabo, for example, writes of a yield of 300 times the quantity sown, but modern observation suggests that the truth, though less spectacular, was nevertheless far beyond anything known in Western Europe. G. A. Olivier, the naturalist, who visited the country at the beginning of the nineteenth century, estimated that the yield of barley was some thirty or forty times the quantity sown.[7]

From the very earliest times the rulers of Mesopotamia regarded it both as a duty and as an act of piety to improve the canal system, and during the period when years were commonly identified by the outstanding events of the preceding months, several were distinguished by a reference to the digging of a canal, which was regarded as equal in importance to a victory, the annexation of some territory or the building of a temple. As for the maintenance of the system, orders have been preserved from the royal chanceries to the governors of the provinces in the Empire for the execution of this work. In the first dynasty of Babylon the letters of Hammurabi to his local officials reflect the same preoccupation, which reappears in a summons dated in the month of Siwan in the second year of the reign of King Cambyses, ordering the dispatch of ten men for forced labour on a canal, failing which the official responsible for the canal is to be punished by Gubaru, governor of Babylon and of the trans-Euphrates district.[8]

When the Assyrian and Babylonian Empires finally disintegrated, at the time of Arab invasion and the medieval invasions from the East, the inhabitants, who had dwindled in number, ceased to pay much attention to the canals, which gradually silted up, so that to-day only faint traces of them are visible on the ground. Within the past twenty years, however, thanks to Father Poidebard, aerial investigation has placed an unsurpassed means of reconstructing their plan at our disposal. In a slanting light, slight unevennesses of the earth's surface, imperceptible at ground level, show up, when observed from a low flying aeroplane, in previously unsuspected relief. But there still remains the problem of the identification of the remains with the canals whose names have come down to us.

This recalls an amusing mistake. One canal which was mentioned in the cuneiform texts, and which seemed to have been of considerable importance, had a name which was read as *Zalzallat*. But the texts gave no information either about its course or upon its starting or finishing points. Great efforts were made to identify it. Several ingenious hypotheses were advanced and it was even marked on some maps, until one day E. Dhorme, after recalculating the various possible alternative values of the cuneiform signs, read them correctly as *Idiglat*, which is in fact the name of the great river Tigris. And that was the end of the canal *Zalzallat*.

Even in antiquity many minor canals had to be abandoned. Although their water, heavily charged with mud from the great rivers, was almost as good as manure for fertilizing the fields, the mud itself formed a deposit in the canal beds, more particularly when the sluices were closed and the water was unable to flow and became stagnant. The reeds which so quickly choked the canals required constant cutting and the silt had to be dredged up and shovelled on to the banks. But despite the most strenuous efforts the canal bed would gradually rise and the mud which had been dredged up and dumped on the banks gradually built them up, so that sooner or later the canal ran first at ground level and then above it, enclosed between two earth embankments. At this point prudence dictated its diversion to a new bed dug near the old one.

Fields at the level of one of the main branches of a canal were watered by cutting a temporary breach in the retaining banks of the channels which intersected them, and damming it again with a shovelful of earth when the fields were thoroughly watered. But when the canal ran below ground level, the water had to be raised. In the Hama region of Syria where the rivers are fast-flowing, use is made of the *noria*, consisting of a wheel with buckets fitted all round the edge. As the river turns the wheel these are successively filled and emptied at the required height. These machines work day and night and the air is filled with the melancholy sound of their grinding. In Mesopotamia, however, it was more usual to employ the *shadûf*. This is depicted on the monuments and appears to be virtually identical with what can be seen to-day not only in the same area but all over the East. The *shadûf* consists of a moving pole on a support. A rope, to which is tied the receptacle to be filled, is attached to the longer end of this pole. The operator raises the shorter end of the pole, which is fitted with counter weights, and lowers the receptacle into the water. He then leans on the counter weights. The bucket rises, and is emptied into the pool which feeds the channels

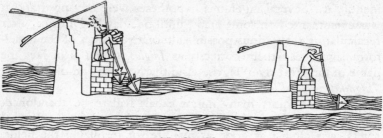

The Shadûf

through which water reaches the fields: and the process is repeated. Often a slight variant which can be made to work by a
draught animal, a donkey or an ox, is employed. The bucket
dips into the water under its own weight, the animal pulls on the
rope which passes horizontally round a wheel like that of a wind-
lass, the bucket is emptied as before, and, as the animal comes
back to its starting point, the bucket falls once again into the
life-giving water.

Navigation

From waterways to navigation is a natural transition. The
changes in the beds of the Tigris and Euphrates, and the currents
which caused the loose bottom to shift, barred them to navigation
by vessels of deep draught for the greater part of their length.
But the vessels of remote antiquity were, in general, not of this
nature; they were mostly large boats like the lighters now used in
Syria for unloading bigger vessels. It was usual, on account of
the small number of natural harbours and the almost complete
lack of ports capable of giving protection, for vessels to heave to
for the night and shelter beneath some promontory which protected them from whichever direction the wind might be blowing:
while very frequently boats were wheeled to the water's edge by
their crews, a revealing comment upon their size at this period.
It was this kind of boat which plied on the canals, hauled by a
rope, and certain bas-reliefs, particularly the bronze panels on
the gates of a palace which have been discovered at the modern
village of Balawat, depict a line of men on the bank hauling
heavily laden craft. In the same way the Code of Hammurabi
specifically refers to the ferry, which doubtless then as now
travelled along a rope stretched from one side of the river to the
other.

Alternatively, in calm water like that of the canals, boats were often propelled by poles, a method of which many representations are extant. This may well be the origin of the Akkadian word for a sailor, which is composed of the sign for a boat and that for going and coming, to signify the ceaseless movement from bow to stern and back again of the man wielding the pole.

Finally these large boats were sometimes roughly rigged with sails, probably consisting, as in the Far East, of matting. In our period the place of the rudder was taken by a great oar at the stern, or indeed might be dispensed with altogether (see Pl. XV). Judging by the texts dealing with the cargoes which the boats carried, their capacity seems to have been small: thus in the time of the third dynasty of Ur we know of boats on the canals carrying from about 55 to 155 bushels of grain.[9]

Among the many texts on the subject of waterborne trade there are some, dating from the Sumerian period (considerably earlier than that covered by this book), which deal with boat construction. These employ a very extensive vocabulary much of whose meaning is at present unknown. Its mere existence is, however, evidence of the importance which navigation had already assumed by the third millennium B.C. We must remember that what we dismiss contemptuously as 'technical terms' and therefore negligible are, properly regarded, witnesses to the wealth of a language and to the level of civilization of the nation which uses it. Measured by this criterion, as by so many others, the civilization of the Sumerians was astonishingly highly developed.

Since the building of a boat was a considerable operation, those who required one often had recourse to hiring. For example, in the seventeenth year of the reign of King Nabonidus, a certain Muranu rented a boat with a capacity of 150 *gurs** for the use of the temple of E-anna at Uruk for 5½ shekels of silver, for one month, from the sixth of Elul (August–September) until the sixth of Tisri (September–October). The temple authorities paid in advance and the contract laid it down that if the capacity proved to be less than that stipulated, the payment was to be adjusted accordingly.[10]

---

* Either 600 or 300 bushels, according to the value of the *gur* (see p. 88). [Translator's note.]

The Coracle and the Kelek

There were two types of boat peculiar to Mesopotamia which have survived until the present day. They are the coracle and the *kelek* (Pl. IIIa).

The coracle was a kind of round basket, like that used by labourers for carrying earth and bricks on their heads, and the name was given to boats of this shape. It was virtually a basket of plaited rushes, flat-bottomed and not very deep. The bottom was covered with skins and caulked with oakum and scraps of wool, all tightly compressed and mixed with fine earth and bitumen, which ensured that it was watertight. The boat was propelled by one or two men with sculls and the whole art consisted in getting it to travel forwards without spinning round and round. When the boats were loaded with miscellaneous cargoes, the gunwale was only a few inches clear of the water. The coracle sailors do not hesitate to cross fast flowing rivers like the Tigris, but they are generally used only for carrying goods up and down the river. The coracles depicted on Assyrian bas-reliefs are absolutely identical with those to be seen in use to-day.

The *kelek* is a raft made either of the strongest of the reeds which grow densely in the marshes and which are tall enough to hide a man completely, or, preferably, of the best wood which the builder can get hold of locally. Its buoyancy is increased by having inflated goatskins attached to its under surface, which render it capable of carrying a considerable weight. The loaded raft then floats down the river with the current, being both propelled and steered by a pole, until it reaches some point in southern Mesopotamia. There it stops: the cargo is unloaded, the *kelek* is dismantled, the wood (which is scarcer in South Mesopotamia than in the North) is sold, the goatskins are deflated and loaded on donkeys and the sailor, transformed into a caravan driver, returns to his starting point and there begins the whole process afresh.

Not everyone owns a boat, but everyone often has occasion to cross one of the network of canals which are frequently too wide and too deep to be fordable: and provided that they are not too heavily laden, they can use 'floats', which are simply a mass of reeds bound together at each end and flattened in the centre. You cannot cross on them dry shod, but they will not sink.

Finally, unskilful swimmers could entrust themselves to

goat-skins.   These, like those used by water carriers and by water sprinklers in the East, were made of the skin of an animal whose head and hoofs had been cut off, and thus preserved its natural shape.   The skin was inflated whenever necessary, and by grasping it or placing it beneath his chest, a Babylonian could cross without risk of drowning.   Bas-reliefs exist which depict an Assyrian army crossing a river by this method (Pl. IIIb).

The skins were in daily use for a variety of purposes, such as holding oil or wine.   A tablet of the third year of King Nabonidus of Babylon is a receipt for 'a dozen inflatable skins'.

Fishing

The canals were also useful as a source of edible fish, and fishing is often referred to as an occupation.   In the river estuaries near

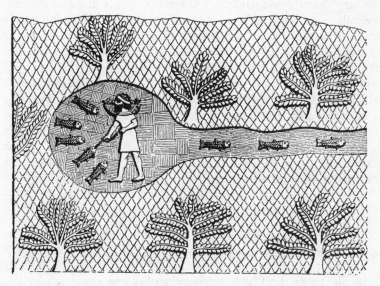

A Fishpond

the Persian Gulf, the catch was sent for sale in the towns of the district, but towns which were too far away for this had to make do with fish from the canals and from ponds.   An Assyrian bas-relief shows a little round pond fed by a stream and the sculptor has been careful to make clearly visible the fish which it contains, as though they were on the surface.   Fishing was generally done on a line, but various kinds of net were also employed, and these supported a lively trade which we shall meet again when we come to the basket makers. The pond depicted on this particular relief is so regular in shape that it may well be a special stew fed by a branch stream from a canal. There is another bas-relief some 2000 years earlier in date than the Assyrian period, on a monument in the Royal Tombs at Ur, known as 'the standard', with a number of little figures in mother-of-pearl on a background of lapis lazuli. The scene portrays a procession of porters, either tributaries or perhaps slaves, loaded with the spoils of the victory which the monument commemorates. Among them is one bearing some huge fish.

Gardens

From a description of the canals upon whose waters the country's fertility depended, it is a short step to the gardens and the cultivated areas, whose importance increased proportionately to their distance from the towns. To judge from the gardens round Baghdad and the oases of North Africa, where soil and climatic conditions are similar to those in Mesopotamia, they must have consisted of rectangles of cultivated land set amongst irrigation ditches, and sheltered from both sun and wind by fruit trees, themselves overshadowed by a few palm trees. The produce of these gardens is recorded in texts and monuments and we have a contemporary description of one of them by the scribes of King Marduk-apal-iddina of Babylon, commonly known as Merodach-baladan.

The Garden of Merodach-baladan

The text makes it clear that this was not a royal park but a kind of vegetable garden. Not only does it give useful information about the varieties which were eaten at that date but it also casts light on the method of botanical classification employed by the Babylonians. The plants are grouped by species (or rather what the writer judged to be the same species) and are classified either by reference to certain common characteristics or simply by reference to their use. Thus garlic, onion and leek form one group and the aromatic herbs such as mint and basil another. A third consists of seasonings like saffron, coriander, rue (also greatly liked by the Romans), thyme and pistachio: assa-foetida is mentioned and so are the gourds or melons which grow in such wide variety in the Orient. There are greenstuffs, too, such as lettuce and, possibly, endive: and there is a striking number of strongly scented herbs like fennel and a kind of carrot. The vegetables include lentils and, among the less delicate varieties, beets and kohl-rabi. Besides these, the Assyrian lists include some which remain unidentified, while others can only be guessed at. The fruit trees include date palms (we shall have more to say later about the date trade) and pomegranates, which not only yielded a drink but were sufficiently highly prized to be set before a king, as can be seen on a bas-relief from Khorsabad which depicts all the preparations for a palace banquet; there are medlar trees, too, apricot trees, plum trees, peaches (native to Persia and known in Latin as the 'Persian apple') and finally fig trees. There are many varieties of fig, which ripen successively from June until the autumn, but the inhabitants of the Orient recognized that their varieties were inferior to the Attic fig. All these fruits grow mainly in the area of central Babylonia and of Assyria where the climate suits them. Herodotus must, it seems, have travelled in Mesopotamia at a date when the fig tree, vine and olive tree were actually being introduced but were still uncommon, for though he remarks that they did not exist there, they are represented on the Assyrian bas-reliefs, e.g., the fig tree on that from Khorsabad.

Oil was extracted from the sesame plant, which had been grown very extensively from earliest times, since at the period of this book the olive tree had only become acclimatized a few centuries earlier. The stock was improved by intensive cultivation and it did particularly well in Assyria and the neighbouring countries. It is depicted on bas-reliefs, and Assyrian soldiers, while on their campaigns, made a point of uprooting olive trees in order to impoverish the enemy's territory. At this date the vine had only recently reached Assyria. There are texts which refer to the sale of wine, and vines are shown on bas-reliefs in the British Museum dating from Ashurbanipal, entwined round the trunks of trees in a garden where the king is eating, and even in a game reserve where wild animals were preserved for hunting.

Farm-yards

Farm-yards were attached to the gardens, and monuments and

texts record the usual occupants as ducks and geese. (A tablet dating from the third dynasty of Ur, about 2000 B.C., mentions a supply of fowl for the birthday of the king's daughter.) The Mesopotamians designed stone weights in the shape of a duck with head and neck twisted so as to rest on its back. During the second millennium B.C. the hen was acclimatized only in Syria, but by the Persian and Assyrian periods it was common in Mesopotamia. An inscription of one of the Pharaohs recording the precious, or at least curious, objects which he brought back from a campaign in Syria speaks of 'the bird which lays an egg every day'.

In the neo-Babylonian period the cock is found among the animals depicted on intaglios, while the Sassanians introduced it into the decorative motifs on their textiles. Doves usually nested in holes cut directly in the house walls, and this arrangement is found in a terra-cotta model, now in the Louvre, of a temple from Cyprus, where the temple of the goddess at Paphos sheltered a vast flock of doves.

The wild birds, which were however sometimes kept as pets, included the ibis, the crane, the heron (of which seven varieties have been counted), which frequented the marshes, and the pelican, which was trained for fishing, while the fields were the home of thrushes, blackbirds, sparrows and larks. Quails were rare, though they were very common in Syria, but partridges and francolins bred in the country and we can see the latter being hunted with the bow on a bas-relief from Khorsabad of the time of King Sargon II, now in the Louvre (see Frontispiece).

By contrast, there were many birds of prey, including vultures, falcons and owls, from which the aviaries required protection, while the fields of ripe cereal crops had to be protected from the ravages of crows and mice.

Large-scale Agriculture. Cereal Crops

It is time to consider the big estates where large-scale agriculture was practised. The staple crop, which the inhabitants of Mesopotamia meant when they spoke of 'grain', was barley. This crop grows wild: we have already described the scale of its yield, and in certain localities it provides several harvests during a year. It was not only the most common of the useful natural products but also the most abundant, and in the absence of money as a medium of exchange, barley grain served as the accepted standard of value. This fundamental function of cereals in human affairs was recognized again at a critical moment in French history: for when the Institute was reorganized at the close of the eighteenth century, the penalties imposed upon its members were fixed in terms of 'myriagrammes of wheat'. Most naturalists believe that the starchy grain known as spelt was indigenous in Mesopotamia, but was never as common or as important as barley. Millet also was eaten.

Spade and Plough

Small plots of land were dug with spades made of a hard stone, chipped round the edges into roughly the shape of an ace of spades. Tools of this kind have been discovered in the Qatna district of Syria. In large fields, however, the Babylonians used the plough, which is frequently depicted on surviving monuments. The ploughshare itself, the forepart of which, seen from the side, was triangular, was made not of iron but of hardwood sharpened to a point or perhaps tipped with a sharp stone. The

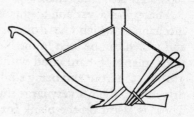

Plough with seed-drill

plough carried a vertical shaft ending at the top in a kind of box, which must have been a seed drill, so that the seed could drop down the hollow shaft and fall to the bottom of the furrow. Mesopotamian religion touched life at every point and symbols which conveyed a religious significance to the Babylonians are now often interpreted as being merely decorative motifs. Thus the figures of a lion, an eagle pacing with folded wings, a plough and a fig tree, which are recognizable in the remains of a mural decoration discovered near some temples at Khorsabad, are quite certainly four religious symbols, or attributes of divinities. The plough is often represented on boundary stones bearing deeds of gift of land and dating from the Kassite epoch (second half of the second millennium B.C.). Indeed one of these stones is inscribed in the name of the god whom the plough symbolizes, the Sumerian god Ningirsu, who later became god of battles, but was at this date still an agricultural deity. On the same stone, together with the remainder of the inscription, is what I take to be an ear of corn which bears the name of the goddess Shala, a Sumerian divinity later identified with the goddess Babu (or Baba), otherwise known as 'the lady of the corn ear'.

Threshing the Grain

Harvest was followed by threshing. There were two alternative methods. The Egyptian one was to use a flail, and the god Osiris, a divinity of agriculture, commonly carries a flail as if it were a sceptre. The other, which was also employed in Egypt and which the Babylonians seem to have preferred, was to tread out the corn, which was spread out on the threshing floor and was then trampled by the hooves of a number of oxen or donkeys moving round and round, until the grain was completely separated from the chaff.

There was a variant of this latter method, involving a simple mechanism which the Romans knew by the name of *tribulum* and which can be seen in the Near East to-day. This consists of a thick plank of hardwood with a notched surface resting on the ground, the front end being slightly raised, and the notches having driven into them a very large number of jagged splinters of stone. There is a seat on the plank for the driver of the animals pulling the *tribulum*, which revolves on the threshing floor until the grain is separated from the chaff. It is all the more likely that this device, which is still in use in the area to-day, was employed by the Mesopotamians of the late Assyrian period, since there is evidence of its use locally at a far earlier date.

Among the royal tombs of Ur was one called the Queen's tomb, in which were discovered the remains of a vehicle drawn by wild asses. This formed part of the funerary offerings which included servants and animals ceremonially sacrificed for the occasion, while the 'King's tomb' contained the recognizable traces of the body and wheels of a chariot. The vehicle in the Queen's tomb, however, seems to have had no wheels, no trace of them having been found. The reconstruction of the remains by their discoverer, Sir Leonard Woolley, suggests a kind of sledge or fairly tall wooden chair on short runners, with a raised point at the front. This is a very unusual type of vehicle, which can only be tentatively compared with the funerary sledge of the Egyptians, itself a memory of a distant past when the wheel was still unknown. Sir Leonard's reconstruction, however, which is the inescapable conclusion resulting from a meticulous observation of the existing remains, amounts to an elevated seat, with short runners. It is therefore entirely unlike a sledge, the main features of which are a low-slung body and much longer runners. In profile this reconstruction far more closely resembles the *tribulum*: and it is noticeable that much of the evidence from the tomb is suggestive of objects of magical significance and associated with fertility cults, such as jewels in the shape of ears of corn, pomegranates, and bulls. In this environment a *tribulum*, if it is one, would not be out of place.

After threshing was over, the grain was stored in silos. The evidence of impressions of very ancient cylinder seals from Susa shows that farmers had arrived very early at the best shape for a silo, namely, high and cylindrical: a shape indeed which has remained unaltered to the present day. Some of the silos are shown with a ladder attached, to enable the grain carriers to climb up and empty their sacks into the top, while there was no doubt a little trap door let into the bottom so that the required quantities could be quickly drawn off. It should be noticed that these silos rest upon a latticed wooden foundation, no doubt as a protection against both the dampness of the ground and also the attacks of rodents, some kind of barrier being fixed to the uprights.

Sale and Loan of Grain

The trade in grain which, together with dates, formed one of the staple articles of commerce, naturally gave rise to a large number of documents such as receipts, loans, taxes payable in grain, exchanges, and records of expenditure on grain for consumption by servants or live stock. The following are a few examples:—[11-14]

(*a*) 'Measures of barley to be supplied in one single payment in the month of Siwan, at the temple of E-anna at Uruk, and in accordance with the measure appropriate to E-anna. In the 32nd year of King Nebuchadrezzar's reign.'

(*b*) 'A simple acknowledgement of a debt of barley: but, since it amounts to 136 *qurru**, there are two guarantors.'

---

* = approx. 540 or 270 bushels, according to the value of the *qurru*. [Translator's note.]

(c) 'A promise to exchange barley against an equal quantity of dates, at E-anna, where the documents are to be kept and returned when the transaction is completed.'

(d) 'A debt of barley. If it cannot be repaid in grain, then to be repaid in silver at Babylonian rates. In the tenth year of King Darius' reign.'

Finally there is a report recording the requisition of some labourers sent to Babylon to guard a quantity of barley, and a warning to them that in the event of any insubordination they will be answerable to the governor of Babylon.[15]

The numerous texts which deal with loans of grain, whether for food or for sowing, are most helpful in our attempts to establish a firm chronology, since they almost always include a clause to the effect that the borrower is to repay the grain by a given date, at harvest time. Now since the Babylonians used a lunar calendar, their months consistently fell slightly in arrears and were only occasionally in a true relationship with the seasons. On the other hand while, as has been said earlier, it is possible to calculate astronomically the date of an eclipse, or of an occultation or a heliacal rising of the planets, these phenomena recur periodically and a choice may lie between two or possibly three alternative dates. As an example, if we imagine that we are using a lunar calendar with months shorter than their real length and that we do not know which of two alternative dates to choose, if we find 'the grain is to be repaid in the month of August at harvest', we can immediately discard the date when 'August' fell in the winter, in favour of that when it came at the proper season: and the calculation based upon the dates given in the tablets enables us to select one single date from a number of apparent alternatives with a fair expectation of accuracy.

Live Stock. The Donkey

The help of a really useful working animal can double a man's output. It is therefore important to know what animals were available to the Babylonians for this purpose.

Then as now throughout the East, the donkey, which had been known since the earliest times, was by far the most generally used for hauling or carrying. It was never fully replaced by the horse, which always remained a 'noble' animal and one of which no breed like the modern carthorse was known. Not until the Sassanian period were good weight carriers successfully bred, capable of bearing both a horseman in full armour and their own caparison, which covered them with metal plates. At their first appearance, during the first dynasty of Babylon, we find horses drawing fighting chariots. One of the reasons for the success of the invasions of Asia Minor by the Hittites, of the Caucasus by the Hurrians and of the Zagros by the Kassites, was that they brought their horses with them from the high plateaux and that their fast moving chariots, which represented a weapon hitherto unknown, were effective in use and demoralizing to the enemy. Later on, but only during the Assyrian period (and no doubt as a consequence of the invasions of the horse-riding peoples who conquered Western Asia in the second half of the second millennium B.C.), mounted infantry became a recognized element in the army and this soon developed into true cavalry.

The Wild Ass and the Horse

During the third millennium B.C. the wild ass was used for the military purposes to which the domestic donkey was obviously unsuited. Herds of these animals, of the species known as onagers, roamed freely through the countryside. They were hunted by the Assyrian kings, and the British Museum reliefs show them flying headlong before a shower of arrows. The Greek writers, especially Xenophon in his account of the March of the Ten Thousand, noted that they were still to be seen. The onager stands slightly higher than the donkey, and has distinctly larger ears than a horse. Its tail, like a donkey's, is long and fleshy, whereas that of a horse is short and only looks long because of the length of the tail hairs. Obviously when the picture is as small as the engraving on a cylinder seal, it is extremely difficult to discern differences of this kind, but on larger scale sculptures the characteristic tail is always recognizable. In the Royal Tombs of Ur, the repository of so many treasures, a rein rest has been found decorated with a statuette in electrum which unquestionably represents an onager, while an examination of the remains of the animals which were harnessed to the 'sledge' (or *tribulum*) of the Queen has proved them to be onagers beyond the slightest shadow of doubt.

When horses grew common in Mesopotamia, they came from

the north and north-east. The inhabitants knew this well enough for, having no Sumerian word for them, they described them in a periphrasis translatable as 'ass of the north-east' or 'mountain ass'. This was indeed the region from which they continued to come, and they were reputed to be among the finest in Asia Minor or the table lands of Persia.

We can read in Herodotus of the value placed upon the 'Nisaean' horses from Media,[16] which were larger than other breeds. By the Persian period, the horse had long been acclimatized, and the Satrap of Babylon, who ruled the wealthiest province in the Empire, owned a stud of locally-bred horses which—Herodotus is again our authority[17] — contained 800 stallions and 16,000 mares.

The breed whose characteristics have been preserved on the monuments of Mesopotamia was a medium-sized animal, light of build and slender of limb, whose forequarters stand slightly higher than its hindquarters, a feature always carefully recorded by the artist. The Louvre contains a well preserved bronze bit, believed to be of Assyrian origin, hinged and with curved side pieces.[18] It is so heavy and large that it must have ruined any horse's mouth and it is difficult to believe that it was used on animals as highly bred as the Assyrian horses. Unless indeed it was a votive bit, it is tempting to suggest that it belongs to the later Sassanian period when the horses were of a much heavier breed. Probably the earliest horse to be acclimatized in Mesopotamia was slightly different from that known in Iran, in the southwest of Elam. This latter was a small horse from the steppes with a head resembling that of a camel and a short and straight mane, known as Przwalski's horse. A small mother-of-pearl picture of one has been excavated at Susa.[19] It must have been related to the breed whose harness trappings have been discovered in what are known as the Luristan tombs, after the district in Persia where they were found. Many of the tombs contained the bit of the occupant's horse. Occasionally it was ceremonial, but more commonly it was made for use. These bits were very elaborately engraved, and consisted of a straight bar linked with two very broad side pieces attached to strips of leather. It should be noticed that the distance between the two side pieces, which is governed by the width of the horizontal bar, would only fit small horses with narrow mouths, i.e., quite different animals from that suggested by the bit in the Louvre. Except in North Mesopotamia, horses were not stabled at all during fine weather but were kept in large courtyards, in which stones have been found fixed at intervals in the ground and fitted with a ring to which the horses could be tethered. The remains of a stable, alleged to be that of Solomon, have been discovered at Megiddo in Palestine, which under the monarchy was a busy transit point in the horse trade.

The evidence of the bas-reliefs shows that whether Assyrian horses were to be ridden or to draw a ceremonial chariot, they wore a most elaborate harness, covered with plumes, fringes and bells (Plates X, XIII). We shall return to this point when we come to describe the court and the Assyrian army (p. 125).

Cattle

A number of different species of cattle were known in Mesopotamia. First, there was *bos primigenius*. This variety, which was widely distributed, had large horns which grew straight out from its forehead, then sweeping backwards and finally curving again and ending in tips which pointed forward. It was the most common breed and was the ancestor of the oxen of modern Mesopotamia.

The second variety was *bos bubalus*, or the buffalo, with horns jutting forward from its forehead in a great curve. This was native to Asia Minor and reached Mesopotamia at the time of the Akkadian dynasty, where it lived mainly on the plateaux. It is fierce by nature, and can still be seen in large numbers in the Tigris and Euphrates basins. It is, however, less widely distributed than *bos primigenius*. It seeks shelter from the heat by plunging up to its head into any water hole which it can find, leaving only its snout exposed for breathing.

A third variety, now extinct, was the huge and savage bison, which slightly differed from, but had affinities with, the American bison. It was in fact probably dying out even by the beginning of the historical period, for its memory was commonly associated with the legendary heroes, and it is often depicted beside them on the monuments recording their exploits. (Pl. IV.) The great winged bulls, the tutelary genii which guarded the gates of Khorsabad, represented a memory of the bison, which can be recognised by the thick hair covering chest, neck and flanks; and the forequarters of the bulls which are represented on the

capitals of the columns of the Persian period at Susa or Persepolis
are derived from the same source. The bison, which was far the
most dangerous animal in Mesopotamia, began to disappear first
in the south. Some specimens were preserved in the Imperial
parks in Russia until the Revolution and a certain number are
still most carefully preserved in Poland.

The last variety was the hump-backed ox, which came originally from India. It probably did not become common until the
late period, but there are some monuments which prove that it
was not unknown, even if rare, at a very early date.

Sheep. Goats. The Milk Industry

Many varieties of sheep and goats were bred in extremely large
numbers in Babylonia, as we can see from the earliest monuments
onwards. One breed had no horns, another had long hanging
ears: a third had horns which seemed both to grow from one
point. This third variety, which is that always depicted on the
early monuments, was dying out at the beginning of the historical
period.

Mention of cows, ewes, and goats brings us to the milk industry.
A bas-relief from the temple at Al 'Ubaid, dating from the first
dynasty of Ur (first half of the third millennium B.C.) shows its
different stages. Near a shed made of reeds (for the method of
building see p. 26), the cows are being milked, and the Mesopotamian fellah, the milker, sits, as he does to-day, not beside, but
behind the cow or goat. When all the milk has been drawn, it is
put in a large narrow-necked jar and rocked by the cowman with
a regular movement. This takes the place of churning. When the
butter has clotted, the milk is poured off into another vessel
through a strainer, in order to catch the butter, which is tightly
packed in a wide-mouthed jar. These different processes are
performed in the country to the present day.

In Assyrian all fat is described simply as 'fat'. When the phrase
is unqualified or is accompanied by some term implying excel-
lence, it means butter. Other forms of fat, like that derived from
the sesame plant, are explicitly described. Some of the butter-
making processes which we have just described are depicted in
an abridged form on certain cylinder seals: sometimes there is a
row of little circles beside the shepherd and his flock, and these
represent pats of butter, or rather, of cheese.

When the flocks were of a substantial size, each animal would be branded with its owner's mark. Flocks owned by temples were marked with the symbol of the divinity who owned them: thus those belonging to the god Marduk were marked with a spade, and those belonging to the goddess Ishtar with a star. On the eve of the outbreak of the 1914–18 war all the flocks belonging to the Sultan were still branded with a crescent.

There is little to be said about the pig. It was not forbidden on religious grounds, as it has been since by Islam, but it was not bred as intensively as it is in Western Europe to-day.

The Camel

No survey would be complete without a mention of the camel, which had been known in the country from the earliest times. It had originally been introduced into Mesopotamia from Arabia, but it was not widely used till the first millennium B.C. and more especially the period of this book. While it was still comparatively unfamiliar the Mesopotamians used a periphrasis to describe it, as they did for the horse, calling it 'the ass of the sea' or 'the ass of the south'. It is seldom mentioned in any texts and it looks as though at this date the donkey was still regarded as

Loading a camel

more suitable for large-scale caravan transport. The camel continued to be closely associated with the nomadic Arabs, and a tribe might come, in case of necessity, complete with their camels. When first the kings of Assyria, and later those of Persia, wanted to invade Egypt, which involved crossing the deserts between that country and Palestine, they came to an arrangement with the Arabs who undertook, by means of their camels, to supply the army with provisions and water. The punitive expeditions against the Arabs by the Sargonid and neo-Babylonian monarchs resulted in the capture of large numbers of camels, the price of which consequently fell very low in the Babylonian markets.

All these tame animals were looked after by shepherds assisted by their dogs. They were housed in cattle pens where they could find shade in the heat of the day and, even more important, protection against the wild beasts which were always eager to attack the flocks.

Shepherds and Sheep Dogs

Shepherds leading animals from their flocks, and carrying a whip with a handle of thick plaited leather and a long lash, are often depicted on cylinder seals. Their sheep dogs, whose powerful build, large heads and heavy dewlaps recall 'Bordeaux mastiffs', are often found upon terra cotta plaques, but the best likenesses, which show their characteristics in great detail, can be seen in the sculpture in the British Museum of the preparations for a hunt, dating from the reign of Ashurbanipal, or in the votive statuette dating from the reign of King Sumu-ilu of the first dynasty of Babylon, now in the Louvre.

The countryside was not entirely safe, and we know, from a receipt dating from the fourteenth year of the reign of King Nabonidus, that shepherds and their flocks were guarded. This document records that 'four and two thirds minas of silver have been dispatched to pay for supplies for forty archers attached to the shepherds from the month of Elul to the month of Adar'.

Sales of Live Stock

There are numerous texts which throw light upon every detail of the rearing and trade in live stock. We know, for example, of the part played by veterinary surgeons who were certainly in existence as early as the reign of Hammurabi. Not only were they paid on a fixed scale for the different operations which they performed, but there was also a scale of fines to which they were liable if an animal was injured or killed through their carelessness or simply if their treatment did not effect a cure.

Champion beasts of both sexes in the prize-winning class and pedigree breeding stock had individual names. One bull, for example, was called 'Sharur-abi' which means 'the god Sharur is my father', or, more simply and descriptively, 'Canefield Glory'. (See also p. 168).

Smaller live stock was sometimes classified by the colour of its coat. Thus a text reads '18 ewes, 21 lambs, 70 female lambs, etc., say a total of 325 head of white; 10 large kids, 75 goats, a total of

85 head of black: in the thirty-sixth year of the reign of King Nebuchadrezzar'.

A great many receipts for dead animals exist, and, when there is no question of their being presented to a temple, they may have been the edible ones. The explicit reference in the following text to the cause of death suggests that this may be the case. 'Besides the rest of the small stock, one ewe has been killed. Iddina received it. In the twentieth year of the reign of King Nabopolassar.'

This section may end with some quotations from litigation about domestic animals. 'Judgement relating to the theft of an ewe branded with a star, from the stock belonging to Ishtar of Uruk, included in the flock of the farmer of the goddess: stolen by X . . . and Y . . . in the first year of the reign of King Cambyses and seen in their possession. The animal is to be returned by them. The officer commanding Uruk, the administrator of the E-anna, the assembly of (free) citizens of Babylon and Uruk have ordered that at the end of the month of Tammuz thirty head of small stock besides the ewe branded with a star, which was seen in their possession, are to be returned to the goddess Belit by X . . . and Y . . ., who are responsible for seeing that this is done. In the first year of the reign of King Cambyses.'[20]

Or again: Subject of litigation. 'One ewe which has kidded and one goat, together comprising two head of stock branded with a spade and a writing stylus (symbols of the gods Marduk and Nabu) belonging to the flock of the farmer of the god Nabu, were removed from the dwelling of X . . . The tribunal has summoned X . . . who deposed "on the sixth day of the month Ab, in the fourth year of King Cyrus' reign, the two animals were sold to me for two and three quarter shekels by the farmer of [the god] Nabu." The tribunal summoned the farmer of [the god] Nabu, who deposed "I sold these two animals to X . . . for silver and no one else but X . . . bought them from me. I sent the money to my centurion."* In the fourth year of the reign of King Cyrus.'[21]

Wild Animals. Hunting

The wild animals against which protection was required were

---

* This refers to the customary division of the population for purposes of levy into groups of ten, twenty or a hundred, according to their occupation or profession. [Translator's note.]

lions, panthers, wolves, hyenas, foxes, wild boars and jackals: and as we have already seen, where farming was practised on a large scale, armed guards, charged with the duty of providing defence against robbers and wild beasts, protected the shepherds. These animals generally attacked the flocks and herds in the farmyards or, as the wild boars did, in the cultivated fields, and, unless they were wounded, would not usually stand their ground against men. This was true of the lions, which were of a smaller species than the African variety and are now extinct in Mesopotamia. Later in this book we shall describe lion hunting under the kings of the Sargonid dynasty; on the impressions of early cylinder seals they are shown at bay against hunters who are launching showers of heavily feathered arrows or thrusting at them with hunting spears. At the same time attempts were also quite commonly made to catch wild animals alive with the object of making them into household pets and taming their young. This must account for the use of the curiously pointed arrows which were still in use at the period of the Royal Tombs of Ur, in which a number have been discovered—triangular in shape, the point being replaced by the slightly concave base of the triangle. This kind of arrow could stun small animals on impact and thus simplify their capture, while larger animals would be weakened by repeated loss of blood and so be taken comparatively easily.

Traps were also used, consisting of concealed ditches dug in the paths leading to water holes, which animals of every kind, seeking to relieve their thirst, would make for with fatal consequences.

Some animals could, however, be tamed as pets, among them gazelles, antelopes, huge herds of which roamed the country, and ostriches, which were still common in the Assyrian period. One of the most popular traditional themes in sculpture of the late Assyrian period is the fight of the hero against wild beasts, whose place is frequently taken by the ostrich.

Road Transport

Our description of life in the countryside turned our attention to navigation on the canals, and it is also relevant to overland transport. But whereas in the modern world the increase in weight of the loads to be hauled makes their transport ever more dependent upon a steady increase in the number of roads, we have seen this to be by no means true of the conduct of commerce in antiquity, when, apart from a few great roads between important centres—and we do not know what they were really like—there were no roads in the modern sense, but only tracks worn by the traffic which created them and virtually dictated by the nature of the ground.

In desert regions, advantage was taken of the firmness of the soil, but elsewhere tracks twisted in order to get round obstacles, particularly the marshes, and approached rivers in the vicinity of fords. When the original surface had entirely disintegrated through wear and tear, a new path was, if possible, made close beside the old one, failing which a completely new track was gradually created.

Transport vehicles in the Assyrian period were, generally speaking, few in number and extremely small, being to all intents and purposes merely small carts capable of carrying little more

Prisoners in a cart

than a few sacks. Apart indeed from fighting chariots (pp. 124–6) it is evident that even the vehicles which carried the army's stores were hardly more substantial, and that the baggage train consisted for the most part of the kind of light carriages depicted upon Assyrian bas-reliefs. Prisoners were followed by small two-wheeled carts, drawn by oxen or donkeys, carrying the women, the children who were being taken off to captivity, and a few household objects.

Caravans

The principal means of transport, however, continued to be the caravan. The animals travelled in single file over difficult ground,

and the donkey drivers themselves carried their share of the load.
The introduction into Mesopotamia of the camel, which could
carry so much greater loads than the donkey, had a tonic effect
upon the caravan-borne trade. We can see how much this meant
in a later period (first centuries A.D.), from the prosperity of
Palmyra, by examining the scale of customs duties which the city
published: this scale lays down the taxes payable on goods carried
by donkey and by camel respectively, and the latter is about five
times the former. The rapid growth in trade in Assyria was
powerfully assisted by the fact that camels, which before the
Assyrian period had been worth roughly one and two thirds
minas of silver, became so common as a result of the military
campaigns and raids carried out by the Sargonid dynasty, that
eventually they cost only half a shekel.

EVERYDAY LIFE

The Morning Greeting

Given the fundamental differences in temperament between the
Babylonians and the Egyptians, we can hardly be surprised by the
fact that we scarcely possess any of the innumerable little documents, meticulously detailed and sometimes breathing an agree-
able sense of humour, from which we derive our detailed knowledge of the latter. Egyptian tombs are full of scenes of everyday
life with some words of humorous comment: even in death they
kept their sense of humour and their zest for life. In marked
contrast, when a scene of Mesopotamian domestic life finds its
way on to a bas-relief, it is only incidental to the main theme,
which is always the glorification of the gods or of a king. There
is no apparent interest in the common people as such, and the
little light which is thrown on some aspects of family life comes
to us incidentally. Thus it is from a curious medical text that we
can infer that Babylonian families kissed each other when they
said good morning. The intoxicating effects of alcohol were well
known, and medical opinion took them seriously, treating drunkenness as though it were a case of actual poisoning. The formula
gravely declares 'If a man has drunk too much strong wine, if his
head is confused, if he forgets his words and his speech becomes

blurred, if his thoughts wander and his eyes are glassy, the cure is to take (here follows a list of eleven drugs), and to mix them with oil and wine at the approach of the goddess Gula (the evening): in the morning before sunrise, and before anyone has kissed the patient, let him take the draught. He will recover.'[22]

The Toilet. Hair and Beard

The bulk of any account of the toilet will be taken up in a description of the comparatively well-to-do. As we shall see later, the palaces and the rich households had their bathrooms, but the ordinary working folk performed their hasty ablutions on the canal banks or in the water cisterns in the courtyards, occasionally varying the routine with vapour baths after the Scythian fashion, which consisted of pouring water on very highly heated stones in a sealed room, massage and the use of terra-cotta instruments which took the place of the strigils (scrapers) of the ancient world. All levels of society, however, except the very lowest, regarded it as an essential feature of their toilet to anoint the body and the hair with oil. This served the double purpose both of softening the skin, which was irritated and chapped by the dry atmosphere and the all too frequent sand storms, and of destroying vermin in the hair. The oil stifled the nits and the parasites, which were as heavy a scourge in ancient Mesopotamia as they are to-day in the East and in many western countries as well. It is quite remarkable how commonly, as the bas-reliefs show, people of all classes wore a full beard and thick hair.

The Sumerians were clean shaven: the Babylonians, however, wore beards, those of the populace being short and those of high officials long and square cut. This was, indeed, the fashion among most men of mature years, in marked contrast to the smooth lips and shaven chins of a considerable number of male citizens. When the Assyrian bas-reliefs were discovered, these beardless, somewhat full-faced men, revealing a slight tendency to fat, were no sooner noticed than they were taken to be eunuchs, who were a regular feature of eastern courts. On the other hand scholars also pointed out both that there were a great many of them and that they often comprised complete military units, and at last it was generally agreed that the difference was merely a conventional way of distinguishing the ephebes, or young men (which would account for the frequency of their appearance among the servants and the soldiers) from the older men who must have comprised the veterans in the army.

Leaving aside the members of the court and high officials, whose way of life we shall examine in the second part of this book, a comparative study of the bas-reliefs shows what a variety of hair styles existed in Mesopotamia in the Assyrio-Persian period. The style favoured by the native inhabitants, though on a smaller and less elaborate scale, seems to have followed the fashion set by the palace, while that patronized by foreigners, with whom the country was swarming in consequence of the slave and caravan traffic, was simpler and less sophisticated.

Soap

No description of the Babylonian toilet would be complete without mention of that indispensable product soap, under the disappearance of which on to the black market France was smarting a few years ago. Pure, high quality soap was unknown to the Babylonians, but they had either a home-made mixture or one which was on sale generally and replaced the home-made product. As early as the third dynasty of Ur, the clay tablets mention, among the allowances assigned to certain individuals, the oil of a plant which has been identified as a kind of rush, the ashes of which contain soda or potash and are still used to-day for laundry work. By mixing these ashes with oil and pure clay a product resulted not unlike the soap in occupied Europe. As we all know, it was less a detergent than an abrasive.

The Barber

Our discussion of hair and beards leads on to the profession of barber (*gallābu*), whose name in Sumerian meant 'the high hand'. He not only did the work of a modern barber, but he also shaved both the priests and the devout in the manner prescribed by ritual, as well as the slaves, either so that the tonsure might be an identification mark additional to the usual brand, or to prepare the skin where the brand was to be applied. A symbolic significance attached to a person's being thus shaved : the laws tell us that if a son or an adopted son renounced his parents with the words 'you are not my father, you are not my mother', they might have him shaved and sell him as a slave.

Masculine Dress

When we come to consider the clothes worn by Babylonian men, we have the description by Herodotus not of court dress but, which is more to our present purpose, of the clothes worn by the man in the street. It was, however, even more characteristic of travellers of his age than of those of to-day that Herodotus, with his subjective point of view, should try to express himself in terms intelligible to his Greek audience. In his own words, the Babylonians wore 'first of all, a linen tunic which came down to their feet, then a second, woollen, tunic, and, on top, a white cloak. They wear sandals, peculiar to Mesopotamia, which bear some resemblance to the boots worn in Boeotia. They wear their hair long: they wind turbans round their heads and they scent themselves all over. Each man carries in his hand a seal and an elaborately worked staff, carved with some device such as a ram, an ewe, a rose, a lily or an eagle: no one carries a staff without its individual device'.

The custom of carrying a staff, described by Herodotus, is attested by the evidence of the bas-reliefs. These, however, portray only the most important personages and notably the king, and the stick in question is not a walking stick but a tall staff, symbolical of power. None of the representations which we possess, however, shows any trace of elaborate working. There is no direct evidence to show whether free men, whom there was no occasion to depict upon bas-reliefs, apart from those who formed part of the royal entourage, were in the habit of carrying staffs, but it is likely enough that they did so, for the practice is not unknown in certain areas of the Semitic world, for example in Abyssinia.

This description applies mainly to the well-to-do section of the population, as one might meet them in the streets going about their business. The clothes worn by artisans and labourers, however, were much less elaborate, consisting of a knee-length tunic with half-sleeves, caught by a belt at the waist. This tunic was worn not only by artisans, but also commonly by foreigners. Workmen engaged in transport or building are often shown on bas-reliefs wearing these clothes. By an odd coincidence, of the two colossi of Khorsabad, which are believed to represent the hero Gilgamesh, one is wearing this simple tunic, while the other is wearing in addition a long half-open tunic reaching to the

ground, below which the first tunic is visible. (Pl. XIX.)
More elaborate clothes often had one of the edges decorated with
a tasselled fringe.

The footwear consisted of flat sandals with an enclosed heel,
fastened to the ankle by a thong passing between the big and the
first toes. We will leave a description of the jewellery which was
worn till we come to deal with palace society. The usual hair
style of the populace was a plain band which passed round the
forehead and kept the hair tidy, or sometimes a very complicated
affair which seems to have been a kind of close-fitting bonnet
made of separate shaped pieces. The care with which the sculptor
shows it as moulded to the head suggests that he was not attempting to depict a turban which is, by contrast, bulky. The turban
was indeed known at this period, but the form worn by the
artisans consisted, not of a long piece of fine material wrapped
round the head, but of a short and narrow strip knotted on top.

Feminine Fashions

Women's dress was extremely simple, being long and con-
cealing the figure. Developments in fashion must in fact have
taken place, but no striking changes are perceptible even over
long periods of time and there was nothing like the rapid variations to which we are now accustomed. In the early Babylonian
period women's clothes, which consisted of garments closely
resembling those worn by men, were remarkable for the fact of
being always slightly more highly developed than men's clothes.
In the earliest phase, in representations of religious ceremonies,
men are often depicted as naked while the lower limbs of the
women are covered by a piece of material gathered into the shape
of a skirt. At the next stage the men wear a piece of material of
varying length covering the lower half of their body, while the
women's left shoulder is covered by the fold of a garment: while
in the final stage of development, when the men wear a garment
which, like the Roman toga, left only the right arm bare, both
the shoulders of the women are covered by the ends of the
material, which is gathered in front.

The Seal

The seal (Pl. V) was an absolutely indispensable possession,
since it was the means by which the authenticity of a document

was established. Every Babylonian outside the lowest classes possessed his individual seal, which might be of either of two different shapes. The earliest known examples date from a period before even the invention of writing. At that date they served as a personal identification mark, being used in a variety of ways not at all unlike official seals of the present day, whose authority is moral rather than physical. When a Mesopotamian left his dwelling, he fastened the door to the doorpost with a cord on which he dabbed a little clay and stamped it with his seal. This would show him when he came back whether anyone had visited the house in his absence. Seals were used in the same way to stamp containers, particularly jars of food, and a large number of fragments of broken seals, which had been used to protect the contents of the jars, have been discovered in the course of excavations. When a jar was filled, the opening of the neck was covered with a piece of linen secured by several turns of string round the neck. The whole was then covered with a layer of soft clay and the owner impressed his seal at various points upon it. It is especially interesting to observe this method in use in the very early period, not only because it is evidence of a definite degree of evolution, but much more because of the evidence which it affords of a psychological condition of belief, which might almost be described as a generally accepted faith in the protection of property by the law. It is when we begin to try to define this law that we find ourselves in difficulty.

It is tempting to think that behind it lies the easily intelligible concept of divine protection, always invoked as a first step by a primitive population. According to this doctrine, the city is the property of the god chosen as its protector. The rulers of the town, even if they bear the title of king, are no more than the viceroys of the god, whose authority, in a material as well as a moral sense, remains supreme. The temple is his dwelling, exactly as the palace is that of the king, and his powers are those of a man, or rather, a superman. The Mesopotamian accepted —and later in this book we shall examine both the concept itself and its consequences—that the representation of an action connotes a reality which lasts as long as does the representation itself: if, then, a seal bore a device which was a sufficiently convincing emblem to be accepted as a representation of the god, and the impression was altered, the first victim of the injury was the god under whose protection the object had been placed: and this would be followed by divine wrath and divine punishment. It is likely enough that this idea may have played its part in the process of protecting property merely by a seal, the breaking of which could, no doubt, moreover set in motion the civil authorities directly responsible for the protection of the population.

The second form which the seal took, equally well and indeed perhaps better suited to the plastic material on which the impression was to be made, was the 'cylinder seal', consisting of a small cylinder usually made of stone or terra-cotta, with some pattern or miniature scene engraved upon the curved surface. If it was rolled on fresh clay, the pattern could be indefinitely reproduced in relief no matter how large the surface to be covered, thus assuring the complete and absolute protection which it represented for the object which bore its impression.

Throughout its long history the inhabitants of Mesopotamia, in this no less than in many other practices, demonstrated their conservative outlook in the form of the seal which they adopted. As early as the protohistoric period the first type to appear was the stamp seal. This was followed almost immediately by the cylinder seal, which remained the only type in use until the end of the late Assyrian period, when it was replaced among the

---

Key to Plate V

1 and 2. Seal and impression of Darius I (actual size).
3. The goddess Ishtar as 'Lady of battles' standing on a lion with a bow in her hand and with palm trees and ibexes. Eighth to seventh century B.C.
4. Seal of Mushesh-Ninurta. King and griffin-demon with sacred tree; above, the winged disc (symbol of the god Ashur). *c.* 850 B.C.
5. Mounted huntsman in military uniform with solar disc and the Pleiades.
6. Winged figure and winged bulls. Eighth to seventh century B.C.
7. Officer eating a hurried meal, standing and holding a bow in his hand. A servant fans the flies. Ninth to eighth century B.C.
8. Cappadocian tablet showing a letter and impression of a seal.

Babylonians by the return of the stamp seal. Both forms of seal were in use among the Assyrians and the Persians. During the two and a half thousand years of Mesopotamian history, the themes of the devices on the seals changed, as they were bound to, but not their spirit, which, in the great majority of instances, remained primarily religious.

Meals. Bread

The meals eaten in modern Iraq will give some idea of Mesopotamian diet in the Assyrian period. No special room was set aside as a dining-room, and meals were eaten from a tray placed either on the ground or on a low stool, as and where hunger dictated, and not at any fixed hour. The meals themselves were for the most part extremely frugal, and the poorer classes can have been no better off in that respect than they are now. The staple food was bread, if that is a correct translation of one of the signs for food. In any event it was the foodstuff which took the place of bread, though we can only guess what it was really like. All that we know is that in Mesopotamia 'bread' was sold neither by the loaf nor by weight, but by volume, which is some reason for thinking that the food in question may have been a kind of crustless floury substance, like the Italian *polenta*. It is, however, quite likely that, even if this was true of the earliest historical period, by the Assyrian epoch bread was baked in the form in which it is still found in the East, namely, in a kind of lightly-cooked pancake, the two sides of which separate in the heat of the oven. A number of different varieties of bread are moreover found at the present time in different parts of the Middle East. One variety is made by sticking flat pieces of dough to the walls of a hot oven to which they adhere until they are fully baked. The nomad tribes, on the other hand, eat bread baked in the shape of large pancakes on a convex metal surface. This is placed slantwise over the fire with the curved surface upwards and the extremely thin layer of dough bakes very quickly. Yet another variety of bread is eaten in Iran. This consists of long flat strips made by spreading a layer of dough on a bed of extremely hot stones laid on a hard and smooth piece of ground. The mass of dough, which is parboiled rather than thoroughly baked, is scorched at the points where it touches the stones. When we were digging in Iran we found that our workmen often ate nothing beyond these last two varieties of bread, which are indeed cruder than the variety first described, though Europeans often prefer bread in pancake form. To vary the monotony, the workmen sometimes ate the two alternately.

We have accounts, dating from the third dynasty of Ur, of the quantities of food distributed on one day in the month to various recipients. They usually received a quantity of slightly over one gallon of 'bread', together with some onions, which were then, as in the East to-day, the normal flavouring for bread. The onions were sold in strings, like garlic nowadays, and were eaten raw like cucumbers.

Drink. *Beer and Palm-wine*

Drink was also distributed at the rate of just over a gallon a head. This consisted not only of a kind of beer derived from a barley base, but also of palm-tree wine, obtained by tapping the top of the trunk of the palm tree and collecting the sap. At this stage it is comparatively innocuous, but it ferments and becomes extremely intoxicating after a lapse of two or three days. The Babylonians made a distinction between fermented and un-fermented liquor.*

Wine

The answer to the question whether the Mesopotamians and Babylonians knew of and drank wine, is that the vine was not fully acclimatized in northern Mesopotamia until the first millennium B.C. From that period onwards, however, not only are there a large number of tablets recording a wine trade, but there were regular vintages, whose popularity varied according to their district of origin, those which aged without fermenting being especially highly esteemed.

The vine was originally regarded as deriving from the mountainous country of the West, notably Lebanon, whose growths are still among the most highly appreciated in the East. In the

---

* There are a number of vegetable juices with a sugar content, e.g., grape juice and the juice extracted in Mexico from the American aloe (agave), called in Mexican *pulque*. When the aloe is about to come into flower, a stem as large as a small tree begins to grow from the centre of the plant, which, if left to reach its full height, will throw out flowering sprays at the top. If, however, this stem is cut when it is beginning to grow, the juice, which would have fed the flower, will flow for several days and is collected in gourds. At this stage the juice is sweet and bluish white in colour, but soon fermentation sets in and it becomes very powerfully alcoholic.

Gilgamesh epic, the hero, in the course of his wanderings to the coast, reaches the marvellous country where the vine grows, and the poet briefly remarks upon the beauty of the shrub whose clusters of 'lapis lazuli' are 'fair to behold'. Gilgamesh has, in point of fact, come across black grapes. It is worth noting that, in his travels, he finds his way to a semi-divine being, a tavern keeper, who advises him to live a joyful life. The same profession is ascribed to a woman who was supposed to have been the founder of an ancient and wealthy dynasty in the town of Kish near Babylon. Since the Code of Hammurabi shows that the actual profession of tavern keeper was not at all respectable, the allusion is clear confirmatory evidence of the existence of a large-scale wine trade originating in the countries bordering the Eastern Mediterranean. During the earliest periods in the Near East, it was usual to associate a successful technical advance or invention with the name of some character who was regarded as its initiator, and in all probability these tavern keepers personified one of the most important forms of commerce between the coast and the interior of the country. It also affords a good example of the fondness of the Mesopotamians, and indeed the Semites in general, for puns. The front of a harp discovered in the royal tombs of Ur is engraved with pictures of a number of animals in human attitudes and engaged in human occupations. The lion is presiding over the gathering, the bear is dancing, and the ass is portrayed as musician, just as he is in sculpture of the Romanesque period. Bringing up the rear is a little gazelle holding a wine jug and a cup, the significance being that in Akkadian the same word *ṣâbitu* is used for both 'gazelle' and 'tavern keeper'.

The Palm Tree

We have already seen that palm-tree wine was regarded as an important feature of the Mesopotamian economy, and we must spend a little time in considering the palm tree itself and its cultivation, since it was one of the principal sources of natural wealth. From the earliest period, the inhabitants knew both how to get from it all that there was to get, and also how to cultivate it. A text dating from the reign of King Shu-Sin, of the third dynasty of Ur, and originating without doubt in Umma, the rival city to Lagash, refers to 'the well watered' palm plantation. This lay between the two towns and was divided into eight sections which belonged to the local god, whose representative for this purpose was the superintendent. The trees in each section were numbered in batches, fruiting and immature trees each being noted, while the absence of any mention of male trees suggests that the pollen was bought from other palm plantations. The text refers to the yield by volume and not by weight, and judging by the number of trees, it seems to be little more in weight than half what would be expected from the same number of trees at the present-day average of about eighty pounds per tree. This suggests either that the majority of the trees in the plantation were young or that methods of cultivation have made a considerable advance since then.

Every part of the palm tree was put to some use. The wood was employed for light building construction, such as roofing where only a small span was required, the plaited fibres formed ropes of remarkable strength, while the leaves were used both for covering the huts made of palm boughs, and, when cut and bound together, make very effective brooms for use against the all-pervading dust of the East. Nor was the date itself a mere sweet-meat, as it is in Western Europe, but a food, and indeed the staple article of diet in those districts where the palm tree grew most abundantly. The dates, which were dried before preservation, were packed tightly into jars inside which they coagulated and began to ferment, which enhanced their nutritive value. Alternatively, they could be mixed with oil, which meant that they could be preserved still longer, while their food value was yet further increased.

There are so many different varieties of date palms that markets in the East offer a wide choice of dates. Their stones, when dried, are used as fuel, especially for metal smelting, or, when ground up, are part of the feed of camels, a fact which will not surprise anyone who has seen the animals eating the leaves of the Barbary fig tree (*opuntia vulgaris*), thorns and all. Finally, the 'palm sprout', the growth at the top of the palm tree, if picked and eaten when still young, is a popular vegetable. It is indeed not surprising that the literature of the ancient world is full of complimentary references to the palm tree. Strabo refers to a Persian song which extolled the three hundred and sixty uses to which it could be put, and Kasvini quotes the following extract from the Koran 'Honour the palm tree, for it is your father's sister: and it has been given the name of the blessed tree because it was created from the remainder of the clay of which Adam was made'.[23]

The fact that palm trees can be of either sex, has led to improvements in methods of fertilization, whereby natives collect the pollen from the conical male flowers and tie it into place on the female flowers. This results in increased yields which would otherwise have been left to chance.

The surface of the trunks is rough, and the normal method of climbing to the top, which is often shown on Mesopotamian bas-reliefs, is for the climber to tie a rope round both the trunk and his body, and then lean back and literally walk to the top, the rope being raised at each step so as to hitch itself on the projections immediately above. This can be seen on a fresco from the palace of Mari dating from the beginning of the second millennium B.C., on which, beside a naturalistic representation of palm trees, there are carvings of long stems from which clusters of flowers are springing at some height above the ground. These stems closely resemble those of the aloe (see footnote to p. 72).

The so-called Fertilization of the Palm Tree on the Bas-reliefs

Some Assyrian bas-reliefs depict palm plantations in process of destruction by soldiers (an early example of 'scorched earth' policy!); others show a scene of which the true significance was at first misunderstood. (Pl. IX.) This depicts some genii carrying a receptacle with a handle, shaped like a small bucket, and holding in their right hand a conical object which they are pointing at a network of lines dotted with palm-rosettes. This is a purely stylized and conventional representation of the 'sacred tree',[24] which is a variety of palm. The reason for this will be discussed in the chapter on religion: all that need be said now is that the palm tree as represented here has shed all its normal characteristics. The palm-rosettes have the general appearance of a fan of feathers or *flabellum*, and the stem has become a flat pilaster surrounded by a kind of trellis attaching the palm rosettes to the body of the tree and linking them in regular tracery.

The fact that, though stylized, the tree is undoubtedly a palm tree, and that the object which the genie is holding resembles in shape the pollen-bearing element of the male palm tree, has led some scholars to the view that these bas-reliefs referred to the act of fertilization from which the country's wealth in food was derived. There are, however, reasons why this view cannot be accepted. Thus the genii are merely pointing the conical objects which they are carrying, in the general direction of the tree, while fertilization depended upon the male flowers being tied down on the female, and not on one light contact. Elsewhere the bas-reliefs show the genii standing behind the Assyrian king and pointing towards him the object which they are holding. On the other hand, remembering that in certain churches in the Mardin region, in the north of the ancient Assyria, the priest uses a holy water sprinkler in the shape of a cedar cone for his sprinklings of lustral water, we may fairly conclude that the two actions have the same significance, and that the bas-reliefs represent ceremonial sprinklings (which were a feature of Assyrian religion) of the life-giving water drawn, it was said, from the mouths of the Tigris and Euphrates; while the container with handles which the genii are carrying is not a basket but a wrought metal bucket, holding the purifying water.

Vegetables, Fish and Meat

A rather better meal than one which consisted merely of onions might have included vegetables such as lentils which, like beans. have always been grown in the area, boiled millet, barley prepared as we prepare rice, and possibly maize; while some botanists have expressed the opinion that sorghum can be identified in the clumps of plants of the corn family depicted on certain Assyrian bas-reliefs. A detailed study of the best preserved sculptures shows that the dishes round which the common people are gathered to eat are topped by what appear to be pyramids of grain, presumably of these varieties. Other common vegetables included pumpkins, cucumbers and melons, whose number and variety astonish a traveller on his first visit to the East (Pl. VI).

Fish, eaten both fresh and dried, was an important element in Assyrian diet. A wide range of edible varieties was to be found in about 2000 B.C. in the market at Larsa, including possibly a few sea fish, which must have been packed in salt for carriage, and some caught in the lagoons, which would present fewer transport problems. Most of the fish must, however, have been caught locally in the canals.

The larger fish were dried by the method shown on Egyptian bas-reliefs, i.e., gutted and filleted and hung on a line, as is still done in Norway. Smaller fish were left in the sun and then compressed into a solid block, from which the required quantity could be cut off. Among other discoveries at Tello were some still easily recognizable fragments of this dried fish.

As far as we know meat was not an important item of diet, and the texts which record the charges payable on a sheep or even an ox suggest that often the animal in question had not been slaughtered but had, for example, been killed accidentally. In most texts, moreover, there is no mention of the carcass being delivered to the butcher for sale. Poultry, on the other hand, was eaten, and during the period of the third dynasty of Ur we find geese and duck being supplied to the palace.

Locusts

Locusts, then as now, were considered to be edible in the regions which lay in the path of their invasion, and a relief from Khorsabad shows servants serving them on skewers, just as frogs are served in France today.[25]

Attendants carrying locusts on skewers and pomegranates

Cheese, Confectionery and Fruit

This may be the place to mention the many different kinds of cheeses and curds. They were served at the palace in a great variety of shapes and many of the moulds used in their preparation have been discovered in the dairy of the palace of Mari.[26]. Confectionery, whether sweetened with honey or with sugar derived from the palm tree, which the Mesopotamians also regarded as a kind of honey, was the subject of a flourishing trade, which included delicacies such as sesame fried in oil. Sesame seed was also used by confectioners.

The varieties of fruit most commonly eaten, other than dates, included grenadines, medlars, apples, pears, apricots, plums, and pistachio nuts—in short, the same varieties as grow in Western Europe (some of which, like the peach and the cherry, come from the East) and which flourished in Northern Mesopotamia. We do not know whether the Assyrians knew of the banana, which is grown on a large scale in modern Syria, but it is at least possible, for there are bas-reliefs which show, among the food on the tables, an object which appears to consist of a number of finger-like sections joined at their base, somewhat resembling a bunch of bananas (p. 132). If so, they were probably imported.

Crockery

The crockery in everyday use, which was of earthenware, included the shapes which recur in every age, plates, deep and shallow dishes, and pots and jugs. Glass was known in the Assyrian period, but it remained a rarity and was not used for bottles or for drinking glasses. Earthenware goblets were used in place of the latter, while instead of bottles there was a variety of jugs, cups, handled vases and narrow-necked jars, which could be sealed with a linen cloth and a clay stopper if the contents required preservation. Fewer wine strainers have been recovered by excavation from this period than from the earliest historical periods when a kind of fermented drink with a heavy sediment of dregs was commonly drunk. This sediment was removed by means of strainers and funnels, the most elaborate examples being found in the royal tombs of Ur, while drinking through tubes is often to be seen on monuments in Mesopotamia. A very unusual form of wine strainer is known from specimens found at Tepe Sialk, near Kashan, and Tepe Giyan, near Nihavend, consisting of a kind of spout, shaped like a segment of a circle and divided in two by a pierced vertical barrier. It was held by a perpendicular handle and could be tilted to the required extent. The wine was poured in at one end and emerged, strained, at the other, while the curve of the vessel made it possible, by adjusting the angle of tilt, to regulate the flow.

Pottery from excavations of the period still includes a large number of vases with more or less pointed bottoms. They must have been made to stand upright in loose earth or else have been placed upon a stand of wood* or a circle of plaited straw, but the simultaneous presence of a large number of flat-bottomed vases makes it hard to see why this far more useful shape had not been universally adopted.

On the question whether the Mesopotamians ate sitting or lying

---

* Or pottery. [Translator's note.]

on couches, we know that the Romans, who sacrificed reclining, alleged that the practice had been introduced from the Orient. Surviving documents on the subject prove that Mesopotamians of the upper classes ate seated (p. 132)[27]. The lower orders either squatted or sat cross-legged on the ground round the dish or dishes.

Strong Drink

As we have seen, indulgence in strong drink sometimes resulted in drunkenness, and there are descriptions, evidently founded upon precise observation, of every stage of the symptoms or at least the warning signs. In the poem of the Creation, during a banquet the gods, under the influence of alcohol, became talkative and excited. In the epic of the hero Gilgamesh the wild man Enkidu, destined to become Gilgamesh's companion, is introduced to civilization by a temple prostitute, and one of the first ideas which he acquires is that of drinking fermented liquor. 'He drank of the beer: he drank thereof seven times: his spirit was liberated and he cried out with a loud voice: his body was filled with well-being and his face lit up.'

In point of fact, what with their drinks made from barley and palm-tree wine, as well as real wine, the Mesopotamians possessed a range of drink hardly less potent in its effects than those of to-day, though not their equal in quality.

LABOUR AND TRADE

Relations between Buyer and Seller

We have observed the daily life of the Mesopotamian, living at home with his family. Now we must watch him in the wider world of business, and for this purpose we will imagine him making his way through the town in search of merchants or craftsmen.

The Babylonian view of the relationship between buyer and seller is clearly implied in the terms in which each is described. The seller is he 'who gives, who delivers', while the buyer is he 'who fixes the price'. This description of the part played by the buyer seems, especially to European thought, in flat contradiction of the whole idea of modern commercial practice. It is, however, in fact strictly accurate in relation to the law of supply and demand which regulates dealings in free societies, and it is in truth the buyer who in the last resort 'fixes' the price, whether he yields to the insistence of the seller (in which case his acceptance of the price admits the value of the object bought or the service rendered) or whether he bargains for and finally acquires it at the price which he offers.

The Doctrine of 'Responsibility'

An extremely important feature was the concept of responsibility in respect of the object sold. By definition the seller tends to divest himself of such responsibility, and the generally observable modern tendency is for shipping or railway companies, whether publicly or privately owned, to disclaim under their regulations responsibility in regard to their passengers, while the State comparatively seldom restricts this disclaimer. In Mesopotamia, on the other hand, the protection of the law was extended at all periods to the buyer of an object or a service. Architect, shipbuilder, surgeon, seller of a slave—the responsibility laid upon all of them was prescribed in the Code of Hammurabi, and in the neo-Babylonian and Persian periods there are examples of contracts which at least represent contemporary legal thinking, if not the actual law itself. From the time of Hammurabi onwards an architect who had been in charge of the building of a house which collapsed owing to faulty construction and killed the owner, was himself liable to be put to death, while if the owner's child was killed in the accident, so was the architect's child. Equally the builder of a leaky boat had to repair it at his own expense and pay compensation for damage to the cargo.

The Organization of Labour in Anatolia

From time to time certain individuals engaged in business, whether free citizens, freed slaves, or even actual slaves appointed by their owners to a specific task, succeeded in outstripping all their rivals. They opened branches and sub-offices, and in short controlled firms in the full sense of the word with interests which ramified through the country and even extended overseas. We can point to at least three examples, from three different areas, of such firms being engaged in a wide variety of transactions and at the same time carrying on a banking business.

At Kul-tepe, in Anatolia, near the modern Kayseri* the business archives of several important merchants have been discovered, preserved in rooms in a huge building which lay slightly outside the actual town, and dating from the beginning of the second millennium B.C.[28] With the help of these tablets, generally described as Cappadocian or old Assyrian, we can reconstruct the operations of a certain Pushukin, who seems to have undertaken every kind of business. If we ask why he and his colleagues in the adjacent offices, all of whom have Semitic names, were established in the Caesarea area, among a population which at that date was not of Semitic stock, the answer is probably that at the period Assyrian influence had spread as far as Anatolia, and that beneath its protection Semitic merchants could engage in business in a wealthy district where commerce was badly organized and which offered the prospect of high profits.

The Aims of Commerce

Moreover, this was not the first Mesopotamian penetration of Anatolia, and we must remember that, behind the recital of conquests and campaigns which we possess, there lay something more than the whim of rulers anxious to enlarge their territories and to satisfy their ambition. Solid commercial motives underlay their expeditions. A half-legendary, half-authentic account of the exploits of King Sargon the First has survived from the Akkadian period, several centuries earlier than the date of the Cappadocian tablets, which enshrines an account of an expedition whose aims were frankly commercial. According to this account, some Mesopotamian merchants had returned to their native land in order to beg Sargon to come and protect them in distant Anatolia where they had settled. The king's generals, no doubt surfeited with campaigning, urged him not to comply, arguing that the distances were great and the route unknown. The merchants offered to lead the expedition themselves. It proved a success, the country was laid under regular contribution, and Mesopotamia had added yet another region to her sphere of influence. The reason for the Assyrian anxiety to control Anatolia emerges very clearly in the thriving businesses conducted by Messrs. Pushukin and Company some centuries later. We should be wrong if we supposed that the gold rushes to California or the

* The ancient Caesarea. [Translator's note.]

Klondyke, or the scramble for precious metals of our own day, are a modern phenomenon. Every age has had its Eldorado, overflowing, or at least believed to overflow, with the wealth its neighbours lacked. Egypt had gold, but no wood : from the time of the Old Kingdom it was Egyptian practice to send expeditions, which were at one and the same time commercial and military, to the Syrian coast to procure the cedarwood of Lebanon in exchange for perfumes, incense and luxury goods. The episode is enshrined in the legend of Isis searching for the body of her husband Osiris, which tells how she taught the women of the country the use of perfumed oils, and the art of hair-dressing, and received in return a huge tree which had enclosed the body of Osiris as it grew.

Mesopotamia too lacked wood and likewise got what she required from the same source. This is the significance of the story in the Gilgamesh epic of the expedition which Gilgamesh made in the 'country of the cedars' (no doubt Amanus), guarded by the giant Humbaba. She lacked metal as well, and we find her merchants travelling beyond the Taurus in their quest for the copper, lead, iron, silver and gold which her own soil could not provide.

Gradually the concept of countries developing in isolation, without contact with the outside world, which represented to some degree the view held by earlier historians of the ancient world, has yielded to a truer realization of the ease of its communications. The caravans, composed first of donkeys and later of camels, moved as rapidly 3,000 years ago as they do now, and they travelled with scarcely less security. The large light-sailed boats which still ply between the commercial ports of Syria, though easily out-distanced by the large steamers which can cross from Beyrouth to Alexandria in a night, scarcely differ from the ships which, perhaps less rapidly but none the less reliably, plied in antiquity on the same run, hugging the shore and lying to each night in the lee of some promontory. The different parts of the ancient East were in touch with each other just as they are to-day: and if travel was less rapid the hazards were little greater. The silk route followed by Marco Polo was already supplying its precious wares to Sassanian Persia and Byzantium. It is a bare century since the steamer has narrowed the seas and naval authority has given them security, and but thirty years since cars first travelled the roads of the Orient. Before then, business was conducted as it had been 4,000 years earlier.

Finally, behind every aspect of commercial expansion, there was one extremely powerful motive, the significance of which we can all too easily overlook. This was the need for spices, which indeed still continues, and for incense, consumed at a prodigious rate by every religious cult, and therefore a product of extreme importance. It was the Egyptians who travelled to the land of Punt (which may have been the Hadramaut and Himyar in South-West Arabia) and brought back with them incense trees, depicted on the temples of Dēr el-Bahrī. It was in response to this need that nomadic peoples settled down to protect and organize the very caravans which they had but lately been raiding: this was the secret of the commercial vigour of the Nabateans and of Palmyra and of the wealth of Himyar and the Hadramaut, who alone remained in possession of gold when their neighbours in Arabia had lost it. At first sight, historical motives might be thought to have altered radically since antiquity: but fundamentally they are the same as they have always been, as we can plainly see, when chance brings to light the reasons for some of the great expeditions of the past.

What, then, was the scope of Pushukin's operations? He dealt in real estate, he advanced money on credit, he dealt in lead, silver, cloth and 'black donkeys', whatever they may have been. Perhaps they were a stronger breed or, since the Mesopotamian donkeys were generally white, the mere colour gave the clue to their origin. Or perhaps the word is simply a Semitic translation of the Asiatic name for the horse, which, though in process of acclimatization, was still fairly uncommon in the Tigris and Euphrates valleys.

The Organization of the Caravan

The Cappadocian tablets throw a good deal of light on the organization and the methods of financing the caravans. The banker-cum-business-man settled his terms with one of the regular caravan owners, or perhaps with an occasional trader, under which the latter collected the animals, arranged for their feeding, and undertook the packing of the goods to be carried. A day was fixed for the caravan to start, and if the trader was behind time his pay was stopped from the day in question. Sometimes the contract stipulated that the caravan owner should convey the merchandise to its final destination, but more often the arrangement was for him to travel to a distant staging point where he handed it over to another caravan owner, who would take it yet farther. The first owner would receive a new cargo in exchange and return to his starting point. Sometimes the caravan owner had to turn himself into an itinerant salesman, buying goods from the countries through which he passed with the proceeds of his sales, in order to sell them again still farther on, and then repeating the process on his way back. The financial arrangements might take various forms. Either the backer might pay all the expenses and take all the profits, paying the caravan owner a fixed salary, or alternatively the latter might take a proportion of the profits. Some security was often demanded from the caravan owner, whose interest in the success of the venture was thereby engaged.

A caravan master would often find himself carrying metal such as lead or silver, which at that period represented merely merchandise and not money. But so close were the links between the different branches of a firm that a letter from a business man in Anatolia might well ask his correspondent in some distant place to deliver grain or metal to its bearer. This is, of course, simply a system of cheques or letters of credit. It is indeed highly probable that the Knights Templars, who have generally been credited with the invention of banking, simply took over and applied to the numerous branches of their Order the methods which had been forgotten in Europe, but which had remained current in the East from the early days.

Business at Nuzu

The second period in which we can get a clear picture of a firm's business activities is during the supremacy of the Asianic peoples known as the Hurri-Mitannians, at Nuzu, near Kirkuk in Assyria.[29] In this case also we owe our knowledge to the archives of a family of business people spanning some four or five generations. Their value to us is enhanced by the fact that since they date from a different period and a different environment from the Cappadocian tablets, they reveal some differences in commercial practice. The great merchant Tehip-tilla, like Pushukin, dealt in everything, but he also ran a separate sideline of his own.

At the period in question the system of fief, under which land was granted by the king, was in force in Assyria. It carried with it the liability to certain forms of service, notably forced labour and military service, but it was held absolutely and could only change owner by inheritance. Tehip-tilla accordingly went in for whole-sale adoption on the grand scale. His adoptive children duly brought him their land, and he in return bestowed on them a present which represented nothing more or less than the dis-guised market value of the land.

Murashu of Nippur

The third era in which we can watch the operations of a great business house is the beginning of the Persian period (second half of the fifth century B.C.), or the end of the period covered by this book.[30] This was owned by a certain Murashu and his children, who maintained hundreds of accounts. The Murashu family were Israelites, and when Nebuchadrezzar captured Jerusalem in 587 B.C. and took the most important inhabitants (including the prophet Jeremiah) into captivity, the Murashus were among them. They managed to prosper during their exile, and their heyday was spent in the city of Nippur during the reigns of Artaxerxes I (464-24 B.C.) and Darius II (423-05 B.C.). The tablets relating to the firm's business are written in cuneiform, but a number of the documents bear, on one side, a summary of the contents consisting of a few words in Aramaic written in ink. At this date only the most highly educated individuals could write cuneiform and Akkadian. The bulk of the population spoke, and, if they could write at all, wrote, Aramaic. Probably the tablets in question were the company's files, and the summary of the contents in Aramaic would enable the clerks to find the docu-ment they wanted and bring it to someone in the firm who could read cuneiform.

There are a number of points connected with the methods of organizing work. Large-scale employers, such as the royal household or a temple, would own slaves among whom tasks would be allocated. There would in these circumstances be no document to record the work actually accomplished, but if the work represented a payment in kind to which king or temple were entitled, some formal demand may have been put forward and we may be able to learn of it from the tablets. No trace remains of day-to-day transactions, but a contract, a promise to sell, a promise of payment by a given date, the letting of a house or a garden, the remission of a debt in whole or in part, the delivery of merchandise to a third party nominated by the buyer—all these cases may have occasioned the drawing up of a formal document which will help to increase our knowledge.

Despite the subordinate condition of the workers, their employers do not seem *ipso facto* to have had unlimited rights over them. We have already seen (p. 42) a summons calling attention to the consequences of negligence. At this period laws were needed to ensure that work was properly carried out.

Rates of Pay

There were no fixed rates of pay, and it is difficult to judge their value with any accuracy, since, in the absence of money, all payments were made in barley. This was meant to maintain the worker, any balance which he did not eat being exchanged for other necessaries. By the time of the Sargonid dynasty and the neo-Babylonian and Persian periods, contracts were drawn up in terms of silver, which, though perhaps not actually minted coinage in the modern sense, was no doubt at least in the form of little slabs or ingots stamped with some symbol guaranteeing their weight. The evidence is however insufficient for more than a rough assessment of the relative values of goods and services.

Forfeits

There was one more, but less common, type of payment, which tended to disappear towards the end of our period. This, as applied for example to a workman, consisted in giving him the raw materials he needed for the work he was doing, and letting him retain, as payment, any surplus remaining after the proper execution of his task. Thus, during the Akkadian monarchy, an armourer received a certain amount of metal to make helmets, together with oxhide for the lining, and wool for the inner padding. At that date helmets completely enclosed the head and would have injured the wearer unless they had been padded. When he had completed the stipulated quantity of helmets, the craftsman kept as his pay the surplus metal, leather and wool. The text recording this transaction makes it possible to calculate the weight of a helmet of this date and to judge that it was about the same as that of the helmet worn until recently by the dragoons.

Finally, since the great landowners, such as the palace or the temples, owned most of the country, the owner often took care to specify the shops from which his dependents bought what they required. He often indirectly paid his workmen by various distributions of provisions, a method which was common during the third dynasty of Ur. We have already cited the tablets recording the allocation to each recipient of what we call bread, of fermented liquor, sometimes of dates and of a certain amount of oil and soda ash, no doubt in lieu of soap (pp. 66, 72).

Overseers

No matter by which of these methods work was organized, a large number of overseers were obviously required. At the period of Urukagina, who was a noted reformer, there were, by his own account, no longer overseers of ships or of herds in the whole of the area which was under the authority of the city of Lagash. We have a pretty good idea of those who existed during the third dynasty of Ur, typified by 'the man with the stick'—a title which conjures up a vivid picture. Moreover, the kings of the Assyrian period took good care to leave a pictorial record of the transport of the huge winged bulls which flanked the gates of their palaces, among the other great tasks which they commanded to be executed. A bas-relief in the British Museum shows the official in charge of the operation perched on the colossal figure to which long lines of men are yoked, and carrying his trumpet, just like a modern foreman with his whistle during the laying of railway lines or electric cables (Pl. VII). At the end of our period gangs of workmen were under the charge of overseers whose titles reflected the number of men—ten or a hundred—under their orders.

The Cost of Living

No inquiry into this topic can of course do more than provide a mere set of figures; it can give no useful basis of comparison with modern conditions. We must begin by setting out the system of weights and measures most generally used in Babylonia and Assyria. This qualification is necessary because there could have been no universal system of the kind at a date when the

Mesopotamian cities exercised a greater degree of independence than did the cities of medieval Europe. In the Middle Ages, for example, the *livre* of Tournais and the *livre* of Paris were both in current use, and old and new systems of measurement existed side by side. Even to-day, the bushel, the 'setier',* the perch and the 'quadroon' are still in use in France alongside the units of the metric system. In ancient Mesopotamia indeed, besides the units in local use, there was a series called the 'king's weights', which the royal household might or might not use according to whether it was paying or receiving. In the Persian epoch the great banker Murashu, whom we have met before (p. 85), had his own system of weights and measures. Making allowance for the period and the country, we find the following units of measurement embodied in contracts. (All English equivalents are approximations.)

Table of Weights

1 *she* (grain)			$\frac{3}{4}$ grain ($\frac{1}{600}$ oz.)
1 *shiklu* (shekel)	=	180 *she*	$\frac{3}{10}$ oz.
1 *manû* (mina)	=	60 *shiklu*	18 oz.
1 *biltu* (talent)	=	60 *manû*	67 lb.

In the neo-Babylonian period, the *she* was no longer used as the basic unit, and small quantities were expressed as fractions of the *shiklu*, the smallest being $\frac{1}{24}$ *shiklu*, or one *obol*.

Table of Volumes

1 *sila* (or *qa*)			$1\frac{1}{2}$ pints
1 *massiktu* (or *pi*)	=	60 *qa*	11 gallons, or $1\frac{1}{3}$ bushels

(in the neo-Babylonian period the *massiktu* was reduced to 36 *qa*).

1 *imêru* (donkey load)	=	100 *qa*	$18\frac{1}{3}$ gallons, or $2\frac{1}{4}$ bushels

In Babylonia the *qurru* (*gur*) of 180 *sila* (= 33 gallons or $4\frac{1}{10}$ bushels) was used; but the *sila* was often reckoned at about $\frac{3}{4}$ pint, which would make the *gur* about 16 gallons or 2 bushels.

* A measure of liquid and grain: about two gallons or twelve bushels. Similar anomalies will occur to the English reader. [Translator's note.]

Measures of Length

1 *ubânu* (finger)	⅔ inch
1 *ammatu* (elbow) = 24 *ubanu*	15½ inches
1 *kânu* (cane) = 6 *ammatu*	7 ft. 10½ in.
1 *gar* = 12 *ammatu*	15 ft. 9 in.

In Babylonia the following measurements were also used:

1 *ashlu* = 10 *gar*	157½ ft. (52½ yds.)
1 *bêru* = 1800 *gar*	5¼ miles

Measures of Area

1 *musarû* = 1 square *gar*	27½ sq. yds.
1 *iku*	⅚ acre
1 *buru*	15 acres

Areas of land were also expressed in terms of the quantity of grain required to sow them, i.e., in *pi* and *imêru*.

It is clear from these variations, of which only the main ones are noted in these tables, that comparisons can only be made in very broad terms.

The Standard of Exchange

The basic medium of exchange, as we have already explained, was barley, and in the early period this was how the purchase price of silver or lead was expressed. Its place was gradually taken by silver, measured not in terms of a coinage, which had not yet been invented, but purely by weight. The invention of money is generally ascribed to Lydia: but the decisive moment was the first occasion when business was transacted in terms of small silver ingots stamped with some device (the 'head of Ishtar' or the 'head of Shamash'). Sennacherib (706–681 B.C.) was actually striking coins of small denominations when, as he records in his Annals: 'I caused a mould of clay to be set up and bronze to be poured into it to make pieces of half a shekel' (= ⅐ oz.) The first coins with a wider currency in Western Asia were Persian 'darics' (called after King Darius), but from the moment that they were 'invented' these coins exercised the same functions as bullion in the Western European economy during the past thirty years, never leaving the State treasury except when used in settlements between two countries or for the payment of mercenaries. All other transactions were conducted in terms of silver, either by weight or, from the date of the Seleucid monarchs onwards, in a minted coinage. Silver was the standard of value: and if a debt was repaid partly in gold and partly in silver, the proportion of the total paid in gold was expressed in terms of silver.

In the period of the neo-Babylonian Empire, an examination of the contracts reveals the following ratios of value between silver and gold and silver and other metals—[31]

Silver	Gold	Date
15	1	4th year of King Nebuchadrezzar
12	1	7th year of King Nabonidus
8	1	7th year of King Nabonidus
10	1	8th year of King Nabonidus
13 and 8½	1	8th year of King Nabonidus
		(N.B. these two transactions took place on the same day).
12	1	11th year of King Nabonidus

The only possible explanation of these variations is that they reflect the assessment of the relative proportions and purity of the gold and silver respectively present.

The comparative value of one unit of silver, in terms of other metals, was: copper, 180; lead, 40; Aegean iron (from Cyprus), 240; iron (from Lebanon), 361. This suggests that lead was second in value to silver. The price variation between Aegean or Cypriot and Lebanese iron reflected a difference in quality, and the same reason lies behind five-fold variations in the value of lead. These points need constant emphasis: we must remember that the mere reading of a contract can give us no precise information about the proportions and the degree of purity of the various metals concerned, while all too often we do not even know the scale that is being used. One of the few things that we can say with some certainty is that the weight of a shekel is roughly that of an American 'quarter' (25 cents), or very slightly less than 1 penny (⅓ oz.)

Value of Commodities

We know the price of certain commodities.[32] In the neo-Babylonian period a *gur** of dates cost a shekel, but by the Persian

---

* In this section the *gur* is taken as equal to about 4 bushels, but the reader should remember (p. 88) that in some transactions its value was only 2 bushels. [Translator's note.]

period it cost two shekels. Originally barley was the same price as dates. Later on, it became more expensive, but the price was subject to considerable fluctuations during the year, falling a great deal at harvest time. Garlic was sold by the string, and a contract dating from the reign of Cyrus refers to a single consignment of 39,500 strings. Sesame remained expensive, costing between eight and twelve shekels a *gur*, or about three times as much as barley, while sesame oil cost over a shekel for a quantity which varied from as little as thirty-six *sila* (54 pints or 6¾ gallons) to 145 *sila* (216 pints or 27 gallons), but was generally nearer the lower figure. The vine was already grown in northern Babylonia at this date, and this wine competed with those imported from the Tur 'Abdin district (the ancient Asallu) and from Syria. Good quality wine from grapes (*karânu*) was worth more than eight shekels a jar, whereas the finest date wine (*shikaru*) sold for less than one shekel. Plain wool (*shipatu*) sold at the rate of 2 minas (2¼ lb.) for a shekel during the Persian period, while purple dyed wool cost anything up to fifteen shekels. There is no evidence in surviving contracts about the price of flax and linen, though Strabo (Book XVI, 1, 7) later referred to its manufacture at Borsippa, near Babylon.

The price of an ox was somewhere round twenty to thirty shekels, that of a ram or a goat, about two shekels. A donkey was expensive, averaging some thirty shekels.

From fifty to one hundred baked bricks cost 1 shekel, and so did 600 minas of asphalt (6 cwt.).

Wood, as might be expected, was expensive. In the reign of Nebuchadrezzar, twenty-four cypress logs cost 27 shekels and five talents (3 cwt.) of cedarwood cost ½ mina.

There is a good deal of evidence about the price of metals, and a single transaction covers the following quantities:—

10 talents (6 cwt.) of copper from Cyprus for 3 minas and ⅓ shekel of silver.

37 minas (40 lb.) of lead for 55½ shekels.

16 minas and 15 shekels (17½ lb.) of dyed wool for 2 minas and ⅔ shekels.

55 minas (60 lb.) of lapis lazuli for ½ mina and 6⅔ shekels.

130 minas (1 cwt. 30 lb.) of Cypriot iron for ½ mina and 2½ shekels.

257 minas (2½ cwt.) of Lebanese iron for ⅔ mina and 2⅔ shekels.

The following table shows the variations in the price of slaves though here again we cannot assess this in terms of modern money:—

In the reign of	Average price
Nebuchadrezzar	40 shekels
Nabonidus	50 shekels
Cyrus	60 shekels
Cambyses	1½ mina
Darius	1⅔ mina
Xerxes	2 minas

The value of real estate rose steadily. Whereas in the early period 100 *gar* (slightly over ½ acre) were worth 1 shekel, by the reign of Nabonidus the same sum would buy only about ten or twenty *gar* (260 or 520 square yards). In the reign of Cyrus a garden of 250 square yards cost more than two shekels and little short of three by the time of Darius.

A house with a little land sold for 15 shekels per unit known as the 'cane' before the Persian period: under the Persian monarchs the price was over forty shekels.

Finally, here are a few miscellaneous prices of clothes and household utensils. A robe, 2 minas; fifty small tools, 2 shekels; eleven copper bowls, 1 shekel; two separate lots consisting respectively of one iron spade, one axe, and two unspecified tools; and four chairs and three beds, each lot for 2 shekels in the reigns of Nabonidus and Cyrus.

Rates of pay varied widely. Two temple guards received 34 shekels for a spell of twelve days. Under the Persians, a slave was paid 3 shekels a year, which was the same sum as was paid to four workmen not specifically described as slaves.

Since so few people had capital with which to buy, renting was very common. A boat could be hired for ½ shekel a day, which had become 1 shekel in the time of Darius. This price made allowance for the fact that the boat would be in constant use, whereas if it had been sold, it would have been laid up for certain periods and would not have been worth more than one or two minas. An ox could be hired for 10 *gur* of barley a year, or about ten to twenty shekels: a cottage or a shop for 2 *gur* of barley a year. Finally, the watering of a plantation of palm trees was paid for with a quarter of the date crop, on the principle that the size of the crop would be proportionate to the watering.

The general impression that one derives from the thousands of neo-Babylonian contracts which survive, is that from then until the Persian period there was a clear rise in the cost of goods, land and houses.

Thus Mesopotamia, like the world to-day, was no stranger to rises in price: and we hear the same complaints about high prices, while even the smallest attempt at deflation was strongly objected to, since rates of pay had not the same paradoxical freedom of movement as they have to-day. Mesopotamian legislators made several attempts to fix prices, but a closer examination makes it clear that any success they may have had was quite fortuitous and that they were doing no more than recording with satisfaction the low prices of certain commodities; while for the rest their calculations were no more than good intentions more or less divorced from reality. One is reminded of the dream of Henri IV of France that every Frenchman should be able to eat his chicken for dinner on Sunday.

We need do no more than recall the reformer Urukagina (first half of the third millennium B.C.) who secured a considerable reduction in the fees which the priests were charging for funerals, viz.: 3 measures of drink, 80 loaves of bread, 1 kid, and 1 bed; instead of (as previously) 7 measures of drink, 420 loaves of bread, 120 measures of grain, 1 robe, 1 kid and 1 bed. To confine ourselves to a later period we find Sin-gashid, King of Uruk (who reigned in the first part of the second millennium B.C.) anxious to establish a price of 1 shekel for 3 *gur* of grain or 12 minas of wool or 10 minas of copper or 30 *sila* of oil. Shamshi-Adad I, who reigned during the time of Hammurabi (beginning of the seventeenth century B.C.) records that in his day the regular price in the city of Ashur was 1 shekel of silver for 2 *gur* of grain or 12 minas of wool or 20 *sila* of oil.

Translated into modern terms, and making allowances for the respective weights in the two reigns, these figures would be:—

Sin-gashid: 21 bushels of grain or 13 lb. of wool or 11 lb. of copper or $5\frac{1}{2}$ gallons of oil $=\frac{2}{7}$ oz. of silver.

Shamshi-Adad I: 14 bushels of grain or 13 lb. of wool or $3\frac{2}{3}$ gallons of oil $=\frac{2}{7}$ oz. of silver.

This suggests that in the reign of Shamshi-Adad I there was a considerable rise in the prices of grain and oil, while the prices of wool and silver remained steady. Over a period of many centuries the prices of metals were always changing. Even to-day indeed, while the price of gold is at least sometimes relatively stable, this stability is due to international agreement: by contrast the price of metals like copper, exposed to the effects of the law of supply and demand and sensitive to the factors involved in production, is liable to frequent and violent fluctuations.

Copper and Bronze

It is important to keep clearly in mind the dates of the first introduction of different metals. By the beginning of the historical period, copper was known in Mesopotamia, its sources being Armenia, the Caucasus or Cappadocia,[33] but not bronze, which is an alloy mainly of tin and copper. Although analysis has shown minute traces of tin in certain examples of metal dating from this period, further research reveals traces of other metals as well. All are merely impurities.

When bronze first makes its appearance, in the period of King Gudea and the third dynasty of Ur,* it is sometimes alloyed with antimony, sometimes with tin. Its discovery gave Mesopotamia an extremely valuable metal, both hard and also adaptable to a wide range of purposes, and by the time that iron became a common article of commerce, in about the eleventh century B.C., it was adaptable only to a narrower range of uses than bronze.

Iron, Gold and Silver

The first kind of iron to be worked was meteorite iron, recognizable by its nickel content. It was however replaced by mineral iron.

The sources of both gold and silver, as of the other metals, lay in the north, and as in modern Europe, they remained rare and 'luxury' metals throughout Babylonian history. Continual efforts were made to refine silver and to increase its resistance to the changes which it underwent so readily. Generally as the names which they gave their metals show, the inhabitants of

---

* Bronze was known at the time of the Royal Tombs of Ur, *c.* 2500 B.C., although analysis has shown that examples of the tools and weapons made then contained very little tin. [Translator's note.]

Mesopotamia gave pride of place to gold 'the strong and shining and durable'. Next came silver 'the shining white'. Originally, as we have already seen, silver was simply a commodity, whose value was expressed in terms of barley. This concept was gradually superseded by that of the equivalence of a given weight of silver to the value of goods sold: finally, under the neo-Babylonian and Persian Empires, values were often expressed in terms of shekels of silver. We have already seen the difficulty inherent in having for each separate transaction to weigh the goods on one side of the scales and the silver, representing an equivalent value, on the other, and how the necessity of ascertaining the purity of the metal led inevitably to the shekels being stamped with a mark which guaranteed their quality. The first day that that was done, the principle of money had been discovered.

As a result of excavation we have considerable knowledge of the contents of the workshops of metal workers, armourers, bronze founders, vase-manufacturers and goldsmiths, and of the details of their industry. A considerable part of their activities was concerned with the manufacture of armaments, and we will examine these more closely when we come to consider the army.

The Casting and Gilding of Statues

Statues and bronze surface panels made by bronze founders still survive, and their manufacture demanded the solution of various technical problems which are nowadays negligible. A small-scale piece does not suggest any special difficulties, but it is quite another matter with, for example, the statue of Napir-Asu, Queen of Elam, now in the Louvre, which, even in its present mutilated condition, weighs nearly two tons. The size of the crucibles and furnaces used in modern foundry work makes it a simple matter to keep a far greater weight than this at a constant temperature when the molten metal is poured off. But at the period when the statue was made, in the second half of the second millennium B.C., a whole battery of crucibles must have been required, all simultaneously heated to the same temperature and so arranged as to be successively emptied into the matrix without losing heat in the process. Success must have been the outcome of innumerable false starts and failures. In actual fact the statue of Napir-Asu was probably first cast in two sections, forming the front and the back respectively, and then soldered together, traces of the process being filed away. Despite its considerable thickness, it was not thought to be sufficiently solid, and this was remedied by pouring more metal into the interior of the statue, which had to be turned upside down for the purpose. The first step was to pour some molten metal into the upper part of the statue and then to superimpose upon it a great weight, which was intended to force the molten metal to spread itself evenly. Then still more molten metal was poured over the mass in order to fill the lower part of the statue. The attempt was, however, not wholly successful, and although enough was poured in, the metal filling evidently only partially adhered to the inner surface of the statue. In the course of a sack of Susa, the head, the shoulder and the left arm were knocked off with a blow from a club, these being the parts of the statue to which the metal infilling had not properly adhered.

The degree of technical skill evinced in this statue and in the bas-reliefs suggests that the science of metallurgy had attained a stage analogous to that which remained general until roughly the end of the nineteenth century in Western Europe. But before this stage was reached there was an earlier stage in which sheer manual skill was employed to surmount the difficulties in default of the techniques at our disposal. There is no need to describe in detail the primitive method of carving a statue in wood or in easily-worked bituminous stone and then covering it with thin plates of malleable metal, burnished in order to make them fit closely over the sculpture and fixed in place with tiny nails.

Vases and Jewels

Metal vases in repoussé work were made by hammering from behind the surfaces which were to stand out in relief. If spouts were required, they were either soldered on to the bodies or alternatively fixed in place with large-headed nails, the heads themselves forming an element in the decoration.

Depending on their thickness, bas-reliefs or surface panels were worked either in repousse or by engraving cast metal with a chisel. At the period of this book articles sold by jewellers included rings, earrings, bracelets, and hairbands. They also sold a few brooches, but the nature of work-a-day Assyrian dress, which tended to hang long and straight, made them luxury goods.

Earrings were made in the shape of rings, of bunches of grapes,

Ear-drop

of cones partly covered with a granulated pattern of varying fineness, or of animal or human heads. They were generally made of a very thin leaf metal, frequently in a setting with brightly coloured stones and in particular different varieties of agate, which were found in an attractive range of shades.

Rings might be either plain or engraved, and were often set with a stone. An unusual contract has survived, dating from the thirty-fifth year of King Artaxerxes' reign, which exemplifies the doctrine of responsibility which we have mentioned earlier. The firm of Murashu had ordered a ring set with a precious stone (which may have been an emerald, since its name is not unlike the Hebrew word for that stone, of which we know the Greek translation), and the jeweller gives a guarantee that if the stone comes loose from its setting within twenty years he will pay an indemnity of 10 minas of silver (about eleven pounds).

Bracelets were made in every variety of shape, either in an open spiral or a plain circle, and with open or closed ends. The ends, if open, were carved in some such pattern as an animal's head, while, if closed, they were nearly always decorated with the favourite decorative Assyrian motif, reproduced almost *ad nauseam*, the single or double rosette. This had a symbolical signifi- cance, associated no doubt

Bracelet

with the sun, and was also extremely common on the metal bands which were worn across the forehead to keep the hair in place.

The Potter

The market was the scene of many other crafts beyond those already mentioned in this survey, one of the commonest being that of the potter. The inhabitants of Mesopotamia used clay not only as the raw material of their houses and of their written documents, but also of their pottery. Parallels can be found

among Mesopotamian ware for almost every shape still in
common use, for once a utensil has proved its usefulness, it is
never abandoned, and the basic shapes of drinking vessel, plate
and bowl will endure as long as mankind.

This was however not the sum of the potter's activities. He
also made great jars like those used for storage in oil-producing
countries, which served a variety of purposes, such as storing
food and water: and he even made household equipment like
ovens. He also competed with the carpenter and the basket
maker in the manufacture of coffins, the size and precision of
which always afford evidence of great skill on the part of the
maker. These coffins are sometimes shaped like square vats with
lids, and sometimes boxes wholly enclosed except for a kind
of dormer window in the upper part of the lid, closed by a little
glazed cover, the different panels of which were decorated with
various figures, especially of divinities. Sarcophagi of this type
first make their appearance in the neo-Babylonian period, become
more common in the time of the Persians, and reach the peak of
their popularity under the Parthian Arsacid monarchs.

The Basket Maker

We have made a number of references to basket making. This
craft was closely related to weaving, since a number of products
might be made by either process. The sails of boats might, for
example, be made either, as one would expect, of thick canvas
or of woven fibre, as they still are in the Far East: and the same is
true of the matting which used to be hung by way of decoration
on the lower parts of the walls of houses and secured by long
thick terra-cotta nails with curved points. Other objects manufactured by the basket maker included the round hampers so
common in the East (which gave their names to the round
boats, see p. 46), boxes, and even seats; for the raw material
used by the basket maker ranged from rope-like fibres to the
largest reeds, these latter being exceedingly hard and used either
in their natural state or cut into boards. The cheapest kind of
coffins were made of woven rushes, and so were the crude boats—
or more accurately floats— which consisted merely of a truss of
reeds tied together with cord at each end and braced amidships
with cross bars (see p. 46), which would give their passenger a
wetting but would not allow him completely to sink. During the

third dynasty of Ur, the price of matting seems to have been fixed by reference to the number of fibres in a given area.

Cloth Merchants

A wide range of materials was to be found in the clothing quarter of the bazaar. Until about 1000 B.C., Mesopotamian dress consisted of an undergarment rather like the modern petticoat, called 'the garment of modesty', over which were worn rectangular pieces of material cut to the required size, which could be draped in various ways, the whole ensemble being invariably held together by a large pin. In the Assyrian period, a tunic, or more accurately a number of short-sleeved tunics, were worn one over the other. It looks as if the fashion of wearing stitched clothing, which was normal in the countries bordering Mesopotamia, must have been introduced from abroad during the second millennium B.C., to be followed at a later date by trousers.

Clothes were decorated with embroidery. This was so much a native speciality, that in the ancient world it became generally known as 'Babylonian work'. The kings' robes and those of members of the court were lavishly embroidered all over.

The newer form of dress left small scope for the flowing draperies of the earlier fashion: but a memory of it lingered in the sash which was worn slung across the chest and over one shoulder, with daggers thrust into its folds.

The Confectioner

The confectioner was to be found in the bazaars in the ancient world no less than in the modern. It is true that the surviving business documents hardly mention him, but we can safely infer his existence from our knowledge of the confectioners attached to the temples, who made the sacred cakes which were eaten in large numbers at the times of religious festivals and the cakes which the worshippers of the goddess Ishtar crumbled and left for her doves. We have already described (p. 50) the little model temple in terra-cotta from Cyprus, the front of which, with its regular pattern of little cavities, is an actual dovecot: while coins from Paphos, which bear the device of the temple, show the birds, which are also mentioned by the ancient writers. The principal materials used by the confectioner were different kinds of flour made from barley, wheat or millet, palm-tree sugar, honey, butter made from the milk of ewes or goats (more rarely from cows' milk), sesame seed and sesame oil, and rose-water.

The Seller of Songs

The list of trades is far from complete: but there is one among the minor trades which seems always to have been popular and to which a text provides a clue, namely, the seller of songs, whether sacred or secular. There is a text, earlier in date, however, than our period, which consists of a collection of song titles or their first lines. Here are a few of them:—

'He appeareth, the god of fire, the Lord of battles . . .'

'Thy love is as the scent of cedar wood, oh my Lord . . .'

'Come to the king's garden: it is full of cedar trees . . .'

'Oh gardener of the garden of desires . . .'

'Ah! how plenteous she is, how gleaming . . .'

'In the streets, I saw two harlots . . .'

It is time now to describe the intellectual professions practised by the inhabitants of Babylon. Their services were called upon every day, but they drew deeply upon learning and religion. We shall therefore first examine the great principles underlying beliefs which governed their activities, and then describe their careers.

CHAPTER II

KING AND STATE

The Royal Palace

BEFORE embarking upon a description of the life of a king of Babylon or Assyria, we should try, so far as our knowledge of the royal palaces allows, to reconstruct the physical setting within which he lived and moved. Their main outlines are already known to us, and excavation has revealed such part of them as survives, often comparatively well preserved. They were built of unbaked mud bricks, like the ordinary houses, and time has taken its toll of them. The upper parts were the first to give way, collapsing in ruins inside and outside the walls until the shell of the lower part was completely blocked. The immediate result was that the fallen rubble formed a protective layer covering the remains of the palace, and while we may know nothing of what the upper floors were like, at least we do know the ground plan and possess the lower part of the walls. We have a number of examples of these palaces at Nimrud (the ancient Kalah), at Nineveh and at Babylon, but many of them were abandoned after being severely damaged in war and sacked, or even completely destroyed by fire. It so happens that Khorsabad, which was the first to be discovered, was also one of the best preserved, and since it has been more systematically excavated than the remainder, we may regard it as typical for the purposes of our description.[1]

The Palace of Khorsabad

King Sargon the Second, long, though erroneously, believed to be a usurper, but actually belonging to the royal line, decided to build a palace outside Nineveh, the ruins of which face the modern Mosul, where the summer heat is stifling. The site which he selected was that of the modern village of Khorsabad. He called it Dur-Sharrukin, or Fortress of Sargon, and here, where the atmosphere was cooler and less oppressive than in Nineveh, he gave orders that the building of his palace and of a town should proceed concurrently. Within a few years the work was completed, but Sargon, whose reign was almost at an end, can scarcely have lived there. The probable fate of the palace is shown by the slight traces of fire which are everywhere visible. No doubt it suffered the fate of many other palaces, and it has in fact yielded hardly any easily movable objects which could have been removed by looting.

The Excavations

The story of how the excavations came to be begun and carried on is worth recalling. The French consular agent at Mosul was Botta, who was born at Milan during the period when that city was united with France under the Empire. In his daily walks he used to cross the river and scramble over the mounds which were scattered along the farther bank, where the wind and horses' hooves often used to expose fragments of ancient buildings. They were too insignificant to have attracted much attention, but Botta, who was an educated man, kept abreast of the controversies then current about the site of Nineveh, and he was encouraged by Mohl, the secretary of the French Asiatic Society, to undertake further investigations. He decided to make some trial soundings on the site and began to work at his own expense, but, for reasons which will appear later, his finds were insignificant. Disappointed, and nearing the end of his resources, he was contemplating abandoning the work completely when he was assured by some inhabitants of the village of Khorsabad, about ten or eleven miles from Nineveh, that they had come across some large statues in the course of building operations. Botta made his way to the spot and began digging there in March, 1842. He had been extremely lucky in his selection of his starting point, for on the very first day he struck the outer wall of the palace, and the science of Assyriology was born.

In the light of these results, the excavations were officially sponsored and were subsidized by the French government. The sums involved were not very large, but the franc of the time had not been devalued, and the cost of living in the East was trifling. The Sultan granted a *firman* confirming the concession for the excavations, but there was still the greed and stupidity of government circles at Mosul to contend with. Sometimes the excavation trenches were regarded as military fortifications: on other occasions the extremely unpretentious house belonging to the expedition was considered to be a dangerous fortress, and diplomatic intervention was quite often required. The site of Khorsabad was, in fact, partially cleared and the ground plan was recovered, but, following the accepted opinion, it was drawn on a symmetrical plan, since to the European mind the idea of an asymmetrical palace was (quite erroneously) inconceivable. A Frenchman named Flandin was given the task of drawing everything that was recovered from the ground, and this resulted in the magnificently produced collection of plates entitled 'The Monument of Nineveh', following the tradition of the earlier collection devoted to Napoleon's Egyptian expedition. For Botta believed at the time that he had found the site of historical Nineveh, whereas in reality he had been too precipitate in abandoning it.

It was at this point that the British authorities, who were anxious to enter this field, arranged to take over the site of Nineveh which the French had abandoned, and an agreement was reached under which France nevertheless reserved part of the area. As soon as they began to dig the English exposed the palace of Nineveh, lying only a few inches below the level at which Botta had given up. This was where the difficulties began, for while Botta and Rawlinson, the director of the English excavations, were both out of the district, Rassam, who was in charge of the actual digging, one night explored the part of the area which was reserved to France, and immediately came upon the richest part of the ruins, namely the palace of Ashurbanipal and the 'library', which the British Museum with justice regards as one of its principal treasures. Rawlinson, who was an honourable man and was much upset by what had happened, did his best to allay understandable French resentment by presenting France with several fine duplicate examples of pieces discovered in the English excavations.

In the meantime Botta had concluded his own excavations and, after incredible difficulties, the antiquities selected by the expedition were conveyed to the Persian Gulf by raft and boat and thence shipped to France. On arrival they were exhibited in the Louvre, first of all in the suite of rooms now occupied by the vessel from Amathus*, and subsequently in the suite decorated by Percier and Fontaine facing the church of St. Germain l'Auxerrois, where they still are. King Louis Philippe, to whom therefore we owe the first Assyrian museum in Europe, formally opened the collections in May, 1847.

The Republic of 1848 abolished the consular post at Mosul and there was a break in the excavations, full advantage of which was taken by the foreign expeditions which poured into Assyria. When order had been restored in France by the Prince-President, it once again became possible to think seriously about resuming the excavations, which the academic world, anxious to make good lost ground, was insistently demanding. Victor Place took up the work where Botta had left off, and found fresh monuments which required transporting to the Louvre. But on this occasion luck was against him. The rafts and boats, laden with antiquities, were threatened by native brigands who followed them along the banks. For protection against their attacks they had to stand out into midstream, where they were at the mercy of the cross currents of the flood-swollen waters. They sank practically without exception and almost all the fruits of this series of excavations were lost for ever in the depths of the Tigris mud.

When the excavations first began, the mound containing the ruins was occupied by a village. This was removed to the plain while the excavations were in progress and was restored to its original position after their completion.

Botta's choice from the great number of bas-reliefs which the expedition had dug up was limited by transport difficulties. Thus he was obliged to leave behind those of the reliefs which had been damaged by fire, while he selected the most spectacular of those which were well preserved, like the winged bulls and the monumental colossi. After the necessary drawings had been made he filled the excavations in again, burying in the process the majority of the monuments which he had exposed.

There is no doubt that Rassam's enterprise, to use no stronger word, had robbed France of a priceless treasure, for there is every reason for thinking that, knowing the results which the English had obtained in their concession, the French would have resumed excavation in their own.

But France once again fell behind at Khorsabad when, between

* A town on the south coast of Cyprus. [Translator's note.]

the wars, the Americans secured the concession for the site direct from the Government of Iraq.

The American expedition reopened Botta's old workings. By using his plans they were able to avoid abortive starts, but serious harm had been done to the fire-damaged bas-reliefs by their brief exposure to the air in 1842 and several were found to be past saving. On the other hand the excavation of areas hitherto unexplored showed that the site comprised not only a royal palace in the fortress of Sargon but also a royal town within the main circuit of the walls, which included not only the king's palace but also that of the grand vizier and the residences of other high officials. The expedition was also able to establish the fact, already suspected as a result of the preliminary investigations by Botta and Place, that the town was never fully occupied, for the palace lasted too short a time to become the focus of a large population.

The Plan of the Palace

The first stage in the building of the palace was to take all the precautions exacted by religious belief, to which we shall return later. Then a terrace was built to form a kind of platform designed to raise the structure above the path of the water which might otherwise have undermined the walls when the river and its tributaries were in spate after the snow had melted. Half the palace, including the entrance, lay inside the walls enclosing the town, while the remainder, which was fortified, projected beyond them, thus forming a bastion jutting forward into the plain. The terrace was made of unbaked bricks and for added stability was built with sloping sides. It contained an extremely advanced system of internal drainage which ensured that all moisture was led off into large sewers. The whole of this construction, built in baked brick, has been discovered. The sewers are roofed with slightly ogival vaulting, and consist of a series of slanting courses each resting on the one below, in order to obviate the need for scaffolding, since wood was still scarce in this part of Mesopotamia, while the drains themselves were jointed terra-cotta pipes. This particular feature of Assyrian building is well preserved and was excellently designed; much of the system could indeed be used to-day with little or no repair.

The courtyards were surfaced with flat bricks or with a layer of bitumen or rammed earth. They sloped slightly inwards towards the centre so that water could drain away easily.

Ramps were cut in the sides of the terrace in order to afford access for draught animals and chariots, while foot travellers from the town approached by a broad and monumental staircase. A walk along the terrace beside the palace led to the walls surrounding the town. Towers were set at intervals in these walls and all round the top ran a broad road which both commanded the horizon and was sufficiently wide to allow troops to be rapidly deployed for defence.

The façade of the palace presented the appearance of a solid windowless block decorated with huge apotropaic figures, designed to exert a beneficent and protective influence over the building, and consisting of pairs of winged bulls, good genies guarding the doors, whose looks alone were guaranteed to terrify and keep away all evil doers.

The gateway jutted forward from the rest of the building. It opened into a passage in the wall (see the description of the city gates on p. 38), which had been especially thickened at that point, and this eventually gave access to an interior courtyard. This was an open square with a large number of rooms opening on to it and was used by any messengers, merchandise and troops required by the palace. A rather narrow passage opening off it led to a second courtyard. This, unlike the outer court, was not square but rectangular, with three separate entrances, divided by two massive pillars, on the longer inner side. These led into a rectangular chamber, smaller than the courtyard, and containing the *podium* or raised dais of the king's throne. A healthy alarm was induced in the foreign princes who were admitted into the king's presence by the base of the throne, which was decorated with various representations of the king's wars and victories, such as a pyramid of the heads of his conquered foes piled high before him. There was also a third courtyard with symmetrically placed entrances which must have been used for official purposes. We must remember that the whole of the building, shown on Botta's plan as being in a straight alignment, was in fact slightly trapezoidal in shape and tilted to one side. This should occasion us no surprise, since we now know that our modern ideals of symmetry and balance (though this is no longer quite true, for in their pursuit of novelty, the modernists have not hesitated to hark back to a forgotten past) meant nothing to remote antiquity.

Store rooms opened off the courtyard, in which the excavators found still preserved the great oil and food storage jars, the stock of paint required for the maintenance of the palace and iron in the form of small bars. This last was still in good enough condition when discovered to be used by Botta to make the tools which he needed for the excavations—picks and shovels and tyres for wheels of the vehicles in which the finds were conveyed to the river.

Yet another passage led to a group of buildings consisting of a series of courtyards adjoining three identical buildings, each with an entrance and a single chamber, and, at the far end, an alcove with a brick bench. This was promptly identified as the harem, containing the apartments of the three principal queens, while the brick bench must, it was supposed, have been piled with soft cushions and have served as the bed. This identification seemed all the more appropriate since Moslem law lays it down that, when a man marries more than one wife, they are all to be treated with strict equality, and the three identical buildings were entirely in conformity with this principle.

In addition, however, the courtyard was richly decorated with blue, green and yellow enamelled bricks and with pictures of an eagle, a lion, a fig tree and a plough. The entrance was embellished with columns of carved wood, covered with a coat of bronze which was in turn surfaced with gold leaf to represent the trunk of a palm tree. The inscriptions which were discovered make it clear that it led to the private palace chapels, and the raised benches were not beds, but altars. The existence of a *ziggurat* adjoining this group of buildings was in this context perfectly natural.

Secondary Palaces

Near the end of the palace away from the town, the excavators found a kind of low rectangular terrace reached by a few steps. This has never been conclusively identified, but I am tempted to see in it the remains of a structure derived from abroad, about which the kings often boasted in such phrases as 'I caused a *bît-hilâni* to be built after the manner of the Hittites.' It has been suggested that the *bît-hilâni* were buildings with windows, which existed in Syria while still unknown in Assyria: but from the evidence of the remains in North Syria, *hilâni* always

contained rectangular chambers with a flight of steps leading up
on one of the long sides. Behind the flight of steps two columns
supported a pent roof, thus forming a room with one side open,
while a second room which opened behind the first, was more
probably intended for living purposes. The rectangular terrace
at Khorsabad may perhaps represent the remains of a building of
this character.*

On the side facing the town, the palace was adjoined by other
large and magnificent dwellings, the most imposing being that
occupied by King Sargon's brother, whom he had created his
grand vizier. It is built with the same general lay-out of numerous
courtyards, some surrounded with store rooms, some with bed-
rooms and others again with reception apartments. Facing this
house there were other buildings, their precise purpose unknown,
though no doubt of an official character, as well as a temple
dedicated to the god Nabu, the scribe of human destinies and god
of writing. This temple, with its outer and inner shrines
approached through a great courtyard, was built upon an artificial
mound level with the terrace of the king's palace. The two buildings stood side by side and were joined by a small stone bridge
with an ogival arch.

Gardens and 'Hanging Gardens' of Babylon

The whole group of buildings, including both the king's
palace and the neighbouring royal residences, was enclosed on the
town side by a boundary wall containing two gates of the normal
type, so that the palace area was effectively isolated on every side.
At Persepolis, which was the capital of the Achaemenid dynasty,
holes are visible cut at intervals in the rock of the palace esplanade.
These must have been filled with earth, and trees planted in them
to form a garden. The same arrangement can be seen at Ashur
in Assyria, where Sennacherib ordered a very extensive garden
to be planted. A description of the garden of King Merodach-
baladan was given earlier (pp. 48-9) when we were discussing
Mesopotamian vegetables. There is no reason to doubt that
similar amenities were provided at Khorsabad, but the soil of the
city is light with no underlying stratum of rock, so that no trace
of ancient vegetation could possibly have survived.

* See H. Frankfort 'Origin of the Bît-hilâni' in *Iraq*, XIV, 2, 1952. [Translator's
note.]

Antiquity unhesitatingly included the 'Hanging Gardens of Babylon' among the 'Seven Wonders of the World', though what excavation has revealed of them affords little grounds for such enthusiasm. They were probably terraced and were set on a small hill beside the palace, flanked by the Processional Way and near the Ishtar Gate. On this small hill, traces of wells have been discovered, which suggests that an endless chain of buckets was used to raise the water to the highest point of the terraces. The terraced construction, itself elevated by the siting of the gardens on the summit of a small hill, made the tops of the trees visible above the walls from a considerable distance, and this no doubt helped to perpetuate the tradition of the 'hanging gardens'.

We cannot, however, leave the subject of gardens without realizing that, besides cultivating gardens for purely utilitarian purposes, the kings of Assyria enjoyed creating botanical gardens, containing collections of non-indigenous species—notably the plants and trees of the Amanus mountains. In much the same way the Egyptian kings instructed their expeditions to collect and bring back the rarest species. A *kudurru** from Susa, now in the Louvre, and known as the 'unfinished *kudurru*' because it is decorated but not inscribed, depicts a procession of foreigners escorting the products of their native lands, prominent among them being a box containing a shrub covered with flowers. The figures are also leading animals, since the kings of Assyria were very fond of zoological gardens in which they kept the rare specimens which their vassal subjects had brought, and which were the object of diligent search. A bas-relief dating from the reign of Ashurnaṣirpal (9th century B.C.) depicts some tributaries bringing monkeys, while the gifts which the subject peoples of Assyria are shown bringing to Shalmaneser on the 'black obelisk' include a variety of horned animals perhaps the most prominent of which is an elephant. When the King of Assyria was campaigning westwards and had made his way as far as the Mediterranean coast, he did not fail to make a short sea voyage in order to symbolize his mastery of the ocean, and one of the narrators of the event adds that he captured 'a sea animal called a dolphin'.

Decoration. Bas-Reliefs

The royal palace was, in essence, little more than a huge

* Boundary stone. [Translator's note.]

pile of clay, a raw material intrinsically unsympathetic to artistic detail: but it was the repository of the royal treasures of Assyria. Earlier in this book we have discussed what the bas-reliefs can tell us of the magnificence of the furniture, while the floors were spread with carpets, of which we can get some idea from the carved thresholds. The walls of the less important rooms were decorated with plinths, bands of contrasting colours, spirals and occasionally imitations of marble. But the chief glory was the wealth of the bas-reliefs displayed in the ceremonial apartments, which form the backbone of the Assyrian collections in London, Berlin and Paris. They consist of panels of alabaster, gypseous and very fragile, since when quarried the stone still contains its natural moisture and hardens as it dries. Unfortunately it tends to form plaster by a process of calcination, and throughout history the natives have used it for this purpose in their own buildings.

Large slabs of this stone were built into the lower parts of the walls of the rooms. They were never used for the friezes of which the Greeks were so fond, and in practice such heavy pieces could never have been securely fixed to the unbaked clay of the walls, but would have been bound to fall and to bring down the wall surface with them. The slabs were always placed as panels at ground level and have often sunk slightly into the ground under their own weight. Various features, such as the joins, suggest that they were carved after being fixed in position. So enormous must the total area of these reliefs be (they are calculated at Khorsabad alone to cover nearly $1\frac{3}{4}$ acres) that, at first sight, the imagination reels before the potential strength of an empire which could accomplish so much in so short a space of time; for the building of Khorsabad took only about five years. But we must realize that the work was specially organized with an eye to the greatest possible economy of effort. The decorative schemes for each room, and the general themes, were designed by creative artists. The work, at what might be called the drawing-board stage, was then taken over by craftsmen who both rough-hewed the stone, and each concentrated on his personal speciality. Thus one would do nothing but embroidery, while another would confine himself to carving the details of hands or feet. The fact that the whole relief was carved in silhouette accounts for our finding, as we do on Greek vases, the hands and feet of a number of the figures reversed.

The reliefs were not painted all over, but heightened with occasional touches of colour, especially on certain dress ornaments, while the wall above was either lime-washed or very often decorated with painted geometrical patterns of stripes, triangles and the ever-recurring friezes of rosettes: with lotus flowers or buds; or, finally, with a disc or a rectangle with a concave side, flanked by genies or bulls. The basic themes of the reliefs were strictly limited. One was the king's hunting, a sport which certainly occupied a considerable part of the monarch's time. In a summary of his hunting expeditions Ashurbanipal puts the number of beasts he has killed at thirty elephants, 257 wild animals slain from the chariot, and 370 lions killed with the hunting spear.

Other themes were banquets, the reception of tributary races, and finally war, which might be described as a staple Assyrian industry. We shall find that when we come to consider this subject, we largely rely upon the wealth of documentary evidence provided by the bas-reliefs.

In Babylonia, on the other hand, decoration took the form not of bas-reliefs, but of panels of enamelled bricks. Fragments have been found in the great audience chamber in the palace of Nebuchadrezzar, in the form of vertical dark-blue bands on a lighter background, ending in a kind of capital with two out-turned volutes of yellow ochre. Ancient historians record that the walls were decorated with hunting scenes, and though no remains of them have been found, it is intrinsically quite probable.

The Provincial Palaces

So far we have confined ourselves to the setting in which a king of Assyria resided when in his capital, but he also owned palaces in which he could stay when visiting the provinces. One of the best preserved is that of Tell Ahmar, the ancient Assyrian Til-Barsip, in the north-west of the Assyrian Empire, situated where the river Euphrates bends sharply near Carchemish.[2] Architecturally the palace is unremarkable, having the usual courtyards with rooms or apartments opening off them, and no apparently coherent ground plan: while the passages seem designed to impede communication rather than to facilitate it. But the unusual feature was the complete absence of the bas-reliefs found in the capital, the decoration consisting solely of paintings which reproduced all the themes of the bas-reliefs. There is little doubt that the cost of building and decorating palaces like Khorsabad or Nineveh was very substantial, despite the use of prisoners of war, costing nothing but their keep, for the transport of the building materials, and the employment of far more craftsmen, forcibly removed from their native lands, than of creative artists. The available money had to be kept for the palaces in the capital, and this meant that the provincial palaces must make do with decorations which were simpler and less laborious and did not involve the problems raised by the transport of stone over long distances.

The paintings of Tell Ahmar have unfortunately perished, and the only specimens to have reached museums are few and fragmentary. During the excavations, however, Cavro, the architect of the Thureau-Dangin expedition, which had found the paintings, copied and restored them with great care, so that we possess an exact replica of the decorations of the palace. When this reached Paris, it was first exhibited for a short time at the Orangerie, and then removed to the Colonial Museum, thus giving further proof that the Louvre has not the space to house and display the whole of its collections. There is no doubt that the short-lived scheme for an Oriental museum, which was conceived in the optimism of the armistice, will one day have to be revived.

The inner surfaces of the walls were first made as smooth as their mixture of unbaked clay and chopped straw allowed, and then coated with limewash, while the design was painted in outline and then heightened with colour, though never painted all over. Most unfortunately, however, the limewash has almost entirely disintegrated and perished in the course of time, with the result that the design no longer shows up against its background, while the scraps that have been recovered are valueless except as archaeological evidence. We must remember this fact while considering them in more detail. Here, as elsewhere, the artists have worked with infinite pains to reproduce the decorative themes of the main palaces, and we see the king, seated on his throne and wearing his full regalia, receiving ambassadors and tributaries. One scene shows a tame lion crouching at the foot of the throne. These animals were frequently kept as pets in antiquity. The account of the indecisive battle of Kadesh in Syria, in which Rameses II of Egypt was opposed by the Hittites, describes the valour of the Pharaoh fighting practically single-handed against a horde of foes, but aided by the prowess of his pet lion! Other scenes depict the royal hunts, with their familiar moments of drama and their lions in mid leap. At this period scenes of warfare had not yet come into favour as a subject of decoration, but during a subsequent restoration of Til-Barsip in the reign of Ashurbanipal, when the wars of the monarch were a popular subject, an attempt was made to treat a dashing charge by Assyrian lancers in this manner. But no doubt this was not acceptable and it was painted over with a theme more in harmony with the existing decoration of the palace.

The Americans have discovered important remains of paintings in the palace of the grand vizier at Khorsabad (as we have said, he was also the monarch's brother), one representing the king standing in an arcade in the form of a stele, a scene often reproduced in sculpture in the royal palaces.

The matter may be summed up by saying that sculpture was virtually confined to the largest and most important palaces.

The Concept of Monarchy

At one end of the social scale were the common people whom we have watched at their daily tasks, at the other the king, his court, and the governing classes. The gap between them was too great to admit of any comparison, and obviously a day in the life of the king could not bear the slightest resemblance to that of an ordinary man. Unfortunately we lack the document which we should most like to possess, namely a diary kept by a member of the court like that of Fanny Burney, but although all our evidence is necessarily indirect, we know how almost every hour of certain days was spent by the king, and for the rest, we know his principal occupations.[3]

In our period the Assyrian and Babylonian monarchy derived its strength from a solidly established tradition. First and foremost, monarchy represented the only possible form of government, and however much the monarch might be subordinate to some superior power, the absence of a ruler would have been inconceivable. This is made clear by some short notes by a scribe about certain enemies of the Empire, invaders lurking in the mountains to the north and east, or wandering over the steppes which bordered the Mesopotamian basin. The writer says contemptuously that they had 'no house' (meaning that they lived in tents) and 'no king'. At this date the conceptions of monarchy, whatever the personal characteristics of its holder, and State were inseparable.

The Rules Governing Accession to the Throne

Our knowledge on this subject implies the existence of a highly developed state and religion. We can, however, infer the existence of a more remote period, thanks to an extremely ancient poem which describes the customs obtaining far earlier. This tells the story of the hero Gilgamesh, legendary king of Uruk, who was a kind of Babylonian Hercules and whose exploits are sympathetically recounted in an epic poem (Pl. XIX). Gilgamesh himself, sprung from the union of a mortal and a goddess—and here is the hint of a more distant tradition—is portrayed as a man of prodigious strength, with all the brutality of the savage. He oppresses his subjects, but at the same time he is their born protector, taking up arms against any threat of harm to his people. He launches a campaign against the guardian of the cedar forest, i.e., Lebanon or Amanus, which is a reference in mythological terms to real expeditions intended to open the trade routes to commodities like wood, which were not native to Mesopotamia. He guards his subjects' flocks from wild animals: he is a fearless hunter. He epitomizes the qualities of a primitive chieftain, as the tough and full-blooded guardian of the interests of his community. A memory of this distant epoch is perceptible in the fact that the right to hunt had long been enjoyed by the nobility alone. When the King of Assyria hunted lions with bow and arrow, he performed in sport what had formerly been his duty as monarch.

The Divine Nomination

During the middle of the first millennium B.C. succession to the throne depended not only upon royal descent, but also upon nomination by the gods. The belief had no doubt originated in the frequent and sudden stresses and strains to which, particularly in the East, the hereditary principle was subjected, but its roots reached far back into the past. It was universally known that royal authority rested with the gods, and this was symbolized by the headdress and the weapon, which, as emblems of power, were laid before the throne of Anu in the sky. The point is made clear in another poem (p. 208) in which Etana plans to journey to heaven to steal these emblems by force. He makes the journey with the help of an eagle which he has rescued from its enemy, a serpent, but like another Icarus he is destined never to reach heaven, and overcome by dizziness he falls to destruction on the earth. When the throne was unoccupied, either because a dynasty had come to its close or because of a barbarian invasion, the kingship was regarded as having 'reascended into heaven'.

At this point it was for the gods to mark out the man of their choice. From the earliest period the monarchs based their title upon having been thus chosen: different gods might be invoked in different political centres, but it was generally Enlil, the ruler of the earth, to whom the final appeal was made. Later on, this power naturally passed to the god who ruled the city, and this led to appeals being addressed to a very large number of gods by kings claiming to be the object of divine choice. By the middle of the first millennium B.C. when the individual cities had been absorbed in the two great states of Assyria and Babylonia, their respective gods, Ashur and Marduk, were regarded as having chosen the king, the divine choice being signalized by the god's having looked kindly upon the infant king at his birth: thus Hammurabi recalls that Shamash the god of Justice looked on him then 'kindly, with his bright eyes'. By an extension of this idea, the king could be chosen at the moment of conception. 'The goddess queen of the gods', in Sennacherib's words, 'chose me while I was yet in the womb of my mother who bore me.' The king could even be chosen long before birth. When in the second millennium B.C. the Elamites captured and carried off the statue of the goddess Ishtar in a successful campaign, the goddess 'chose' to be brought back to E-anna, about 1,500 years later, by him who was destined to be King Ashurbanipal of Assyria. The choice had to be accomplished by 'a name propitious to royalty, a good name'. Eannatum, who lived in the first half of the third millennium B.C. and to whom we owe the Stele of the Vultures, already boasted of this appellation. From this it follows that though it was important to belong to the royal line, if only because legitimacy eased the way to inheritance, this was not in itself enough the supreme importance attached to the divine choice. Usurpers

like Neriglissar of Babylon or Lugal-zaggisi, who ended the
supremacy of the Akkadian dynasty, based this claim upon the
favourable regard of the gods and a propitious name.

The divine nomination necessarily meant that the individual
selected as king was the personal representative of the god who
ruled the town, a kind of viceroy appointed to govern in place of
and on behalf of the god. Thus the king had always retained a
double responsibility, both for the cult of the god and for the
successful conduct of affairs, the latter function being in truth
only one aspect of the former. For this reason, in the archaic
period the rulers of the towns assumed the title of 'viceroy'
(in Sumerian, *pa-te-si*, which is now read as *ensi*), and only
gradually assumed the title of king (*lugal* meaning 'great man');
while their assumption of additional ceremonial titles such as
'King of the Four Regions' (the four points of the compass) or
'King of the World', symbolized by the areas lying to the north
of Mesopotamia and inhabited by unconquered tribes, was merely
subsidiary to their fundamental character, as the chosen of god
and his earthly representative.

The King of Assyria was not a God

The King of Assyria made no such claims to personal divinity
as the Pharaohs of Egypt or even the Hittite monarch who
ordered himself to be addressed as 'Sun Majesty, my Sun'. No
doubt obsequious courtiers would make a point of telling the
king that he was their Sun, and we find a woman called 'Hammur-
abi-Shamshi' or 'Hammurabi is my Sun': but we must realize
that while the king might be 'the light' of him who invokes him,
he was not the god who was its source, and it is extremely rare
to find an example of a monarch claiming identity with the god
Shamash. Only in certain limited periods of Mesopotamian
history, such as the third dynasty of Ur, and then perhaps under
Egyptian influence, did certain monarchs prefix their names with
the sign which connoted divinity, while by the end of the Assyrian
and during the neo-Babylonian periods, the practice had long
been obsolete, surviving only in the form of a curious conventional claim to be the son of this or that goddess: an assertion
which could hardly carry conviction, since the king's mother
could be seen at the court. The Egyptian Pharaohs did not
hesitate to claim divine descent, despite the fact that everyone

had known their predecessors on the throne. Certain Mesopotamian monarchs, like Agum-kak-rime and Idin Dagan, claimed
to be 'of the race of the god Shuqamuna' or 'son of the god
Dagan', but this must have been a purely formal title, for King
Gudea of Lagash describes himself successively as the son of
Gatamdug, Nina, Nin-Sun and Baba: while during the late Assyrian period we find Ashurbanipal on different occasions claiming Ninlil, Belit of Nineveh and Ishtar of Arbela as his mother.
We should see in this merely a distant memory of the divine
origin of monarchy and divine selection, and an assertion that
divine power had endowed a king with every perfection from
before his birth.

Two qualities were pre-eminent among all those supposedly
inherited by the king, namely strength and understanding, the
latter being especially important. The possessor of wisdom and
knowledge had received the gift of 'great ears'. It was quite
natural that a monarch should be thus endowed, since he was not
merely of divine descent but had been suckled by a goddess.
Ashurbanipal himself had this fact recalled to him by the god
Nabu, who appeared to him in a dream while he was anxious
about the outcome of a campaign. The god reminded the king
that he, Nabu, had entrusted the king as an infant to be suckled
by the goddess Ishtar and he added 'of the four breasts against
thy mouth, two thou didst suck, and in two thou didst hide thy
face'. This episode has the added interest of showing that the
idea of many-breasted goddesses was already current in Mesopotamia, as it was later in Asia Minor and Rome, without any
need to look for a specifically Egyptian influence. In the latter
country Hathor, the goddess of fertility, is further represented as
a cow.

The heir to the throne, supposedly born and suckled by a
goddess, was educated as befitted a prince, and grew up under the
eye of his tutors. The proper education for a child of noble birth
is, I think, summed up on a neo-Hittite bas-relief in the Louvre.
This shows an elaborately dressed little boy standing upon the
knees of a seated woman wearing a long veil, which covers the
back of her head and reaches to her feet. This proves her to be of
high rank, since no servant was permitted to wear a veil of this
kind. Towards the edge of the upper part of the relief, beside the
figure of the little prince, the artist has carved a falcon, with a

cord tied round its foot, and beside it a closed book, which must represent tablets with inner surfaces of wax, which were used for writing Aramaic characters. These two symbols—the chase and learning, physical and mental discipline—seem to me the perfect epitome of the ideal prince's education.[4]

The Nomination of a Successor

At the proper time, the reigning monarch summoned the leading citizens and even some of the common people and formally presented the prince as his heir. They all swore to accept him and amid scenes of enthusiasm the heir apparent then entered the *bît-ridûti*, or house kept for the exclusive use of the legitimate heir to the throne. Both Esarhaddon and Ashurbanipal were appointed heir apparent in this manner and both mention specially the crowds who were present at the ceremony, which may have been swelled by delegations from all quarters of the empire. A similar scene is depicted upon another neo-Hittite bas-relief which was found at Carchemish on the Euphrates, north-east of Aleppo. This shows the king holding his son by the hand and presenting him to the army. The prince's younger brothers are standing behind and the smallest of them is trying to walk, while a nurse is carrying the youngest born, whose pet animal has been brought along as well.

A formal ceremony of this nature was not left to the unfettered choice of the monarch, but could only be performed after the gods had been duly consulted by the priests and had given their consent. As soon as it had taken place, the heir to the throne could act for his father at certain functions and could command military expeditions. Thus, while still only heir apparent, Nebuchadrezzar raised a contingent of troops to accompany the Medes, with whose assistance his father was hoping to make himself master of Assyria. There is a mutilated letter in the Louvre in which he seems to be summoning his followers.

Naturally enough when a usurper, 'no man's son', seized the throne, his champions were forced to omit any reference to the question of legitimacy and to confine themselves to the summons from the gods to the throne, and the favour with which they regarded him. An early example of this was the great Sargon of Agade, who was brought up by a gardener, a fact to which the king refers, adding merely that while he was a gardener he was beloved of Ishtar and ending 'I wielded the royal power for so many years'.

The Coronation

After the death of a monarch two kinds of ceremony, one civil and military, and the other religious in character, attended the coronation of his duly appointed heir. The latter took place in the temple of the god Ashur in the city of the same name. The new king took his seat upon his throne and while the servants advanced, bearing it on their shoulders, the priest of Ashur beat a tambourine and cried out 'Ashur is King', no doubt in order to identify the new king with a manifestation of the god. On entering the temple, the king descended from his throne, prostrated himself at full length on the ground, and set out the censers for the god, at the foot of whose statue he laid a garment, gold and silver, which became the property of the priest. After this the sacrifices were begun. We should not overlook the central part played in the ceremony by the king, who performed the functions of a priest, especially in arranging the table for the sacrifice which was dedicated to the use of the god Ashur. When, however, he had completed this rôle, the priests proceeded to the coronation ceremony proper which, by contrast, emphasised his character as earthly representative of the god. During this he formally received the crown and the emblems of royalty which had, until that moment, been arranged in front of the altar of the god, in imitation of the insignia symbolizing power, which were believed to lie upon a table before the throne of Anu in Heaven.

The King, by now the anointed of the god, then returned to his palace in the midst of the general acclamation which was assured him by the distribution of largesse. There, seated upon his throne, he received the homage of all the nobles, while each high dignitary laid before him his badge of rank and office—staff of authority, purse, or harp, for the chief musician was always a person of great consequence in Oriental courts. They did obeisance to the king, who commanded them to observe the duties of their office. Within the last few decades this ceremony was brought curiously close to us by the formalities which attended the coronation of the Sultan of Turkey, during which the general superior of the dancing Dervishes presented the new Sultan with the scimitar of

Othman as the symbol of his power. There are brief passages which suggest strongly that there must have been close parallels in the enthronement ceremony in Babylon. It is possible that the two types of royal insignia, head-dress and sceptre or weapon, which are distinguished in the texts, may be intended to recall the twin aspects of the king as ruler in peace and leader in war, and that this double panoply may symbolize the two kingdoms of Sumer and Akkad, which were united under single rule in a very early period. Once it was accepted that the king was the god's viceroy, the weapons which were formally presented to him symbolized his obligation to defend the god: a task all the easier to perform as the divine weapons conferred invincibility upon him.

A fragment of a stele in the British Museum, dating from the reign of Tiglath-pileser, depicts two hands emerging from the solar disc which represents the god, one holding a bow and the other beckoning to the king. The implicit idea, of the god's inviting the king to take up his weapon, was one which had long been familiar in the ancient East; in Egypt, for example, as early as the reign of Tutankhamen artists had depicted the rays of the sun in the form of arms embracing the monarch.

We shall find, when we come to consider Assyrian religion in detail, that true believers were always preoccupied with the need to retain divine favour, which they regarded as the only reliable form of protection. This was equally true of the king, and when he says in his inscriptions that the gods regard him with a kindly eye, or when he even boasts of enjoying the love of the goddesses and, as he often does, proclaims himself to be the beloved husband of one of them, the emphasis is more than a mere assertion of dignity. For an inhabitant of Mesopotamia words created facts, and facts acquired reality by virtue of utterance. Besides this the part played by the king in certain ceremonies no doubt gave him good grounds for making this particular claim.

The Secular Duties of a Royal Day. The King's Dress

The scene is set: how did this character, half secular and rather more than half religious, pass his day? In the East even the rich woke earlier than is usual in Western Europe, so as to make the most of the relative coolness; and on waking, the king would proceed to his toilet[5] in the bathrooms which every palace in antiquity possessed as a matter of course. He would be surrounded by a throng of servants, hairdressers and barbers, and his clothes would be brought to him. His dress was in a sense subject to priestly approval, since 'hemerology', or the science of favourable or unfavourable days, laid it down that on certain days the king should not change his clothes, and for others prescribed garments of a particular material or colour. Normally he wore a long embroidered short-sleeved tunic of wool or cotton, or even, possibly, of linen or silk. The wool would be dyed plain or parti-coloured: cotton, made from what the Assyrians called 'tree wool', was the source of highly valued materials which took dye very well, particularly the purple in which the Phoenicians traded so widely. They had the secret of matching the exact shade required as it dried in the sun, ranging from lilac and almost pale rose to deep purple. Some scholars believe that linen was used: but though the surviving commercial documents constantly refer to transactions in wool, we do not meet linen, which suggests that it must have been imported and can never have been common. Silk was already being produced in China at this date. It may have been known as a rarity even in the neo-Babylonian period, travelling stage by stage along the road which was later to be known as the 'Silk route'. We must remember that the ancient world, despite its lack of modern instruments and chemical reagents, was perfectly capable of recognizing the naturally rare raw materials, though they may not have been superficially attractive. Small quantities of iron have been found in the Pyramids: and although it may not have come into general use on the Mediterranean coast and in Mesopotamia before the first millennium B.C., it was already being exported by the Hittites during the second half of the second millennium B.C. One of the foundation tablets of Sargon's palace at Khorsabad is made of magnesium carbonate, and an offertory vase from the Royal Tombs of Ur, which was thought worthy to be placed beside gold and silver, was of calcite. Both these stones are rare in Mesopotamia.

Over his undergarment the king wore an open tunic, richly embroidered and fringed, and a belt, either broad and flat, and worn under a leather baldrick carrying a short sword, or in the form of a twisted scarf with a dagger thrust into it. The embroidery, of metal thread and different coloured wool, must have been a wonderful sight, for, as we have said earlier, Mesopotamia was famous for this work.

'Babylonian work' embroidery has completely perished, unless possibly a fragment is discovered one day in some tomb in the preservative climate of Egypt. We can, however, get a reasonably accurate idea of it from the Assyrian monuments, which we can accept as reliable evidence. The artists employed both patience and scrupulous care in reproducing what they saw, and their imagination was kept under strict control. Indirect proof of this fact is to be found in the Sassanian sculptures in the great grotto of Taq-i-Bostan, near the modern Persian town of Kermanshah. The king who was responsible for the creation of this work of art—some scholars believe him to be Chosroes II* (A.D. 590–628), and others Peroz (A.D. 457–484)—is shown on the bas-relief wearing a tunic covered with embroidery, a prominent feature of the pattern being the dragon-peacock, a fabulous monster with the forequarters of a wild animal and hindquarters ending in a plume of feathers patterned like a peacock's tail. This occurs frequently as a decorative motif in Sassanian art, and the artist might well be supposed to have transferred it to a bas-relief, which he thought needed decoration. It so happens that European museums and collections are full of examples of Sassanian materials. They were all the more eagerly sought since they were of silk, which was not then made in Europe, and during the early middle ages they arrived there in large numbers and in a variety of ways, some by commerce, some as royal gifts, and some as costly shrouds for the relics of saints. Two specimens now in the Museum of Decorative Art in Paris carry identical decoration, which is similar to that on the king's tunic at Taq-i-Bostan, one being woven in two shades of green, the other in dark blue, green, violet and cream.[6]

We can therefore rely on the accuracy of the artists when they depict the King of Assyria wearing garments covered with elaborate embroidery. One bas-relief of many will serve as an example (Pl. IX). On this, as elements in the pattern, we see a winged genie in the attitude of rapid movement, holding in one hand a cup and in the other a garland composed of a plaited spiral ornament which, on the evidence of other reliefs, we can safely assume to represent the waters of the subterranean abyss.

* Known as Parviz. [Translator's note.]

Below is the sacred tree with its horizontal branches, flanked by two winged genies, who are sprinkling it with lustral water. These motifs are surrounded by other scenes depicting, in addition to the sacred tree and genies with the winged bull, a group containing a winged genie, head and chest facing to the front, and apparently kneeling, but actually in the conventional attitude of running, and grasping in each hand the paw of a lion which has seized a bull and is biting its breast. The whole design is symmetrical and is surmounted with a border of lotus buds and shrubs decorated with palmettes, from which flowers are growing.

The king's hair was dressed in the shape of a fez, over which was stretched a piece of material with knotted ends which hung down the back. On his feet he wore open sandals, which left the front of the foot bare, with a loop for the big toe and fastened to the ankle by a thong which passed between the toes.

The king's beard, part of which was false, was waved, and dressed in horizontal rows of curls. His hair was parted on top of his head and hung, luxuriant and curling, over his shoulders (Pl. XIV). Although we have few documents from which we can follow the precise developments of this fashion under the late Assyrian dynasty, the broad outlines are fairly clear. The hair was worn shorter in each successive reign, while the king's head-dress, which in the time of Ashurbanipal is little more than a simple fez, has by the last of the late Assyrian kings come almost to resemble a dervish's head-dress. Its top always had to be pointed.

Jewels and Weapons

The jewellery displays little originality. The traditional cornelian, onyx and agate were the most commonly used stones. Open-ended or closed bracelets were worn on arm and wrist, with massive earrings which were worn by men and shaped as pendants, crosses or bunches of grapes, hollow and elaborately worked. The closed bracelets, and head bands, which could be worn with or without a tiara, were invariably decorated with a motif of a single or double button-daisy, while the ends of open bracelets were beautifully worked into the heads of heifers, ibexes or lions. The same motifs were generally used for the handles of the knives which were thrust into the belt. The

necklaces were of large golden beads, which might be either
round or shaped like an hour glass with either a smooth or a ribbed
surface, and were interspersed with cornelians, or various other
stones or even glass paste. With so limited a range
of materials, any merit possessed by such ornaments
depended upon their composition and they relied
for their effect upon the constant search for novelty.

The monarch's ceremonial armour, as distinct from
his fighting armour, was exceptionally magnificent.
The sword was broad and short and was enclosed in
a scabbard decorated with a pattern of two crouching
lions opposed. This motif had been in use since the
earliest period and had formed the handle of a copper
dagger found at Tello, and now lost. This was one of
the earliest examples of hilts shaped like lions with
the blade emerging from their mouths.

The handles of the knives which were worn in
the belts were very finely engraved, and two, orna-
mented with rosettes, plaits and flowering shrubs, can
be discerned on the same bas-relief as the embroidery
described in the preceding section. Both clothing and
weapon are decorated with precisely the same reliefs:
so much so, that one wonders whether the embroidery did not in fact consist of woven gold or silver
thread, but possibly of thin plates of metal, engraved
and worked in relief, like the gold leaf from Mycenae,
but far more elaborate.

The bow must have been constructed of rare wood,
and each end was tipped with ivory, generally carved
in the shape of a duck's head, a motif found also
on the uprights of the stools, which somewhat
resemble camp stools. It was equally popular in
Egypt. In Elam, as in Mesopotamia, stone weights
were made in the form of ducks with their heads
twisted round and resting on the bird's back.

A sword in
its decorated
scabbard

Royal Chariots

We know of three types of royal chariots. The first, or war
chariot, had a heavy body and large and specially strengthened
wheels. A bas-relief in the Louvre dating from the reign of Sargon

shows that the shaft, designed for a team of four horses, had a special reinforcing bar because of the jarring to which it would be subjected.

We possess considerably more representations of the ceremonial chariot, one of the best known examples being that of Ashurbanipal, copies of which are in several museums, including the Louvre (Pl. X). It was constructed on the same general lines as the war chariot, but its wheels, which were studded with iron in order to prevent excessive wear, were set very far back under the body in order to lessen the vibration. The principal difference was, however, that both the body and the reinforcing bar, which was slightly curved, were richly decorated. The horses, which, even when yoked to the war chariots, normally wore a harness decorated with tassels, bells and brasses, were even more elaborately caparisoned when they drew the ceremonial chariots. The most striking feature about the royal chariot was the parasol which shaded it. This was not merely a meaningless embellishment, but was a symbol of the most exalted rank, and was covered with the inevitable embroidery. Two customs in use at the Assyrian court are still practised to-day. One was the parasol, which is still used to shade the Sultan of Morocco, and is granted to certain churches as a mark of honour; the other is the punkah, which can be seen at the Papal court in the form of the *flabellum*, a great long-handled fan of ostrich feathers carried in the Papal procession during great ceremonies.

A third type of royal chariot, which is depicted on a relief from Sargon's palace of Khorsabad, now in the Louvre, might be described as a chair on wheels. In shape it suggested a high-backed armchair and resembled a throne in having the seat supported by one or more rows of tiny human figures in the attitude of so many Atlases, representing the various tributary peoples of the Empire, supporting the monarch. At a later period, the Achaemenid kings developed the idea a stage further, like every idea which they borrowed from Assyria, and the tributaries were made to support not the actual throne, but the base upon which it stood.

One other point is worth noticing about the bas-relief of Ashurbanipal's chariot, and that is the courtier who is standing near it with his hand on one of the spokes, and pushing it, as a mark of respect and obedience. As late as the time of Abdul

Hamid, the last great Sultan of Turkey, when he came out of the mosque on the Friday *Sélamlik** and was ascending the slope which led to the palace, the courtiers elbowed each other aside in their eagerness to push the chariot wheel, though their assistance was quite unnecessary.

Besides his weapons, which he often gave to his courtiers to bear, the king also carried a kind of sceptre, in the form of a ceremonial mace, as a symbol of power. It consisted of a ball of stone or metal mounted on a long handle and ended in a short carrying-thong or a lace tassel.

A second badge of kingship was a pole ending in a metal crescent, with a serrated outer edge. This was a purely stylized version of the 'harpé', which was the name given to the weapon by the Greeks when they first encountered it. It was widely used by the Sumerians and we know all the stages of its development. It began like a shallow sickle and consisted of a bit of wood in which sharp flints were fixed with bitumen. Later, after the discovery of metals, the blade was made of bronze. Finally the whole weapon was made of metal in the shape of the oriental sabre called the yatagan; and as in the yatagan, the cutting edge of the 'harpé' was the outer side of the blade.

On certain occasions both sceptre and 'harpé' might be replaced by a tall stick, which was also a badge of royal power.

The Royal Furniture

The bas-reliefs bear witness to the richness of the royal furniture, which was as scanty then as it is to-day in the East, being virtually confined to bed, table and seats; objects in daily use must have been kept in boxes or wall cupboards, and brought to the king as and when they were required.

There is a bas-relief in the British Museum of a banquet held in the gardens of Nineveh after the defeat of Teumman, King of Elam (Pl. XI)[7]. King Ashurbanipal is half reclining on a couch, at the foot of which the queen is seated on a throne shaped like an armchair. Both king and queen are holding goblets and their relaxation is enlivened by music, while servants fan the royal pair or bring them sweetmeats.

The couch stands very high off the ground, and has a built-up head like those which became fashionable under the French

* Public appearance. [Translator's note.]

Empire. The king, whose lower limbs are covered by a rug, and who is propped upon a cushion, has taken off his heavy tiara, and is wearing only a decorated head-band. In contrast the queen is wearing a low crenellated crown, drawn low on her head, like a fillet. Her hair, like the king's, falls in masses over her shoulders, and her clothes resemble his, except for a kind of cloak hanging down her back which could be drawn across her body. She is wearing not sandals but slippers, and is seated on a true throne with a high footstool before her. The table near the couch, carrying the sweetmeats, is correspondingly high and solid with feet carved with lion's paws, while, as if for the sake of further elaboration, the artist depicts it as resting on a flat base, supported on pine cones pointing downwards. It is generally agreed that pine cones (or rather cedar cones, which were so often used in religious ceremonies), which were commonly used as feet for furniture, were a manifestation of the magic power which attached to the point: in this case they would have been meant to preserve the king against the attacks of the genies of the earth, and to keep evil influences at bay.

The stretchers of the stools and the tables carry friezes decorated with a running pattern of two curved lines shaped like the letter C back to back and joined at their centres by a line. Each half of the pattern represents the volutes of a 'Cypriot' capital which decorate a bronze stand (throne and table) found in the Van district* and now in the British Museum. This is another example of the accuracy of the reliefs.

The king's bow and quiver are lying on a lower table behind the head of the couch, the top of which is decorated at each corner with round bosses carved in the shape of heifers' heads; a motif often found on the arms of chairs.

The king's furniture leads us to consider his eating arrangements. Except where Western fashion has superseded local customs, there are no separate dining-rooms in the East, and food is carried on dishes to wherever the eater happens to be. This is what we see on the Khorsabad reliefs. A procession of servants are carrying the table and the footstool (the Assyrian custom was to eat sitting: the couch described earlier was where the king rested) and water vessels for washing before the meal, some of

---

* In Eastern Turkey. It is now considered to come from Nimrud. [Translator's note.]

which are rhytons shaped like lions' heads. Another procession of servants is bearing pomegranates, figs and grapes, while yet others carry locusts on wooden spits, which were eaten by king and peasant alike (p. 77).

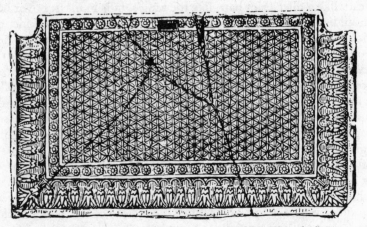

Stone threshold in the pattern of a carpet (from Khorsabad)

It only remains to mention the stone thresholds carved in imitation of carpets. The example in the Louvre is decorated with overlapping circles while the border, bearing the traditional lotus-flower pattern, seems to have been fringed with woollen tassels, like those on a modern carpet.

Ivory

Of some kinds of Assyrian trinkets, which could not have been widely manufactured, we know but little; but since everything intended for the personal use of the monarch was elaborately decorated, we are very familiar with the ivory panels used to decorate the royal chests and furniture. Much has been written about the near-Eastern ivories, which certainly came from a wide variety of sources, whether they were imported ready worked or were carved by foreign craftsmen after import. They exhibit a wide range of influences, but in any event they are miniature masterpieces. We can read in the Bible that during his struggles against Assyria, Hazaël, King of Damascus in the second half of the ninth century B.C., was forced to abandon a ceremonial litter decorated with ivory, and there is reason to think that these are the actual remains which have been found in an Assyrian palace at Arslan Tash, the ancient Hadatu in Upper Syria. Some of the carving is in relief on a solid ground, which suggests an obvious Egyptian influence, while some is of open work, which hints at the Aegean: and other parts again suggest local influences. When we consider also what has been found at Megiddo and Samaria in Palestine, at Nimrud[8], the ancient Kalah, in Assyria and even in the temple of Artemis at Ephesus, it is clear that the ivory industry was greatly dispersed, and generally practised in widely scattered areas of western Asia. De Mecquenem has recovered a considerable quantity of fragments of ivory from the excavations at Susa, simply carved with a circular spiral pattern. This no doubt once decorated a chariot pole.

As for the sources of ivory, we have on the one hand the complacent accounts of the Egyptian kings, dating from the second millennium B.C., of their elephant hunts in North Syria, while on the other those mighty hunters the last monarchs of the Assyrian Empire do not mention the animal at all. But even though elephants may have been extinct by the end of our period, trade with the Far East was firmly established, and it is no doubt eastwards that we should seek the source of ivory: unless it simply came from Upper Egypt.

Entertainments, Banquets, Music, Dancing

The bas-relief of Ashurbanipal in his gardens has already given us some idea of the character of the entertainments. The setting is a garden in the palace of Nineveh, with palm trees, conifers and vines arching high above the royal pair. We are left in no doubt that king and queen are celebrating the defeat of Teumman, King of Elam, by the Assyrian forces, and indeed the relief of the battle, which is also in the British Museum, shows a messenger departing for Nineveh at top speed, bearing the head of the defeated monarch; while in the relief of the celebrations the head itself is stuck in a tree directly facing Ashurbanipal, whose enjoyment of this *fête champêtre* is evidently heightened thereby. (Pl. XI.) The king is often depicted in Mesopotamian art with a goblet in his hand; but this does not always represent a feast, and he is more often preparing to pour a libation of gratitude to the gods for a hunt or a victory in war. Moreover in this particular case the archaeological context admits of no doubt.

Music, of which the inhabitants of the East always have been, and still are, extremely fond, was an essential feature of entertainments like that in the garden of Nineveh[9], and the reliefs show the musical instruments in use in Mesopotamia during our period. Strings, percussion and wind were all known, the first of these including a kind of squarish cithern. This was played while walking, as was a portable harp with a sounding box covered with skin. Similar instruments were known in Egypt, papyrus occasionally being used instead of skin. There was also a kind of miniature mandolin with an extremely small sounding box and strings attached to the end of a very long handle, and similar instruments are still employed in Mesopotamia and Iran.

Percussion was provided by drums of different kinds, ranging from portable timbals to others of very large dimensions. We possess terra-cotta plaques which depict some musicians striking timbals with their hands, while others are carrying kettle drums, apparently much smaller than modern drums, which they are beating with their hands.

Some of the instruments were wholly made of metal, like the hand cymbals, or the sistrum which had long been familiar in Mesopotamia, and was equally common in Egypt. An animal-orchestra is engraved on the front of a harp found in the Royal Tombs at Ur, and the sistrum is being played by what is believed to be a tiny jerboa. Wind instruments comprised a variety of single and double flutes and also, no doubt, pan-pipes.

Musicians playing their instruments appear on a number of monuments like the relief in the Louvre on which four musicians are performing while the army has halted for a rest. Drummer and harpist, cithern-player and cymbalist face each other in pairs, alternately advancing and retreating (Pl. XII).

On a relief depicting the capture of Madaktu in Elam we see the inhabitants of the town marching in procession before their conquerors, the musicians in front and the inhabitants, small and great, marching behind and clapping their hands in time with the music.

Singing and music were often accompanied by dancing, usually in the form still to be seen in the East, especially in Syria, in which two lines of dancers face each other, alternately advancing and retreating while the spectators accompany the music with cries and clapping. There were also dances which, for example, mimed warlike actions, and we possess a terra-cotta plaque which shows two men each carrying a stick somewhat reminiscent of a folding ruler opened at an obtuse angle. I do not accept the view that these are boomerangs, for though this implement has often been attributed to the Mesopotamians, there is no proof that they possessed it. I believe them rather to have been so-called 'dancing sticks', a large number of which have been found in excavations in Egypt. These are flourished in a series of complicated movements by the dancers, who clash them together to mark the rhythm.

Finally a terra-cotta plaque dating from the first dynasty of Babylon shows a curious scene in which a naked woman, holding a kind of lyre, stands on a small stool, while at her feet a male figure wearing a short tunic is crouching in what might be described as a Russian dance, while accompanying himself on a tambourine. We have no clue to the meaning of this scene, which may represent either a ritual dance or a priestess in the rôle of dancing partner, and we can merely infer that some dance of this nature must have existed.

The existence of plaques showing figures in the attitude of boxers suggests that then, as now, boxing was a popular spectacle. It must, however, have been only a carefully rehearsed sham fight, since one of the plaques shows two men beating an enormous drum beside the boxers, in time with their movements.

Boxers and drum- and cymbal-players

Finally, like the Egyptians and the Aegean races, the Assyrians were extremely fond of games resembling the modern draughts, which could be played by one or more players. There is a beautiful set in the Louvre, and a number of others, much earlier in date, were found in the tombs at Ur. The contents of a tomb consisted of what the occupant had most frequently used on earth, in order to provide him with his wonted comforts in the other world: and the frequency with which these games have been found at Ur is eloquent testimony to their popularity in Mesopotamia.

We may sum up the leisure occupations of a king of Assyria as the harem, listening to music, dancing, sedentary games, and the giving of banquets for his nobles. We have a picture of one such banquet on a relief from Khorsabad. The nobles, whose meal is

A banquet of noblemen

set at small tables for four, are dressed appropriately to their rank, namely in a tunic with a long-fringed scarf wound round their bodies, and are sitting on stools before a table on which there is lying a mysterious dish like a pile of ears of corn, faintly reminiscent of a badly drawn bunch of bananas. Their left hands are resting on their knees; in their right, they all simultaneously raise a rhyton in the shape of a lion's head, presumably drinking a health to their benefactor, the king. The odd thing about this scene is that all the guests are sitting on high stools, with their feet off the ground, like people in modern bars. (This should be compared with the practice described on p. 79).

Hunting

Every king was devoted to hunting, and what had once been his duty as protector of the tribe had become a recreation, not free of the spice of danger despite the precautions with which he was surrounded, and repeated to the point of tedium on the bas-reliefs of the numerous palaces.

We do not find the king hunting birds, a sport requiring nothing but cunning, and therefore too trivial to deserve his attention, but the Assyrian population loved it, sometimes shooting at targets, sometimes shooting francolins with bow and arrow. There is, however, a perplexing scene on a bas-relief in the Louvre, which shows two huntsmen practising their art in a forest (Frontispiece). One of them, clean shaven, stands in the foreground:[10] the other, wearing a beard, seems to be some distance off, since he is much smaller than the figure in the foreground, who, however, cannot be the king, despite the scale on which he is carved, since he has no beard and is unpretentiously dressed. The only possible explanation of the difference in the size of the two figures is that he must be a prince, unless indeed on this one relief the Assyrians have uniquely succeeded in realizing the modern concept of perspective (p. 238).

Between the reigns of Ashurnasirpal and Ashurbanipal, i.e., from the ninth to the seventh centuries B.C., Assyrian sculpture seldom varied the conventional representation of a wild beast hunt, and followed the authoritative pattern obediently.

Although the late Assyrian kings did not hunt the wild boar, which later became a favourite sport of the Sassanians, the plains were still the home of wild bulls of the species *bos primigenius*, the ancestors both of the domestic herds and also of the Spanish fighting bulls (bulls of the *ganderias*), as well as enormous herds of wild asses, which supplied Mesopotamia with draught animals before the acclimatization of the horse. The king would pursue the wild asses on horseback and, after riddling them with his arrows, would slaughter them with his bow or his hunting spear, or sometimes force a young one to gallop alongside his chariot and capture it alive.

Wild goats, too, were hunted and caught. We see the hunt

setting forth, the beaters moving off with the huge savage mastiffs, as fierce as their quarry, with sticks and stakes on their shoulders and followed by mules carrying further supplies, so as to make a complete enclosure from which the animals could not hope to escape. This kind of hunting is depicted on cylinder seals from Susa dating from about 3000 B.C.

But hunting in the true sense of the word meant lion-hunting. As we have already said (p. 4), lions of a smaller breed than those of North Africa, but nevertheless dangerous, were still numerous in Mesopotamia at the time of the late Assyrian monarchs, and afforded the kings their favourite sport. Further, the King of Assyria imported really formidable lions, both male and female, from Africa and put them in game reserves where they were left in peace, until the day they were to die, among a jungle of varied trees and luxuriant vine shoots.

Let us imagine the day of a hunt (Plates XIII and XIV). The beaters, their task unchanged through the centuries, drive the quarry towards the hunters, while other servants have captured the lions in the game reserves, and have caged them behind stout wooden bars, above which, at a safe height, a servant is perched in a little cabin with the task of raising the door and releasing the quarry. The lions, maddened by the attacks of the hounds and by the beaters, are eager to fight. They are pursued by the king in his chariot, his driver at his side and a guard standing by, and are transfixed by his arrows: the reliefs spare no detail of the extent of the slaughter. The lions are so numerous that the ground is soon thickly strewn with their bodies. Many indeed are dead, but we possess some reliefs, now in the British Museum, which portray the animals in their death agony. We see one long-maned lion with an arrow through its lungs, sitting with drooping head and coughing up gouts of blood: and an even more famous relief shows the 'wounded lioness', her hindquarters paralysed by an arrow in the loins. Roaring defiance, she gathers herself on her forelegs in a last attempt to drag herself along and avenge herself upon the hunter, threatening him even in the moment of her death.

But sometimes the lion was not mortally wounded, and, in rage, charged his assailant. Then the horses would gallop off with the chariot, and the king, his long hunting spear in his hand, took the full force of the animal's assault and thrust it through.

Sometimes his companion had to assist him in finally dispatching it, for two men's efforts might well be needed against so formidable a foe.

On yet other occasions the king fought on foot, and the pictures which we have of the process are bound to make us doubt their accuracy. As the lion rears up to strike at the hunter's head, the king grasps him by the mane and plunges his sword in his body. This theme evidently found favour: it was frequently employed in the time of Ashurbanipal, and in the Achaemenid palaces the King of Persia often had himself represented in this attitude. Thus, in a representation of a struggle with a fabulous monster, symbolising the conflict between good and evil, the animal is rearing up before the king, while the latter, indifferent to the claws which are tearing his flesh, grasps his assailant by a horn and runs him through with his sword.

And so the hunt draws to an end, and the king can reckon up the day's bag with satisfaction, while teams of servants lift and collect the dead lions from the ground where they lie. The whole scene illustrates the perpetual mixture of truth and fiction in Mesopotamian art. Thus, although the king is by this date no longer carved on a larger scale than his subjects, his superior strength and importance are everywhere implicit. He fights the lion in equal combat and has no difficulty in slaying it, while the lion itself is reduced to a mere game-beast which the king can grasp and hold upright by the mane to deliver the fatal blow. We are reminded how Gilgamesh, the son of a goddess, seized a wild bull by its rear leg, lifted it in the air, and broke its neck with a blow from his heel. But once the struggle is over, we are back in the real world again, and several men are required to carry each of the victims of the day's sport.

But this was not the end of the hunt: to the Assyrian mind the lion was possibly even more dangerous dead than alive, for its angry spirit could pursue the hunter and avenge the victim's death. Thus the final action was for the king, surrounded by his courtiers, to approach the dead beasts and to pour a libation over them in expiation and atonement for the injury which he had done them. The scribe has engraved, as though issuing from the king's mouth, the full text of the ritual, being careful to ascribe the successful outcome of the hunt to the king's tutelary goddess.

The King's Retinue

It was the members of the court, many of whom held some great or small official post in the direct service of the king or his family, who were privileged to attend him on these various occasions. They would include provincial governors and chief officers on such occasions as they were not in their provinces, the officials responsible for the administration of the royal estates, the comptrollers, the cupbearer in chief, the chief steward, the master of the stables, the master of the kitchens, the master of the horse, the master of the music, and other high ranking officers and priests. The most important of the official dignitaries was the grand vizier, who was often a near kinsman of the king, which would at once both gratify him and make it possible to control his actions more easily than if he were governing a distant province. He was the master of the treasury, and responsible both for supplying the needs of court and country, and also for the collection of taxes, which were levied by tax collectors, and took the form of payments in kind, e.g., of barley, wool, wood, horses and live stock, though they were sometimes payable in silver. Thus we find the towns of Arpad, Quë and Magadu taxed at the rate of thirty, thirty and fifteen talents of silver respectively, while Carchemish was assessed at one hundred talents of silver and two talents of gold, though we do not know the length of time to which these payments related.

In addition to this direct taxation, and leaving aside those who benefited under the system of fiefs (which was in existence as early as the second millennium B.C., long before a feudal system) which conferred certain immunities, a system of forced labour for the king's service was in being. The possibility of buying exemption from this varied proportionately to the success of military campaigns and the consequent abundance or scarcity of foreign labour. But as the royal building programmes expanded, so did the demands for labour, with the result that Nebuchadrezzar, whose plans for building, like his conquests, were conceived on the grand scale, none the less found himself obliged to requisition the services of his own subjects in order to execute his plans.

All members of the court had to be paid, and payment usually took the form of food, though clothes and silver were also sometimes given. We possess the following list of the pay received by certain officials during the period of the Sargonid dynasty, which

Plate I.   Huntsmen shooting birds in a forest

Note the bowstring invisible in front of the archer's face.

(Editions 'Tel'.   Vigneau phot.)

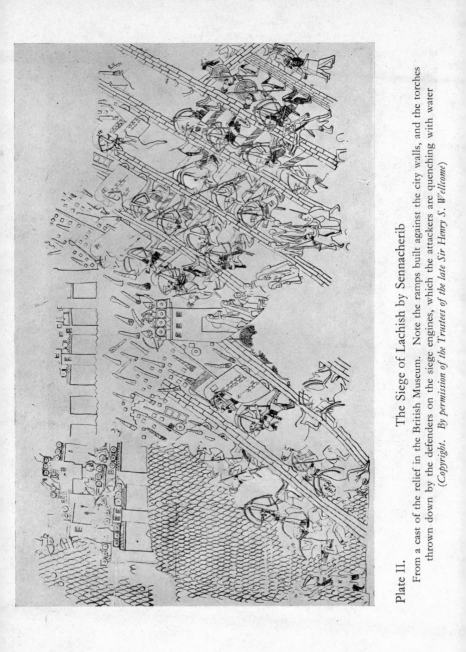

Plate II.   The Siege of Lachish by Sennacherib

From a cast of the relief in the British Museum. Note the ramps built against the city walls, and the torches thrown down by the defenders on the siege engines, which the attackers are quenching with water

Coracle and Kelek

Plate III.   Soldiers crossing a river on goatskins

Plate IV.   Man-headed winged bull
from the palace of Sargon II at Khorsabad
(*Editions 'Tel'.   Vigneau phot.*)

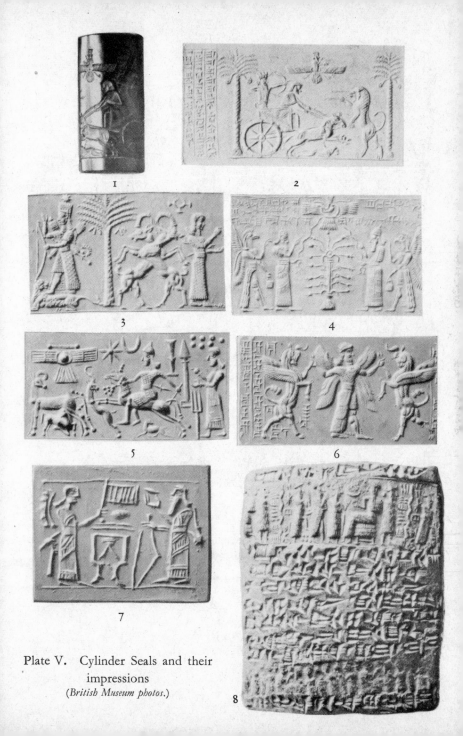

Plate V. Cylinder Seals and their
impressions
(*British Museum photos.*)

Prisoners eating a meal

Plate VI.   Vegetables for a banquet

Plate VII.   Transport of a winged bull to Sennacherib's palace

Plate VIII.   Reconstruction of the palace at Khorsabad

(From Loud & Altman: "Khorsabad", vol II, by permission of the Oriental Institute, University of Chicago)

Plate IX.   Detail of embroidery on King's robes

Plate X. Ashurbanipal in his chariot receiving the surrender of Babylon

(British Museum photo.)

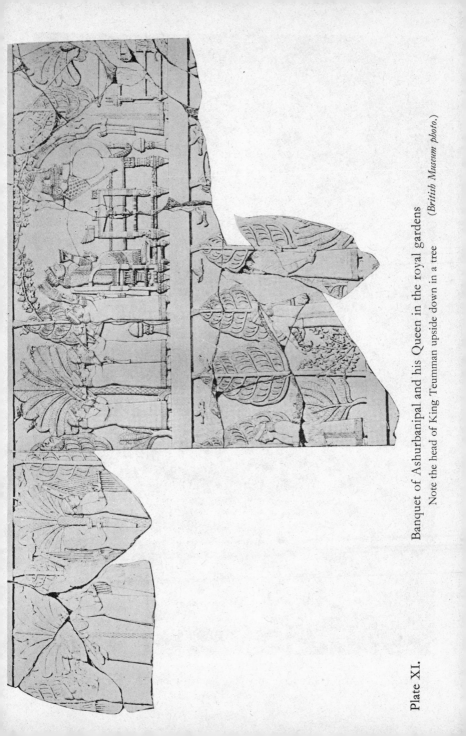

Plate XI.

Banquet of Ashurbanipal and his Queen in the royal gardens

Note the head of King Teumman upside down in a tree

(British Museum photo.)

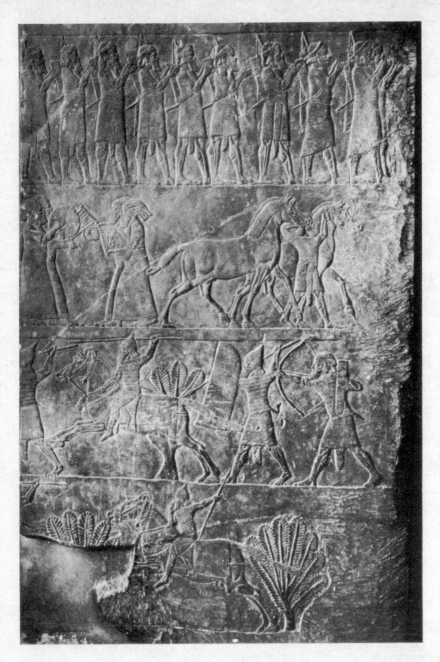

Plate XII.   Musicians accompanying an army on the march
(Editions 'Tel'.   Vigneau phot.)

Plate XIII. The Lion Hunt of Ashurbanipal—I

Plate XIV.   The Lion Hunt of Ashurbanipal—II

Plate XV.   Transport of a cargo of wood from Lebanon: the convoy off Sidon

(Editions 'Tel'.   Vigneau phot.)

Plate XVI.   Assault on a city with a battering ram

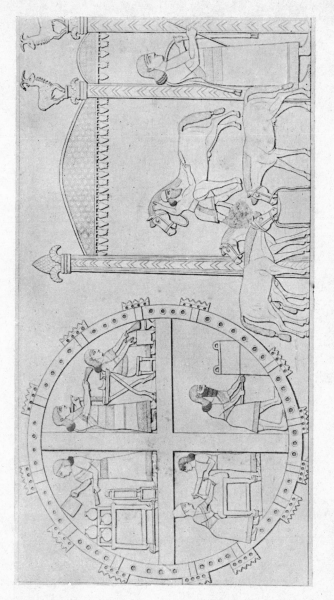

Plate XVII.

Scene inside a fortified camp

Plate XVIII.

The Sack of Musasir by Sargon II in 714 B.C.

Plate XIX. Two statues of Gilgamesh in the Louvre (8th cent. B.C.)
In his right hand he holds the ' harpe '.
The two figures show the two types of male dress

Plate XX.   The use of ladders in the assault on a city

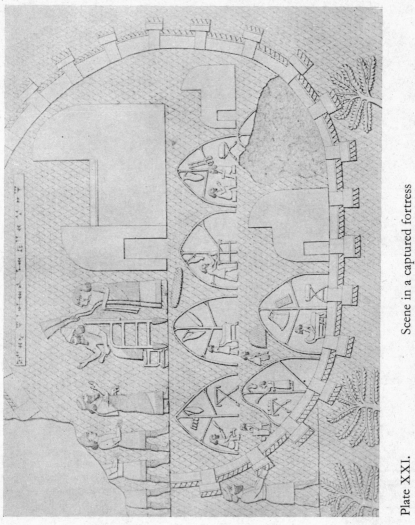

Plate XXI.   Scene in a captured fortress

The king seated on his throne.   Three houses and seven tents

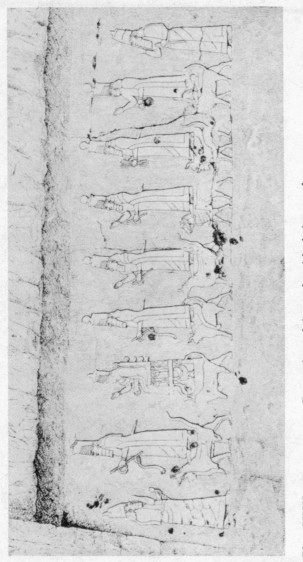

Plate XXII.   Procession of the gods with their attendants

Rock-carving from Maltai, 8th or 7th cent. B.C.   The gods from left to right are probably Ashur, Ninlil, Enlil,
Shamash, Adad and Ishtar

Plate XXIII. Symbols of the gods from the
boundary stones of Ritti-Marduk
(*British Museum photo.*)

Plate XXIV. The demon Lamashtu

A bronze plaque from Carchemish
(*British Museum photo.*)

throws incidental light on the comparative status of their offices:—

Position	Minas of silver	Garments of the best quality	Garments of ordinary quality
Commander-in-Chief	10	5	5
Chief Minister	6	3	2
Chief Judge	3	3	0
Junior Minister	3	3	0
Cupbearer-in-Chief	4	3	3
Palace Chamberlain	5	3	2
Inspector of the Palace	1	1	0

From this we can see that the Commander-in-Chief, or *Turtan*, enjoyed a position of unique importance, which is only what might be expected in a state which looked to warfare as its main source of revenue, while on the other hand the Chief Judge was paid less than the Cupbearer-in-Chief and the Palace Chamberlain.

Despite the fact that the king inspired such fear that special amulets were designed to ensure a favourable reception when the wearer had the honour of being received in audience, and although he was the earthly representative of the god, we shall see that he was a long way from exercising absolute authority in all circumstances, and members of his suite did not hesitate to tell him the truth (p. 216).

Business of State. Diplomacy

At least in theory the king promulgated laws, fixed the calendar and taxation, and made decisions about war and peace, though in practice the preliminary work was done by the court officials, with the assistance of an army of scribes. In the conduct of day-to-day business he was advised by such of his relations as held high office and by certain members of the court, who together formed a kind of council, a system far more highly developed at the Hittite court than the Assyrian. The Assyrian adoption of this custom was probably due to the influence of the long contacts between Assyria and the Asianic and Indo-European peoples. It never appears to have assumed an equal degree of importance in Babylonia.

Apart, however, from the aspects of the king's life which we have examined, there were other calls upon him of vital importance to the Empire, namely, diplomacy and war. The king received the ambassadors and tributaries, large numbers of whom came from all parts of the great late-Assyrian Empire. Seated on his lofty throne in the great audience chamber of the palace, with his tame lion crouched at his feet and surrounded by his ministers, members of the court and guards, the king, wearing full cere-monial robes, solemnly received the ambassadors of the great powers with whose rulers, the 'great kings', he could, by diplo-matic convention, treat as brothers. At the same time as the ambassadors presented their letters of credence, they laid at the king's feet the costly presents which they had brought him, of gold and silver, rich stuffs or precious stones: or paraded before him choice horses from their own countries, specially selected slaves, or rare animals or plants. They would bow deeply to the king, but they neither knelt nor prostrated themselves as they were expected to do at the Egyptian court. It was only the envoys of the small countries, or the numerous tributaries, who could not treat with Assyria on equal terms, who had thus to humble themselves. In the royal Annals the movements of these embassies are regularly recorded in a deliberately misleading manner, while the true motives—the commercial alliances, or the shifting of forces in search of the balance of power—go unmentioned or disguised as homage. A distant monarch—for example, the King of Lydia in the reign of Ashurbanipal—is encouraged by a dream to acknowledge the greatness of the Assyrian monarch and sends him an embassy: whereas, in cold fact, a common front was urgently required against the Cimmerians who were ravaging Northern Assyria and Northern Asia Minor. Sometimes, again, in search of security an embassy might seek or offer the hand of a royal daughter in marriage. Our knowledge of the conventions employed by the Hittites enlightens us on the formalities which governed unions between two royal houses. The two kings might be equally anxious for the match, but neither would show the slightest sign of impatience. The prospective father-in-law would therefore begin by refusing. After a decent interval the request would be renewed, and the number of refusals would be propor-tionate to the dignity and importance of the object of the approach. Finally negotiations would be brought to a head and the bride would depart for her husband's country accompanied by an imposing retinue and bearing rich presents. Coin collections throughout Europe contain numerous medallions struck to commemorate royal marriages, and the practice was followed in a slightly different form at the Egyptian court. From the middle of the second millennium B.C. onwards, when the Pharaohs of the eighteenth dynasty married Mitannian princesses in order to ensure the possession of allies in Upper Syria, they had scarabs engraved to commemorate the event.

The Reception of Tributaries

The second theme on the bas-reliefs is the reception of the tributaries, which was designed to overawe visitors to the royal presence. The king, wearing full ceremonial robes, is shown

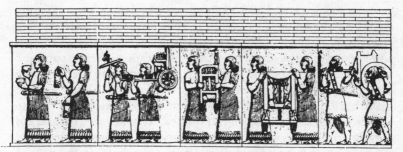

Bringing tribute

standing or sitting, and holding the tall staff which is the insignia of his rank. Behind him are ranged the bearers of his sceptre and his arms and fans, and before him the sponsors of the ambassadors or tributaries who bear gifts or tribute such as delicately engraved vases of precious metal, fabrics, rods of ebony or jewels, or, sometimes, jewel boxes shaped like miniature fortresses, thus symbolizing the gift of their city to the King of Assyria. Sometimes again the envoys have brought chariots and horses. Here and there are a few brief lines of descriptive text.

Tribute of Cedars of Lebanon

The Khorsabad reliefs record one expedition intermediate in character between the offerings brought by the tributaries and the major military operations which we shall describe later. This was the transport by water of a cargo of wood, and though we do not know its precise significance, we are left in no doubt of its importance; for since every detail of the decoration at Khorsabad is designed to emphasize the greatness of the king, we can safely infer that the arrival of this cargo must have been an unusually important event.[11] We must of course remember that the building of the palace was itself an event of considerable importance.

Of the materials required, the clay was already on the site, while stone, of which the architects made only limited use, was, by comparison with conditions in the south, quite plentiful. Wood, however, was scarce, and while the kinds of timber which grew in the north could, like stone, be brought to the site, they did not provide roofing members large enough to span the projected rooms. The pine trees, or more especially the cedars which were the natural wealth of Syria, were the only source of beams o the size required, and indeed the insatiable demands of antiquity ended by denuding the Lebanon and Amanus of their timber reserves, so that nowadays the cedar trees can be counted in ones and twos, while the survivors owe their escape to their association with some sacred spot. The Egyptians had for long been sending expeditions to Syria to procure cedar trees, which they used to make both masts for their ships and mummy cases, while the sap called 'cedar blood' was highly prized. It was only natural for Sargon to turn to Syria for the wood which he wanted, and whether because he acquired it as tribute or because the project set such formidable transport problems, it remains true that the expedition was regarded as of sufficient importance to merit some permanent record.

The first relief shows the gangs of pressed labour, wearing short tunics and carrying long beams, slung on cords from their shoulders, down from the mountain, the slopes of which are visible immediately beside them. This represents the transport of the cedarwood from the mountains to the beach.

The second relief shows the wood being loaded on boats with built-up bows and poops and animal figureheads.

The third in the series is the most interesting (Pl. XV). It shows the flotilla under way: the boats, propelled by long oars, are sailing in line ahead, the cargo of timber being conventionally represented as resting on the bows and the poops, while more timber is being towed by ropes. In the midst of the waves, which are represented by a dense pattern of wavy lines, we can see an assortment of fish, crabs and shellfish, together with a sea god with a merman's body and a good genie accompanying

the expedition in the form of a winged bull. About half-way up
the relief is a very flat island with a fort on it, and a little higher
up, where we might expect to find the shore, a second fort standing on a marked elevation. I consider that this is intended to be a
touch of local colour and represents a real view, and, if I am right,
we must look for some site in Phoenicia with an island at water
level some distance from the shore and a fortress sited on the top
of a hill by the water's edge. There is one site, and only one,
which satisfies these conditions, namely Sidon, the acropolis of
which was the site of the now ruined St. Louis' castle, while the
island, rocky but levelled and flat, was the site of a fortress. This
was the island on which the King of Sidon sought refuge, in his
efforts to escape from the King of Assyria, 'like a fish' in the midst
of the sea. The shellfish which the relief depicts in the midst of
the waves have a special significance, for Phoenicia was the
country of the famous purple dye and Sidon was one of the towns
entirely devoted to the industry. The coast on either side of the
town was raised into positive cliffs largely composed of shellfish
which had been thrown away after use.

The fourth relief is the counterpart of the first, and shows the
unloaded timber being transported up a mountain road. The
meaning of the whole series can be summarized by saying that the
cedars were felled on the mountains and carried in convoy the
whole way up the Phoenician coast: they were unloaded in the
north, and transported by the shortest possible route to rejoin
the rivers and so conveyed to Nineveh.

War

Last, but by no means least, of the king's occupations, were
military expeditions. Their principal features are depicted on the
bas-reliefs, while the more detailed aspects are illustrated on a
smaller scale,[12] e.g., on repoussé bronze panels like those dating
from the reign of Shalmaneser III and found in the small and
insignificant village of Balawat, to which they had been brought
for no apparent reason, since no palace can ever have existed
there.* The panels were fixed with rosette-headed nails on the
wooden leaves of a great double door. Most of them are in the

---

* But Professor Mallowan who has recently visited the site (Spring, 1952), has
observed a large mound there, which may well conceal a palace. The place from
which the bronze doors were removed is still recognizable. [Translator's note.]

British Museum, the remainder being divided between the
Louvre, the De Clerq collection and the Istanbul Museum.

At the Gods' Command

We can reconstruct the wars of the Assyrian kings fairly
accurately with the help of this varied range of documents and
accounts of the campaigns. We are bound to be struck by the
fact that the real motive for starting a war was never frankly
admitted. There is no doubt that then, as now, these motives
were primarily economic, being inspired either by the need for
expansion, or because outlets appeared to be blocked in what was
regarded as a vital direction. But this was never explicitly stated:
and when the king declared war on a neighbouring country he
only did so in obedience to the orders of Ashur, either because the
god himself had commanded it or because the treaties placed
under the protection of the god had not been duly observed. In
the campaigns the king assumes the rôle of the deputy of the god:
he is his general, his dedicated champion. As well we know, the
excuses—provocation, violation of treaties, threat of encircle-
ment—for a declaration of war are the same nowadays as they
were then: ideological factors have taken the place of 'the will of
Ashur'. The preamble to the account of a campaign always contains the statement that it was undertaken at the command of the
god. But more was needed, for the day must be propitious for
undertaking a campaign, and in this connection we may observe
with interest, though hardly with surprise, that a propitious time
corresponds remarkably with what the strategists regarded as the
most suitable season and, consequently, the most favourable
ground conditions with the best prospects of keeping an army
supplied along its lines of communication.

The Army

The royal Assyrian army was based upon conscription, to
which not only all fief holders were liable, but also the contin-
gents of fighting men whom the villages were obliged, as a form
of taxation, to provide. It also included auxiliary troops whose
characteristics were eagerness for booty, readiness to attack and
equal readiness in flight. They were lightly armed compared with
the shock troops, and their special task was to penetrate the

wavering ranks of the enemy, to turn hesitation into a rout and
then to sack the enemy's camp. The shock troops comprised
units of various types. First there were the *qurâdu* or 'strong
ones', who might be described as the bodyguard, consisting of
seasoned warriors responsible for the monarch's personal safety
and regarded as completely reliable. The army's fighting power,
apart from the weapons carried by the lightly equipped auxiliaries,
who had no defensive armour and whose offensive weapons

A Battle

Bearded and beardless soldiers, with conical helmets and round caps

consisted only of clubs and slings, depended upon archers,
mounted lancers, engineers and artillery. Mounted infantry were
employed who rode to their appointed positions, as well as
lancers equipped with a long light lance, sappers to undertake
mining operations or to counter those of the enemy, and artillery-
men to operate the machines designed to open breaches in the
opposing walls (Pl. XVI).

On the bas-reliefs depicting battles we see both bearded and

beardless soldiers performing virtually identical tasks. This is
further proof of the error of the old view, that the beardless
figures represented eunuchs; in fact they merely represent the
young men (the 'ephebes' of Greece), in contrast to the bearded
veterans: the distinction being between regular and reserve troops.

By the late Assyrian period the clothes worn by the troops had
reached their highest pitch of effectiveness, and the long envelop-
ing garments of Ashurnasirpal's period had been replaced by a
short tunic reaching half way down the thigh, which left the
arms half bare. Troops no longer went barefoot, but wore high

Archers and their shield

boots laced in front, while on their heads they wore helmets
whose shape still survives in native Indian armour, fitting closely
round the head and rising in a cone to a sharp point. The laced
boots protected the soldiers' feet against rough ground and prevented bruising, and the shape of the helmet was such that blows
glanced off it without doing serious damage. Sometimes the
helmet was replaced by a close-fitting skull-cap with projecting
cheek pieces, rather like an airman's helmet.

The main body protection consisted of a tall, roughly man-
sized shield, the top of which curved backwards to form a kind of
canopy. It was apparently made of bundles of plaited and padded
osiers, tightly bound together, the purpose of the canopy being
to protect the archer from spent arrows which might fall almost

vertically. It is worth noticing that the effectiveness of the shield was diminished by its unwieldiness, since it required someone to carry it. The normal offensive weapon was the bow; this was singly curved and of medium size. A close examination of the bas-reliefs often suggests that the archer's hand has passed behind his head as he draws his bow, since the taut bowstring can be clearly seen in front of the archer's head, but disappears at the point where it ought to be visible in front of his face. This would represent an almost impossible physical movement, and the true explanation is a simple artistic convention: the cord is not shown because it would not 'look right' in the place where it should in fact be, and if we look at the archer's hands we see that they are in exactly the position in which we should expect to find them (p. 237 and Frontispiece).

The archers were sometimes mounted, and in these circumstances they shot either when their horses were standing still or after dismounting. The cavalry, on the other hand, were armed with a lance of moderate length, and actually fought on horseback. Both archers and lancers were also equipped with a shortish flat-bladed dagger thrust in their belts, while their bucklers were frequently convex so that blows glanced harmlessly aside.

Sometimes the cavalry and the archers wore, on the upper parts of their bodies, breastplating of linen or leather sewn with small metal plates which at the same time allowed freedom of movement and gave them protection. This kind of breastplate was in general use in Europe at the end of the Middle Ages, when it was known as the 'brigandine' or 'brigantine'. The cavalry, though they had no stirrups, did not ride bareback but were seated on a plain saddle-cloth.

Halfway, in a sense, between cavalry and archers, came the chariots drawn by two horses or indeed by more, if their passengers were of sufficient importance. From the military point of view, however, the chariot's value seems to have been limited, since besides the man who actually shot from it, it required a driver and two other people to carry the round shields for the protection of the two effectives. Since the forepart of the chariot was of rigid construction, it could not change direction sharply when near an obstacle, and the correct counter manoeuvre was that of the toreador when confronted by the bull, namely to step aside and let it go harmlessly by.

Sappers and Artillery

The sappers, who played an extremely important part in siege warfare, are often depicted wearing helmets of the same shape as those of Greek hoplites, closely resembling those worn to-day by French firemen or, till comparatively recently, by French cuirassiers—a link with the very distant past. These sappers had the job of undermining fortresses and so opening a breach for the assault. Their method consisted of making and shoring up with wood a sufficiently large excavation under a wall or a tower, and then setting light to the timber scaffolding so that the wall would collapse into the cavity. Meanwhile the occupants of the besieged city would of course be making equal efforts to drive counter mines, by digging a shaft underneath that of their opponents, in order to prevent their advancing it any farther. At the city of Dura Europos on the river Euphrates, which was at one period subject to Palmyra and was later occupied by the Romans, excavation has revealed subterranean traces of the great struggle between the Romans and the Persians in the weapons of defenders and attackers which were crushed in the collapse of the walls.

Contemporary artillery consisted of siege weapons whose character hardly changed until the invention of firearms. One machine consisted of a platform on wheels which would place the attackers at wall level and had to be countered by the normal tactics of an ordinary battle on the ground. Another device, which was covered with leather and was constantly sprayed with water to prevent its being set alight by the blazing tow and torches which were thrown on it by the defenders, sheltered the troops who were manning a battering ram, consisting of a long and heavy beam slung underneath the superstructure, and swung backwards and forwards. The force of the blows could cause extremely serious damage to the walls of a fortress of the period. The defenders reacted to such attacks in the traditional manner, by trying to catch the wooden ram with ropes and chains and so to neutralize it (Pl. XVI).

The army would only take the field during the months which the soothsayers and the auguries pronounced to be auspicious for military expeditions. The king was the commander-in-chief as a matter of right: but if he chose not to assume command his place was taken by the chief general or *turtan*. When the army set out the *qurâdu* marched beside the king. The evidence of the bas-reliefs suggests that the guards were the only troops who were properly drilled, marching with an easy stride and keeping good order in the ranks. At the rear of the columns the chariots and siege engines followed, unless indeed they were built on the actual scene of operations as the particular circumstances demanded. On reaching a river, the chariots and baggage wagons crossed either by a bridge of boats or on light craft, while horses and men both swam, the latter inflating sheeps' bladders, which they put between their legs, and then struck out with their arms.

Camp

During a short halt, the troops bivouacked, but if for any reason it had to be prolonged, a proper fortified camp was built (Pl. XVII). This was generally circular and strengthened with towers, the tents being pitched in the centre. The royal tent was the most elaborate, and was covered, like a modern perambulator, with a movable canopy adjustable against wind and sun. The tents used by the rest of the army, or at least by the officers, were very much like those in use to-day, being round with a central stake for a tentpole. Cookhouses were always provided, and some reliefs show the soldiers engaged upon a variety of tasks, one cutting up a sheep, another drawing up the fire by fanning it with what looks like a small flag, and a third watching an enormous stewpot.[13] Others again would be busy grooming the horses, which were generally left in the open at night, at least during the hot weather. Excavation has revealed rings for tethering horses set in the walls of the outbuildings in the large palace courtyards or sometimes fixed in the ground.

We need not linger over the details of the conduct of a siege. The activities of the sappers and the battering rams were supplemented by the establishment of as close a blockade as possible, with the object of starving out the beleaguered garrison. Spies or anyone else who might attempt to make their way through it were impaled through the throat and exposed in full view of the walls, to inspire fear in the defenders.

Plunder

The capture of the enemy citadel or the entry of the Assyrian monarch through a breach in the walls was the signal for the sack of the city. The battlements, from which boiling oil, flaming

naphtha and stone missiles had been hurled, were torn down, the
chambers of the palace and the houses were stripped of their
contents and fire raged unchecked. When the inhabitants saw
that all resistance was nearly at an end, they would often bury
their precious possessions, though many of them were destined
never to recover them. In the course of time, some of these
hoards have come to light, and
they still do so to-day, when
the objects find their way into
museums: others are lost for
ever. Assyrian greed spared no
fragment of gold or silver.

The king's throne would be
set up before the gates of the city
and the prisoners would be
paraded before him, led by the
monarch of the captured town,
who would undergo the most
agonizing torture, such as having
his eyes put out or confinement in
a cage, until the king of Assyria
set a term to his long-drawn
agony. Sargon had the defeated
king of Damascus burned alive
before his eyes. The wives and
daughters of the captured king
were destined for the Assyrian
harems and those who were not of
noble blood were condemned to
slavery. Meanwhile the soldiery
had been massacring the population, and brought the heads of

Sennacherib on his throne before the
gates of Lachish

their victims into the king's presence, where they were counted
up by the scribes. Not all the male prisoners were put to death,
for the boys and craftsmen were led into captivity, where they
would be assigned to the hardest tasks on the royal building
projects, where the swamps which cover so much of Mesopotamia
must have caused an enormously high rate of mortality. The
remainder of the population were uprooted and sent to the other
end of the Empire, a practice which was abandoned with the

advance of civilization, but has been revived with honour in the twentieth century A.D. Its ostensible purpose was to populate empty tracts of country, but it was also meant to ensure that the newcomers were rootless strangers among the peoples surrounding them, and that if they rebelled they would receive no help.

It was quite common for the youngest members of the royal line to be carried off to the court of the conqueror, and there to be brought up at least in fear, if not in love, of Assyria. From their original status of hostages at the court they might advance to the point of later being called to govern their hereditary possessions as tributaries of their overlord, provided that they proved themselves to be, at least superficially, 'Assyrianized' enough to win the conqueror's trust.

Success in war was followed by celebrations, in which army and people alike joined; thanksgivings and sacrifices were offered to the gods, while a tithe of the natural products and of the valuables and also of the prisoners was reserved for the use of the temples. The practice of slaughtering prisoners, which was not so much an act of revenge as an offering to the gods, was in origin religious. The Assyrian character was too shrewd and grasping to relinquish a valuable capture, but it accepted the obligation freely to offer for destruction part of the capital debt to the gods who had granted the victory.

We possess extremely detailed information about the successful military campaigns, but the compilers of the annals never utter a word about defeats or reverses, while we should always treat their account of the victories with considerable reserve. We possess, for example, three separate official accounts of one of Shalmaneser III's victories, and the number of prisoners varies by 100 per cent.

Sargon's Eighth Campaign

For the purpose of studying a typical military campaign, we may select the eighth campaign of King Sargon's reign, which he conducted in the east and north-east of his dominions. A study of the topography of his campaigns suggests that Assyria regarded the countries on her frontiers as so many storehouses which she invaded in turn on a variety of pretexts, in order to supply the empire with what it needed. The main scene of this particular campaign, which took place in 714 B.C., was the inaccessible Urartu district (the modern Armenia). The king had come to the throne in 724 B.C., which shows that these campaigns were almost annual events.

We should not be misled into thinking that the Assyrian monarch took the decision to initiate a campaign in reliance solely upon omens and upon the choice of a propitious season and dates for military adventures. He had a full-scale intelligence service at his disposal and he made extremely detailed preparations for this Armenian campaign, to which he devoted his whole attention. We possess a number of letters from a high frontier official which are in effect reports on the intentions and the activities of his opponent, and contain every scrap of available information. Thus, in reply to an inquiry from the Assyrian monarch about what the King of Armenia was doing, a letter reports that his arrival has been announced during a religious ceremony. As Sargon had given orders that none of his own adherents was to take part in any ceremonies, the writer assures him that he will always continue to do his duty as he has done in the past.

There was a series of small frontier raids of varying fortune, but the king's main anxiety was always to learn what had become of certain individuals who were considered dangerous and whose whereabouts were unknown.

Information was gathered by the simple method of dispatching spies. These reported that the Armenian forces had massed precisely opposite the Assyrian concentrations. But they added that the troops were grumbling, the country was very difficult, and the rivers could not be crossed either by swimmers on bladders or by rafts. In fact, as we shall see from the official account of the expedition, these difficulties may have been more apparent than real and may also have been deliberately exaggerated in order to lessen the responsibility of those who supplied the information, in case the expedition miscarried. In practice, however, they were all overcome without difficulty and the grumbling of the troops yielded to a genuine enthusiasm.

The account of the campaign, which was found at Ashur, is now in the Louvre and has been translated and critically studied by M. F. Thureau-Dangin. Unlike most royal inscriptions, it is not in the form of an historical account, but, most unusually, of a letter from the king from his residence at Kalah to the god Ashur in his temple in the city of Ashur, giving him an account of the campaign. It is in effect a report to the god, and in summarizing this most unusual text we will draw attention to the significant points.

The king writes in the first person and solemnly addresses his letter directly to the god Ashur, father of the gods, the mighty lord, who dwells in the temple called 'Great Mountain of the Countries', sending his greetings not only to Ashur, but also to the gods of destiny and the goddesses who have their shrines in the temple. He asks to be remembered to the city, and to its people and to his palace, and he wishes complete peace for himself, King Sargon, servant of the great gods, and for his army. The whole campaign is completed: but he commits it to divine protection. 'In the month of Duzu, the month consecrated to Ninurta, the mighty elder son of Enlil, the month which the lord of wisdom had decreed in an ancient tablet as the moment when I was to assemble my army and prepare its encampment, I set forth from Kalah, my royal city . . .'

He goes on to describe the difficulties which he encountered in securing the passage of the rivers, which were in spate, by his troops: and yet the Upper and Lower Zab were crossed without fear by his soldiers, as though they were but a ditch. Then he entered the mountain region, the emblems of the god always borne before him . . . 'And though these mountains were high, covered with every kind of tree and with thick undergrowth, though their terrifying gorges were overcast with darkness like the darkness of a forest of cedars, and no light is ever seen there, yet I advanced.'

The sappers had to be called in to make a road, and with the king at their head, 'chariots, cavalry, infantry all sped over these mountains like eagles'. Behind them came the builders of the camp and the sappers: and last of all 'camels and pack mules scaled the slopes like wild goats born in the mountains'. After this climb the army enjoyed a well-earned rest and encamped on the summit of the mountain.

After successfully crossing a large number of torrents and negotiating a great many high mountain passes, each carefully detailed, the expedition reached enemy soil. The king of the Mannaeans realized his peril and incontinently presented himself

before Sargon, accompanied by his nobles, his elders, his coun-
sellors and his family, offering tribute of live stock and of draught
horses with their drivers and in the phrase hallowed in Assyrian
parlance 'he embraced the feet' of the conqueror. A second local
princeling, equally alarmed, acted as though he were the governor
of an Assyrian city, first supplying the army with wine and flour
and then begging Sargon to restore the former boundaries of his
country, which had been half captured by his formidable neighbours. Thanks to the superior power granted him by Ashur
and Marduk, Sargon announced his compliance with this request.
Assyrians and Mannaeans jointly took part in a banquet, while various princes who had given no sign of their existence hitherto sent
tribute to Sargon, who installed an Assyrian governor over them.

One of the dissident Mannaean princes saw the Assyrian
advance from a neighbouring mountain, and promptly took to
flight with his companions, and never reappeared. He evidently
preferred a whole skin to his palace and the enjoyment of his
wealth, and he left his army to be massacred.

The document then unblushingly enumerates Sargon's personal
qualities, in order to justify the requests which he is making to the
god and to remind him that the king is worthy of his protection.
He is, he says, scrupulous in observing the laws of Shamash, he
hearkens reverently to the word of the great gods, he never trans-
gresses their commandments, he is full of rectitude and compassion, he hates falsehood, he never utters an evil or a hurtful word.
The passage ends: 'Having never yet encountered Rusas the
Armenian in pitched battle, I lifted up my hands to heaven,
praying that it might be granted me to defeat him, to make him eat
his insolent words, and to crush him beneath the weight of his sins.'

The miracle happened. Ashur heard this prayer and the
Assyrian armies, though exhausted by their exertions and despite
the uncertainty of their supply lines, became new men. Such was
Sargon's confidence that he scarcely regarded the serried ranks
of his foes before him. He hurled himself upon them like an
arrow from a bow, inflicted a resounding defeat upon them,
secured magnificent booty, and captured 260 kinsmen of Rusas,
king of Urartu, who, having lost his horses, 'to save his life abandoned his chariot, jumped upon a mare, and led his army in flight'.

One by one the strongholds fell and the cities were enveloped
in flame as the Assyrians burned the crops and looted the gran-

aries. 'As if they were locusts I led my camp animals towards the countryside near the city, and they destroyed the crops that grew there and laid waste the plain.' After the land had been duly ravaged, Sargon began his return march towards Assyria, without having to fight and indeed without encountering any resistance.

King Urzana of Musasir, whose life is described as one of sin and iniquity, who had broken the oath which he had sworn in the presence of the gods Ashur, Shamash, Nabu and Marduk, had revolted against Sargon: he sent no gifts, he did not come to embrace the king's feet, nor did he send any messenger to bring him greetings. Such conduct deserved swift and condign punishment.

The easterly route which Sargon had taken from the opening of the campaign had rounded lakes Urmia and Van and had doubled back to follow the line of the Tigris. This was the point at which Sargon took what appears to have been either a sudden decision, or at least one which he had been at much pains to conceal. He sent the bulk of his troops back home, and, keeping with him only the infantry and a thousand cavalry, struck eastwards, as if aiming for the west coast of Lake Urmia. The ruse was completely successful and the inhabitants of Musasir had no time to put their treasures in a place of safety.

The Sack of Musasir

Once again the mountains had to be crossed by a track which was normally impassable by chariots, and the king's chariot had to be hauled by ropes as the cavalry and their mounts made their way in single file through the gorges. The city of Musasir fell and Sargon ordered the inhabitants to be deported and the statue of the god Haldia, the tutelary deity of the city, to form part of the spoil (Pl. XVIII). The wife, children and family of the king, who had himself fled, formed part of the total capture of some 6,110 inhabitants, twelve mules, 380 asses and unspecified live stock. Sargon himself took up residence in the royal palace, where he broke open the treasury and removed all the gold, silver, bronze, lead, cornelian, lapis-lazuli, ivory, rare woods, royal insignia, ceremonial weapons and plate, which it contained. Nor did he spare the temple of Haldia. He looted all its treasures, including six gold shields which hung round the door, their centres deco-rated with circular bosses in the shape of dogs' heads, a large-scale statue of a cow suckling a calf, some metal bowls which stood at the entrance to the gates, the colossi which belonged to the doorway, and a long and monotonous list of precious objects, the whole being past counting, as the inscription itself says: all this excluding the private loot of the troops.

This particular section of the account of the eighth campaign is more than usually interesting since the actual events are depicted on the Khorsabad reliefs, which were discovered, drawn and then buried again by Botta (Pl. XVIII). They show the temple with its sloping roof (a reminder that the scene is in the mountains) and the soldiers engaged in carrying off the shields, while the great bowls and the cow are standing at the door. At one side, some soldiers are smashing a statue with an axe, while others are weighing the fragments on a great pair of scales with two balances and a beam. When he heard of this disaster, King Rusas, who had fled, abandoned himself to the profoundest grief, for Sargon reduced the whole area to abject misery.

Sargon's letter to the god Ashur concludes with a recital of a number of minor engagements in which the king is described as attacking 'like an angry dog', and a list of the warriors who fell in the battle, whom the chief officer of the palace was ordered to commemorate in the presence of the god. The tablet itself was written by the head of the royal scribes who was both a skilled writer and one of Sargon's ministers, besides being himself the son of a former royal scribe.

The whole account leaves two main impressions upon the reader. The first is that the hyperbolic language in which Sargon describes his own achievements is matched only by the profound humility with which he renders thanks to the god Ashur. In performing his tasks he has been nothing but the appointed of god, concerned only to carry out his orders and owing everything to him. The second is, how clearly the endless and meticulous lists of the booty show the extent to which war was a matter of business for the Assyrians. Plunder was regarded as a prospective source of revenue. It was one of the rare periods when war was a paying concern.

The War against Elam and the Sack of Susa

An example of a second type of expedition, different from that against Muṣaṣir in being primarily punitive, is Ashurbanipal's campaign of 640 B.C. against Elam. As usual the desire for gain was an element in it, but only a comparatively minor one, and it was accompanied by a profound and genuine hatred, and an almost insane desire for revenge. Before taking the field, the king had been gathering intelligence and, when the campaign opened, he was receiving reports of the operations of his subordinate commanders who were engaged in attacking the outlying areas while he was marching on the capital, news of their victories, their booty, and the release of Assyrians whom the Elamites had captured and imprisoned. We have a letter from a liege of Ashurbanipal written from the 'Country of the Sea', bordering on Elam, which gives news of Nabu-bel-shumati, an enemy of Assyria. We may quote a few passages from it:—

'The king, my lord, has restored me to life by the numerous signs of his goodwill which he has manifested to me, who am but the meanest dog, the son of no man . . . What can I do for the king but pray each day to the great gods of heaven and earth that his life may be preserved . . . The king, my lord, has exalted me to the sky . . .' The writer goes on to remind the king that he has made the people of the Country of the Sea swear an oath of loyalty to him, and concludes by informing him of rebellions within Elam which will ease the path of the Assyrian advance. The carefully concealed preparations for this campaign no doubt owed much to Assyrian gold, and an endless series of rebellions and betrayals caused divisions inside the country, which the invader could turn to his advantage.

When the capital was captured, Ashurbanipal took up his residence in the royal palace, where he celebrated his victory and there took possession of the ancestral treasures of the kings of Elam. He seized the furniture, including even that from the bathroom, and he emptied the stables of the gold-bitted horses and mules. We need not linger over the full list, which recalls that compiled by Sargon after the sack of Muṣaṣir, but it is worth looking at the tale of destruction. 'I have destroyed the *ziggurat* of the temple of Susa, which was built of enamelled bricks: I have burned its horned pinnacles of shining bronze. I have carried off to Assyria Shushinak, the god of the oracle of Elam, who dwells apart by himself and whose actions no man has seen, besides the lesser gods and goddesses and their riches. I have carried off thirty-two statues of kings, statues of gold, of silver, of bronze and of marble, together with the colossi that guarded the temple, and the bulls which stood at the gate. I have utterly laid waste the sanctuaries of Elam, and have scattered their divinities to the four winds. My soldiers entered their sacred groves where no man might pass and which no stranger ever entered, and laid bare their mysteries and burned them. The tombs of their kings, from the most ancient to the most recent, kings who had not venerated Ashur and Ishtar my lords, and who had mocked at my royal ancestors, them have I destroyed, made desolate and laid open to the sun. Their bones I have carried off to Assyria, leaving their ghosts for ever without repose, without funeral offerings of food and water."

The whole of the royal family together with the families of the nobles were led into captivity during this destruction of Elam. This took more than a month, and over the ruins of the city Ashurbanipal ordered salt to be scattered and weeds to be sown. Silent for ever were the sounds of happy people, the cries of joy, the tread of household animals; the city site was the home of wild asses, gazelles and beasts of the plain. In the meanwhile Ashurbanipal recovered the statue of the goddess Nana, who had remained in Elam for 1635 years, a place which he regarded as 'not fitting for her' and who was awaiting the coming of Ashurbanipal, which she had appointed, proclaiming that the king 'would lead her forth from this miserable Elam and would bring her to the temple E-anna.'

The great divinity of Susa in his turn also experienced exile, for the king, though with great respect, used force upon him, 'taking him by the hand' in an invitation to depart, and establishing him in the city of Uruk.

The various gods were given the first choice from among the prisoners, the soldiers being absorbed in the Assyrian army, while the remainder 'like sheep' were divided between the temples, the officials and the nobles.

Here we may leave the campaign of Elam, which was conducted with a violence to which history can show few parallels. It was common practice to violate the temples of an enemy, but not to desecrate royal tombs, and Ashurbanipal could rest secure in the belief that he had utterly obliterated a hated enemy.

Warships

We possess a number of pictures of warships. Boats were for

the most part propelled by oars like galleys, though sails could also be used. Their most striking feature was a kind of pointed ram, with a solidly constructed base, which can be seen protruding almost at water level and was used to attack enemy ships.[14] The rowers remained out of sight behind the protection of the bulwarks. Moreover, in anticipation of the practice of a later age, the bulwarks were further strengthened by being lined with the round shields of the soldiers who were carried on board. We have a boastful description of a naval expedition by Sennacherib, resulting from his decision to strike at the riverside dwellers of Elam who believed themselves to be immune from attack. Accordingly, in order to save time, he had a fleet built by his Phoenician subjects simultaneously on the Tigris and Euphrates. A concentration of the two was effected, despite the fact that the rivers were no longer navigable for certain of the boats, by dragging the vessels on to the bank and hauling them along on wheels. It is clear that, whatever the labour force employed in this operation, the boats themselves must have been small. In point of fact, despite the high-flown language of the inscriptions about this expedition, it appears to have had a very limited success.

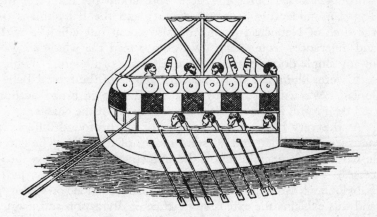

A warship

CHAPTER III

MESOPOTAMIAN THOUGHT

General Concepts

THIS chapter can claim to be the heart of the book. Hitherto we have been examining the actions and customs of the inhabitants of Mesopotamia, and have observed wherein they resemble and wherein they differ from those of other peoples. Now we must attempt to read their thoughts, and to comprehend their view of the universe and of their own part in it; to understand not only their attitude towards the forces by which they believed themselves to be ruled but also how far they regarded themselves as dependent upon them and what they expected of them. This is surely the central point of our whole inquiry, the answer to which will shape our convictions both about the nature of the Assyrians under the Sargonid dynasty and the Babylonians of the time of Nebuchadrezzar, and also about our affinities with and differences from them. We cannot read the whole answer in any single document, but the great mass of literature should, as it were, illuminate the intellectual aspect of the typical Babylonian. We will first try to draw the picture in broad outline and then to fill in the detail in the remainder of the chapter.

At the very outset we must recognize a profound difference between Babylonian and Western modes of thought. The latter is based fundamentally upon the inductive and deductive processes, with analogical reasoning playing a secondary part. Babylonian reasoning was, on the other hand, founded on analogy, and this explains the extensive practice of divination and magic, which were regarded as branches of science, and the sacerdotal aspect of medicine, which was largely another expression of the same idea. Their method of scientific classification, for example, whether in the field of botany or of cuneiform signs, so far as we can understand it, derives from the analogical method;

indeed, the shadow seems sometimes to be in danger of being taken for the substance.

This lies at the root of the fundamental Babylonian belief in the similarity of the composition of earth and heaven, and in their interdependence; and this in turn naturally led to the conviction that every action in the one sphere must necessarily produce its counterpart in the other. Heaven and earth were indissolubly united, but if the obligations enforced by the former were fully and duly discharged by the latter, then heaven could neither disregard nor evade the counterpart to be expected on earth. The use of the words 'obligations enforced' is deliberate and does not imply any exaggeration, since no school of theology that has envisaged the creation has failed to assert that the purpose of the gods in creating man was that he might build temples and practise their worship. There is at least this to be said in favour of so rigid a subordination of man to the divine, that, no matter how precarious his situation, an inhabitant of Babylon could not expect the final catastrophe: the world must continue, since the gods cannot do without human beings.

The Babylonians believed that the creation of the world was followed by the earliest age, described in the Gilgamesh epic (p. 201 *ff.*). During this period the gods, whose abode was in heaven, dwelt also in their temple upon earth, their divine retinue of priests having its counterpart in the king's retinue in his palace. Later, when the gods had finally reascended into heaven, prayer still remained as a link uniting the two worlds, while divination, or the language of 'signs', was revealed to men as the means of communication whereby they might know the will of the gods, whose appearances on earth had become much less frequent. In order to ease man's lot heaven had revealed another method to him, in the shape of magic, and the final proof that, at least at that particular time and place, divination and magic were an accepted element in official religion, can be seen in the fact that the former was conducted under the auspices of Shamash and Adad and the latter under those of Ea and Marduk, accepted as great gods of the Mesopotamian Pantheon.

These circumstances resulted in a strict and unquestioned parallelism between heaven and earth. The Babylonians had some conception, though not a very precise one, of the division of beings into their various natural 'kingdoms', and they allotted every natural animate and inanimate object, as well as everything manufactured, to the sphere of its particular god. A tenuous system of relationships between heaven and earth was established, and the most primitive religious phase, which was expressed in nature cults of fertility and fruitfulness, relied upon a multiplicity of such relationships for its belief that man could expect what he desired from his performance of an action which would provoke its counterpart in heaven; for example, the libation which prayed for rain or flood, or the intercourse of the divinities, in the persons of the priests, to ensure its repetition among the gods and thus the procreation of children.

Further, no school of Babylonian theology ever admitted that the creation of the world could have run counter to what we may call 'The Doctrine of the Name'.

The Doctrine of the Name

The doctrine itself can be summarized in the basic principle that nothing exists unless it has a name. The Creation epic opens with the affirmation that in the beginning Chaos alone existed and nothing had a name :—

'When the heavens above were yet unnamed
And no dwelling beneath was called by a name . . .
When no names had been recorded . . .'

As long as anything had no name, it did not exist, which is no doubt the reason why we read in Genesis (Chapter II, v. 19), that after creating the animals, God called them before Adam so that the latter might name them and thus confer individual existence upon them. The Akkadian phrase denoting universality, 'Everything which bears a name', is itself an expression of this belief. As a mode of thought it has striking similarities with Schopenhauer's theory that neither subject nor object can exist independently of each other, which he illustrates by supposing (as was still quite possible in his own day) the existence in the heart of an unexplored continent of a lake much larger than any known up to that time. He contended that, if no one had ever penetrated to it, the lake, philosophically speaking, had no existence.

The Babylonian view was shared by the Egyptians, who believed that the name of an object shares its essential nature.

In the Book of the Dead the phrases 'I was not carried off' and 'my name was not carried off' are used indifferently; while Plato was inclined to the same line of reasoning and to see in objects a reflection of their 'proper' name. The argument of the Cratylus is that objects have a natural designation, the peculiar property of which is to represent them. It eventually became an axiom of scholastic philosophy that names are the consequences of things. The point is summarized as follows by Lefébvre in his analysis of this doctrine among the Egyptians: 'The name of a person or a thing is an effective representation of it, and thus becomes the object itself in a less substantial and more adaptable form, which is more susceptible to intellectual treatment: in short, it forms a mental substitute . . . the name, which we regard as an image of the object in question, seems consequently to be an essential element or projection of it, in the same natural relationship to it as a body's shadow or reflection.'[1]

Modern society, in exercising public authority, still subscribes to this theory. The nameless or anonymous person is an 'individual', who only acquires a legal existence when armed with an identity card. This shows that the prime consequence of a name is that its bearer becomes known, and to this extent he becomes vulnerable.

The Voice. Personal Names

Experience proves that if you shout a proper name like John or Peter in a crowd, many of the owners of that name will turn round to see who is calling them. The voice, that is to say, is an instrument which can evoke the almost perpetual power that the knowledge of a name confers, though it is limited in practice by the impossibility of perpetual repetition. If, however, the name is written down, the knowledge of the object and, consequently, the influence which that knowledge can exercise, acquires a quality of permanence. The voice calls into action the power conferred by knowledge, while writing it down projects it indefinitely. It is, in fact, a means of perpetuating power.

Since, however, it is accepted that the name of a person or an object connotes the qualities which it expresses, a good quality is naturally attributed to everything which requires a name. This is what the Mesopotamians called 'the good name' and it was originally the equivalent of 'good destiny' since it conferred its good influence on its owner for life. The process was equally applicable to the peasant naming his children and to the prince. Mesopotamian monarchs, who were very ready to claim to be sons of goddesses, are always emphasizing the 'good name' which they have received from them and the favourable words about them exchanged between the gods. 'The god Ningirsu, in the temple of Uruk, spoke favourably on the subject of Urukagina with the goddess Baba'. The whole of this lengthy phrase is a single proper name, which Urukagina, who reformed the city of Lagash, gave to and engraved upon a sacred stone in the temple carved in the shape of an olive. Anyone who repeated it reinforced the action described and thereby caused the donor to benefit.

This is also why Gudea, in his dedication of some steles in the temple built for Ningirsu, calls one of them 'The king of the hurricane, Enlil, who has no rival, looks favourably upon Gudea, the great priest of Ningirsu.'

In the same way streets ('May the enemy never tread it', the processional way in Babylon), canals ('Hammurabi is the source of abundance for mankind') and city gates and walls in Babylon ('Bel hath built it, Bel hath shown it favour') all bore names designed to ensure good influences for the city. The practice naturally extended to people, whose name might be a wish, an assertion of divine favour or a blessing, as the names of Assyrian and Babylonian kings clearly show. Sargon is 'the firmly established and legitimate king', Sennacherib is 'The God Sin increaseth the number of the brothers', Esarhaddon 'Ashur hath given a brother', Ashurbanipal 'Ashur is the creator of the son', Nebuchadrezzar (whose name should never include the 'n' which is commonly inserted in it) and which should really be Nabuchodorosor, means 'Oh Nabu, protect the progeny'. Some of the names even have modern equivalents. Ishtar-ibni and Ilu-bani are in meaning very like Theodore or Theodosius.

The Tone of Incantations

The mere pronunciation of someone's name is, however, in itself insufficient; for a summons, to be obeyed, must be uttered in the proper tone. The voice, in fact, is only effective in certain conditions. The Egyptians, who were well aware of this, used to say that to pronounce their sacred formulae required a 'true voice', not in the sense in which the phrase is used of a singer, but in the sense of 'the proper tone for the utterance of prayers'. This is what the inhabitants of Mesopotamia are trying to convey in their references to the 'proper way' of pronouncing incantations, and they do not in fact use the verb 'say', normally applicable to conversations: the word is *luḫḫushu*, which signifies 'utter' or 'murmur', and can also mean 'chant' or 'mutter'. A special tone of voice for the recitation of prayer, different from that of normal speech, is an almost universal feature of all religions, and Babylonian ritual nearly always specifies its importance in incantations: for example 'An incantation to be recited in a murmur: May the wise men, the priests of incantations, the snake charmers, be enabled to appease thee . . .'

The Power of Writing, Drawing, Statuary, Songs and Dances

As we have said, one way of fixing in perpetuity the power which resides in the voice that pronounces a name was by writing it, and this method was one of the first stages in the process of endowing statues in the temple with life. Many statues of Gudea are now in the Louvre, and many more, of varying quality, scattered throughout the world: but each time one of them was originally placed in a sanctuary, its purpose was to stand eternally before the god in the place of Gudea himself, while the essentially impersonal quality of the stone, despite its physical resemblance to him, was countered by the cartouche, high on the arm or the shoulder, containing the inscription which would identify the statue for all time. The statue stood in the temple of the god, and was dedicated to him: it was intended to take Gudea's place in his prayers to the god, which were inscribed *in extenso* on the front of his garment. If, as was probably the case, the statue had been 'endowed with life' by the 'washing of the mouth' (p. 292) then a new Gudea dwelt within the temple who, if not actually immortal, would at least outlive his mortal original.

So great was the power of the written word, and so unquestioned the gods' universal knowledge, that the prayer need not be inscribed where it could be seen by all and sundry. There is a series of reliefs at Khorsabad with their inscriptions on the reverse, which was always buried in the wall, while when King Bod'ashtart of Sidon strengthened the foundations of the temple of Eshmun with a reinforcing wall, and inscribed his own name and the dedication on each block of stone, he saw to it that each inscription should be on a concealed surface, and consequently invisible. The engraved letters, coloured with a red pigment, still preserved their pristine freshness when the wall was taken down, more than twenty centuries after its original construction. If the usual motive for the concealment of an inscription was the desire to remove it from malevolent eyes, it was sometimes deliberately disguised in order to make passers-by curious to read it. This point is discussed later in pages 169, 187 and 294, when we deal with the cryptographic scripts of the inscriptions on Egyptian steles deciphered by E. Drioton.

Since to know and pronounce the name of an object instantly endowed it with reality, and created power over it, and since the degree of knowledge and consequently of power was strengthened by the tone of voice in which the name was uttered, writing, which was a permanent record of the name, naturally contributed to this power, as did both drawing and sculpture, since both were means of asserting knowledge of the object and consequently of exercising over it the power which knowledge gave. The purpose of the most primitive representations must generally have been to ensure the expected capture of the object represented, as in the cave paintings of Altamira and the bisons carved in full relief in the 'Tuc d' Adoubert',* where they were meant to ensure success to the hunter.

The same fundamental origin and purpose also lie at the root of the songs, in which the power of the voice is enhanced both by the employment of the proper tone and often by their being sung by several voices at once, as well as of the dances which mimed the desired result. This is all part of 'sympathetic magic', a subject treated in more detail at the very end of this book, where we shall discuss magic in Mesopotamia.

The Importance of Concealing the True Name

Since the knowledge of a person's name gave power over its owner, care was naturally taken to prevent it from becoming known. The Egyptians, for example, gave a child one name and called it by another throughout its entire life. The steles of a high

---

* The site of famous cave paintings in the Pyrenees. [Translator's note.]

priest and his wife of the Ptolemaic period record, on the subject of their child: 'He was named Imhotep, but he was called Petubaste.'

This fear may appear to have been without substance, but the Egyptians could provide incontrovertible proof of its truth. When the god Ra grew old and feeble, Isis, who was at the time merely a witch, conceived the idea of mixing some of the god's saliva with earth and making a snake which she placed in the path which Ra must tread. He was bitten in the heel, and in his agony called on Isis, who claimed that she could give him no relief unless she knew his true name. In the face of her insistence, Ra revealed it to her, and thanks to this knowledge Isis, from being a witch, was raised into the ranks of the gods.

In certain circumstances, however, the possession of a second name was not due to any desire for concealment. Thus during the Seleucid period, when it was fashionable to copy Greek names, certain individuals assumed a 'grecianized' name, apparently even, in some cases, by special grant from the king. In these conditions the motive was probably to create a new and enlarged personality.

Despite the reluctance revealed in Assyrio-Babylonian literature to disclose any element in its mysteries, some record had sometimes to be made, and this was done as cryptically as possible. So great, however, was the fear of some indiscreet revelation, even though the written record was meant for the eyes of the priests alone, that it often ended with this sacramental formula: 'the novice may see these rites which thou shalt perform: the stranger, who is not associated with the masters of the oracle, shall not see them. [If this rule is transgressed] may his days upon earth be shortened. Let the initiated explain them to the initiated, and he that is not initiated must not know them: that would be an abomination to the mighty gods Anu, Enlil and Ea.'

The Power of Numbers

A corollary of the power of the name was that of the number, which was also regarded as a method of expression, conferring its own essential qualities on the object to which it related. The inherent property of infinitely varied combination which numbers possess, and the fact that one numerical result could be reached by a variety of calculations, gave them an almost sacred character and led them to be regarded as a kind of language capable of expressing every thought. One of the first manifestations of this power of numbers was the creation of a numerical hierarchy of the gods, whose supreme lord, Anu (and this itself is a sign of its antiquity), was the possessor of the perfect number, 60, and the number ascribed to each of the gods corresponded to the place they occupied in the universal system which they ordered and to which they belonged.

The Mesopotamians next conceived the idea of ascribing a numerical value to each sign in their syllabary so that every name was capable of numerical expression, and it was thus that, during the construction of the palace at Khorsabad, Sargon created a bond of identity between himself and the wall by which the palace was defended, by saying in effect 'I built the circuit of the wall of 16,283 cubits, the number of my name.'[2]

The system was in fairly common use. A text giving a version of the exaltation of Ishtar, dating from the Seleucid period, bears an inscription giving in numerical terms the name of the owner of the tablet and of his father, i.e., '21–35–35–24–44, son of 21–11–20–42.'[3]

The key to this system is contained in an unfortunately very seriously damaged tablet from Susa, originally published by Father Van der Meer, and brought to my notice by G. Dossin, on which the corresponding syllabic values—*me, pa, il, lu,* etc.— are shown opposite the column of numbers. The end of the document affords further evidence of the Babylonian love of alliteration, for opposite the numerical sign for 3600, which bears the name '*shar*', we find the word '*sharru*', the root of which is '*shar*' and which means 'the king'.[4] Again, there is another tablet known as the 'tablet of Esagila',* which has been interpreted in a wide variety of ways. This gives all the dimensions of the temple and the *ziggurat*. At the end of the list of numbers, the scribe has repeated the prohibition on explaining its significance to the uninitiated, and we are forced to conclude that the recorded dimensions are only symbolical and contain some esoteric meaning.

The Mesopotamians must take the credit for having invented this system, known as '*isopsephia*'[5] which was in common use among the Greeks and Romans. These two last were able to perfect it through the possession of an alphabetic script, in

---

* The temple of Marduk at Babylon. [Translator's note.]

which some of the letters were actually used as numerals, so that a value could consequently be ascribed to each letter. They then applied the same processes of reasoning to numerals as they did to names, and conceived the idea of adding together the numerical value of the letters in a word and comparing the result with the value of other words, thus establishing numerical relationships and even identities between words. By this argument Nero was predestined to kill his mother, since the letters in his name 'added up to' the word matricide. This mode of reasoning was much employed by the Gnostics and the Fathers of the Church, who were convinced believers in it. Thus the Holy Spirit revealed itself at the baptism of Christ in the form of a dove, or 'peristera', whose number is 801: while, since the combined value of the letters A and Ω (Alpha and Omega) is also 801, the assertion 'I am Alpha and Omega' must be an assertion of the Trinity. The goodness of God, according to Theophanes Kerameus in his 44th Homily, is proved by the correlation by isopsephia of Theos (god) and Agathos (good), while he also recalls in his 36th Homily that since the nets drew up all the 153 known varie-. ties of fish in the miraculous draught of fishes, and since these fish represent the universal church, Rebecca must symbolize that church, since her 'psephia' is also 153. The method was destined to be forced to its final point by the Rabbis in the Kabbala, who knew it by the name of '*gematria*', which is probably a corruption of 'geometria'.

Spoken and Written Puns

Distant antiquity owed much of its taste for alliteration, and for what we now call puns, both spoken and written, to the theory, or what might more accurately be called the dogma, of the name and numbers. But we are immediately faced with a sharp distinction. To us the phrase 'play on words' means what it says, an amusing pastime without profounder significance. The Babylonians, however, and their spiritual ancestors the Sumerians, took it very seriously. We regard a stone whose shape or colouring reminds us of some other object, merely as a freak of nature, but the Babylonian regarded it as a sign, and a warning of a positive relationship between the two objects, reinforced if they happened to possess similar names. At this period, of course, the capacity for play on the spoken and still more on the

written word must have been confined to the most highly educated
class.

Riddles

The same instinct must also have been responsible for the
taste for the riddles which the various princes used to ask each
other, in their desire to assert their intellectual superiority which
at that date was, or was claimed to be, as highly valued as superior
physical strength. Be that as it may, a refusal to pay the forfeit
which was the price of defeat was often the signal for the more or
less immediate opening of hostilities.

When we come to discuss the Flood (p. 194) we shall have
occasion to quote the answer given by Uta-Napishtim when he
was asked why he was making his preparations for departure.
He duly reassured the inhabitants by a promise that it would rain
kibtu and *kukku* on them—'corn' and 'sound': but the answer
contained both a pun and a riddle, for the words also meant
'grief' and 'misfortune', and it was a question of choosing the
correct meanings.

We find a pedigree bull, which was the apple of his owner's
eye, called Sharur-abi which could mean either 'The God Sharur
is my father' or, less pretentiously, 'Canefield Glory' (p. 60).

In Egypt, during the period of the Hyksos supremacy, according to the papyrus known as Sallier I, King Apepi sent the
following message to Sékenenré, from whom he was separated
by the entire length of Egypt: 'Leave the marsh of the hippo-
potami which lies near Thebes, for the noise thereof reaches to
Avaris and prevents me from sleeping.' Sékenenré did not know
the correct answer and the incident led to war.

Samson had propounded the following riddle to thirty young
Philistines: 'Out of the eater came forth meat and out of the
strong came forth sweetness'. If he lost, the stake was to be a
tunic and a garment for each of them. At the instigation of the
young men, Samson told his wife the answer to the riddle. He
had come across a dead lion with a swarm of bees lodged in its
side (which was odd, since bees do not settle on carrion meat).
His wife hastened to tell the secret to the young men, who
replied 'What is sweeter than honey, or what is stronger than a
lion?' Samson said to them 'If you had not ploughed with my
heifer, you would not have found the answer to my riddle'. Then

the spirit of the Lord took him and he went down to Askalon, and there he slew thirty men and took their spoils and gave the spare garments to those who had answered the riddle.

Tradition relates that the Queen of Sheba, who had heard of the vaunted wisdom of Solomon, came to him from a distant country to test his wisdom and to ask him some riddles.

Akkadian and Sumerian are full of riddles of this kind, which owe their existence to the character alike of the script and the spoken language. In its earliest form, Sumerian writing, which was later adopted by the Semites, was pictographic and ideographic, i.e., the signs represented either an actual object or an idea, and later in this chapter (p. 181) we shall consider how they came to represent multiple objects or ideas. But a Sumerian sign was in its very nature something of a riddle, and the scribes often deliberately wrote it in the form which would tax the reader's ingenuity most severely. Thus, for example, while a proper name like *Marduk-shum-iddin*, which meant 'Marduk has given a name (i.e., lineage)' could be fully written out syllabically, both the words 'name' and 'give' are represented by the sign 'mu', and the scribe might choose to write '*Marduk-mu-mu*'. Similarly *Sin-ahi-uṣur* ('O Sin, protect the brother') contains two elements 'protect' and 'brother' both capable of being rendered by the sign 'pap', and the scribe might therefore write '*Sin-pap-pap*'. An example of this kind is quoted in the section dealing with the reading of omens (p. 287).

In the following examples we can see the scribes using these two features of the written and the spoken language and plunging into recondite etymological research, in order to conceal the meaning of their writings, which must in any case have been incomprehensible to the uninitiated. This becomes less surprising in the light of the practice of their neighbours, the Egyptians, who sometimes used a kind of hieroglyphic code, whereas we should regard the hieroglyphs alone as an adequate safeguard.

'The Garment of Marduk'

G. Dossin has conducted some research upon this subject which, though still in an early stage, is beginning to reveal the ingenuity of the system employed by the scribes. We will confine ourselves to one example of each of what seem to have been the two most commonly used methods (see Bibliography).

The first example shows the scribe apparently thinking at random, but led to an entirely unexpected conclusion by accidentally realizing the possibilities inherent in his terms. Thus, in the poem of the Creation, Marduk is to be invested in the assembly of the gods with supreme powers, and his scepticism leads him to seek some tangible assurance of them. Then the gods:

' . . . placed in the midst a cloak, and said to the god Marduk, their first born; "decree thou the throwing down and the building up* and it shall come to pass: speak but the word, and the cloak shall be no more: speak a second time, and the cloak shall be intact." Marduk spoke the word and the cloak was no more: he spoke a second time and the cloak reappeared.'

No doubt the choice of a cloak for so important a test was the fruit of complicated etymological research. This is proved by a later passage in the same poem: the seventh tablet is inscribed with the fifty names of Marduk, and as the result of elaborate ingenuity the process 'has been carried to the point when it has even given rise to an etymological style'.

The second syllable of the name Marduk was not unlike the Sumerian *tug*, meaning 'cloak', while *mar* can also mean 'place'. This is the point of the 'placing of a garment' among the gods. But this was not all. *Duk* also meant 'to speak' and *mar* also had the diametrically opposed meanings of 'produce' or 'create', and 'destroy'. This explains the latter part of the quotation. There is reason to believe that this was how the scribe was thinking, since in the list of the epithets of Marduk with which the compiler leaves the actual name of the god, those which glorify him as the creator are followed by those lauding him as the destroyer. The influence of this etymological ingenuity is visible throughout the list. Dossin, in his study of the subject, quotes two further phrases from the sixth tablet in which Marduk is briefly described as 'creator, destroyer, full of compassion and pity, and in his commands showing all good will towards the gods': which again must be a carefully-phrased reference to the different meanings of *mar* and *duk*.

These different meanings provided the material of which this

---

* i.e., the establishing of a new creation to take the place of the old. [Translator's note.]

phrase could be composed. Faced with any given word, the scribe uses its component parts like a musician exploring the elements of a musical phrase in a set of variations, pursuing each point to its logical conclusion without ever losing sight of the original theme. Dossin has pointed out the essential artificiality of the practice, which leaves no room for genuine literary skill or poetic inspiration, but is merely an exercise in ingenuity of construction. But while to us this may be true, the purpose of the Babylonian was so to break down one meaning of a word as to reveal several other meanings, and to create a new name by etymological processes; and so, by virtue of the doctrine of the name, to give rise to a new 'reality'. We may regard each of these speculations as an arid exercise, but for the Babylonian it was the equivalent of our discovery beneath the microscope of a new element; it was as real as a human being, it came into existence at the very moment of discovery and the realm of mankind was thereby proportionately enlarged.

But the scribe had other methods at his disposal. We have just seen him squeezing the original sense of a word in order to extract its concealed meanings. Instead of watching him follow them unresistingly let us observe him working on other lines and calling, not word or thought, but writing to his aid.

'*Brg'yh King of Ktk*'

An Aramaic stele discovered at Séfiré near Aleppo preserved the text of a treaty between *Mati'-ilu*, king of Arpad, and King *Brg'yh* of *Ktk*. (There are no vowels in written Aramaic.) A comparison of the treaty with that imposed by King Ashur-nirari V (753–46 B.C.) on Mati'-ilu proved that the same protagonists were involved, but it was difficult to understand why the king of Assyria had assumed so outlandish a name. It was reasonable to suppose that he wished to use a borrowed name in his dealings with Mati'-ilu of whom, justly as it turned out, he entertained suspicions; but how could Ashur-nirari king of Assyria get transposed into *Brg'yh King of Ktk*?

G. Dossin solved the problem by way of the name of the country, which was written in the signs *Kur* (meaning 'country') *Ash* (for Ashur) and *Ki* (the word-ending for the names of countries). Cuneiform signs often, however, have more than one

value, and this is true of the second of this series (*Ash*), which
becomes *Dil* or *Til*. The scribe transcribed these three signs into
Aramaic by the process of merely taking the initial letters,
namely K.T.K.

The explanation of the king's name followed the same lines.
The cuneiform sign of Nirari is complicated, consisting of two
single signs in sequence, *Bir* and *Gab* (or *Ga*). The Aramaic
practice of omitting the vowels led to this being written *Brg*,
while the soft breathing which followed no doubt represents the
vowel '*a*' which was required for purposes of pronunciation.
Finally the '*yh*' was the Aramaic transliteration of the divine
element, and stood for Ashur. Thus the monarch's own name and
that of his country were alike concealed, and it was safe from
any abuse which might endanger his person. This is another
example of the inventiveness of the scribes, whose traditions
still flourished in their schools, not only in Assyria but beyond her
frontiers, at a time when the heart of the country had already
begun to turn away from Assyrian, and particularly from the
cuneiform script, in favour of Aramaic.

There was a third method of juggling with words which it
was desired to keep secret. This was to read them backwards,
either letter by letter or syllable by syllable. V. Scheil suggested that *Gaspar*, the name of a magician king, was really
Rapsag, the name of the office of chief cupbearer at the Persian
court. The name *Sin* might be its Sumerian elements read backwards, i.e., *Enzu*, which turned first into *Zu-in* and then *Sin*:
while by the same process *Gal Lu*, the great man, could be read
as *Lugal*, the king.

Assyrian Symbolism

Every religion which has represented its gods and their actions
in physical terms, has portrayed them in terms of a settled
iconography, according to which the various divinities are
endowed with immutable physical and moral attributes. The
prime reason is, of course, that, by describing the divinity in
accepted terms, all such representations are obliged to conform
to a single pattern, while in addition the figures are designed for
the benefit of the generality of believers, and must therefore
remain constant in order to be recognizable. The practice of
putting a distinctive sign of some episode associated with them,

or of some attribute, beside the figures itself creates a kind of symbols which bring the figure, even if it is not explicitly portrayed, into the mind of the beholder.

This was the practice of the Mesopotamians, who constructed a full-scale iconography. We shall discuss the extent to which their symbols, unaccompanied by any figure, could stand for the gods. But the inexorable relationship between heaven and earth meant that every created object 'belonged' to one or other of the gods, and that each instrument, each object and each element employed in the ceremony possessed its own explanation. This need cause us little surprise if we remember that the memory of these relationships is still kept evergreen by astrology, which still has so many devotees to-day.

Thus in modern astrological belief, Jupiter is a masculine planet, hot, a benefactor: he evokes ideas of justice and religion: he is responsible for tall men, generally auburn-haired: among the professions he corresponds with judges, with men of public affairs and the Church: he is associated with illnesses of the liver and palpitations. Similarly the Ram is a cardinal sign of the Zodiac: he is masculine, and connected with fire: he is responsible for open, frank, independent characters, for thin and brown-haired men of middle height; he governs the head, the face, and illnesses connected with them: he is particularly associated with the countries of England, Germany, Denmark, Palestine and Syria, and the cities of Naples and Florence. His colour is red, his day is Tuesday, his stone the amethyst. And so on for the other planets and signs of the Zodiac.

The Mesopotamians believed in similar attributions. Not only did these import a profounder significance into their ceremonies but they ought to prevent us from regarding them merely as a meaningless rigmarole. On the contrary, every detail was thought out and minutely prescribed, and during a ceremony, a whole new world was revealed to the believer.

Some tablets known as the 'Commentaries' throw a certain amount of light on these symbols. We need not concern ourselves with them all, but can confine ourselves to a few examples for the purpose of illustration.

Thus we know that 'the [libation vessel] *agubbu* symbolises the queen of incantations: the tamarisk, Anu: the crown of the palm tree, Tammuz: the reed, Ninurta: the cypress, Adad. Silver is the moon, gold, the sun, copper is Ea, lead, Ninmah. The censer is the god Urash, the torch is Gibil, gypsum is Ninurta, the seven-headed weapon of laurel wood is the storm'. (Incidentally, superstition still regards the laurel tree as immune from being struck by lightning.)

During an exorcism, different kinds of figures are described as the chest, the loins and the knees of the patient. It is perhaps useless to probe deeper into the subject, but it is possible to imagine that in pouring a libation, for example, in order to obtain rain or spate from the great god of fertility, the use of the libation vessel (*agubbu*) and the placing of a piece of palm wood or tamarisk in the copper bowl into which the libation was to be poured—all these actions might summon the gods for whom they symbolically stood, and the prayer of the believer might be so much the more effective.

KNOWLEDGE

Writing. The Education of the Scribe

Mesopotamian writing presents an especially interesting field of study, for an unusually large number of the written documents survive and writing touched daily life at every point. But its complexity and difficulty, which were far greater than those of most western scripts, meant that it was an accomplishment confined to a very few, notably the class of the scribes, who had assumed responsibility for preserving and transmitting knowledge and who were in practice more or less attached to the priesthood. Scribes could be drawn from all levels of society, but the fact that they included the sons and relatives of city governors and princes is evidence of the esteem in which they were held. We do not in fact possess quite so revealing a picture of the Mesopotamian scribes as that drawn by an Egyptian scribe of his own colleagues, but there is no doubt that the profes-

Scribes

sion was difficult to master and required long studies. There was indeed a saying to the effect that an intending scribe must rise with the sun; but the qualified scribe was widely respected and the same phrase may well suggest (if we are right in seeking for an esoteric meaning) that the scribe of proved skill would shine like the sun. One of Ashurbanipal's inscriptions records that Nabu and his consort Tashmetum have granted him 'great ears' (i.e., great intelligence, which the Assyrians seem largely to have equated with memory), and have enabled him to know and to master the ' "markings " of cuneiform', the word used by the scribe being the same as that used to describe the dappling on a panther's hide. There were many aspirants to so enviable a profession and, though they were admittedly a rarity, female scribes were not unknown. For reasons which will soon appear, scribes specialised in one of various branches, e.g., temples, business, the army, medicine and the priesthood, and they began their studies at a tender age. Almost every excavation includes among its temple tablets some childish exercises, like those found at Sippar and at Mari (Tell Hariri) where the actual school where the young scribes were taught has been exposed. It consists of a moderate-sized room with clay benches fixed to the floor and a number of large earthenware receptacles, whose purpose we shall see later.* The pupils in this school had to repeat phrases which had already been composed for them, and copy them from a model sentence written at the top of their tablet, while they gradually memorized various expressions connected with the branch of affairs in which they were specializing. 'Knowledge' consisted merely of the capacity to produce without notice phrases appropriate to a given situation, and to have mastered them sufficiently to be able to string them together. Each literary field had its individual vocabulary and the good scribe was the one with the most accurate knowledge. Memory, not original thought, was required of him, and he would be asked to do no more than to arrange in the proper order the information stored in his brain. We find it difficult, when we are confronted with works of art such as bas-reliefs or pictures, to recognize the hand of any individual artist: this is equally true of written documents, and no doubt a scribe would not presume to an originality which would have been

---

* For a more detailed description, with photographs, see 'The Oldest School in the World', in *The Times Educational Supplement*, October 31, 1952. [Translator's note.]

regarded as out of place. This explains even more clearly why scribes had to specialize: for while they could become extremely expert within a limited field, they would have been but little use if they had had to be jacks of all trades.

The training schools were generally situated in the ancillary buildings attached to the temples, and in the neo-Babylonian period scribes, whose usual name was *tupshar* ('he who writes on the tablets') are described in the contracts as *shangu* ('priest'), thus enshrining the close and age-old association of official documents with temples. We shall not be far mistaken if we think of a class of scribes as an actual school with the pupils, in the shape of the apprentice scribes, sitting on benches and receiving from their master a tablet inscribed with a sentence which they had simultaneously to memorize and to copy. Their exercises were generally set out in a particular way, usually on slightly convex tablets. This explains the little water-troughs which were placed near the benches: they held the necessary quantities of pure clay, which could be kneaded into cakes of any shape required. During the late Assyrian period, contract documents were generally rectangular, and broader than they were tall, whereas for ordinary letters the proportions were reversed and one surface

Cuneiform writing   (*British Museum photo*)

was always slightly convex, like a small cushion. The tablets used in connection with the temple were slightly larger in size. The actual method of writing was for the scribe to take a writing instrument (usually simply a piece of reed) with an end shaped like the mouthpiece of a flute, and not to trace, but to print the signs on a virgin tablet. The point of the instrument was held more or less flat on the clay and the characters were formed by a series of sharp jabs, with 'tails' of varying lengths depending upon the angle at which the instrument was held. This is why this type of writing, the characters of which resemble nails, is called cuneiform (literally 'wedge-shaped'). The tablet was then left to dry. It was, however, very liable to crumble, and in order to prolong its life indefinitely, it had to be baked in an oven. This converted it into a small brick which was virtually immune to the effects of time or damp, and could only be destroyed by being crushed to pieces.

Anyone who tries to copy anything on clay with a stylus soon discovers that one person's writing is exactly like another's, and that the wedge-shaped impressions have no individuality. In our period, the method used for ensuring that written texts were not tampered with was to place the contract or the letter inside a thin clay covering, which served as a kind of envelope. In the case of a letter the address of the recipient was then written on the outside and it was stamped with the sender's seal. A contract was stamped with the seals of the witnesses, and with a short summary of the text. If the envelope was unbroken, neither letter nor contract could have been tampered with.

Documents of considerable length, requiring several tablets, if written out in full, were kept in piles on racks and the edges were inscribed with the first words of their texts, like the modern method of referring to Papal encyclicals by their opening words.

Cuneiform script is in fact nothing more than a pattern of wedges and lines. It was without any question the most widely used script in antiquity, being employed, though with a number of variations, from the centre of Asia Minor as far as Persia. Egyptian writing, at least in its hieroglyphic form, changed little throughout its history, tending always towards a simplified derivative script, to become in due course, the hieratic and the demotic scripts respectively. The cuneiform script used in any given area, however, once its form became well settled, never showed much variation, although previously it had been liable to very extensive changes.

The Development of Writing

Assyrian was first deciphered about a hundred years ago. Some twenty or thirty years after this, however, a suspicion arose that the script was the debased descendant of some totally different script somewhat resembling Egyptian and Chinese, which had itself radically altered from its original pictographic form. This opinion was reinforced by the discovery of an admittedly small number of tablets suggesting that in an earlier period certain signs had had an entirely different form. Matters remained like this until about twenty years ago when the discovery of documents in recent excavations enabled the question of its origin to be settled.

During a long initial period lasting for at least 1,000 years, Mesopotamian civilization was ignorant of writing as well as of the use of metal.* This is known as the Al 'Ubaid period, and must have closed about 3400 B.C. But though the art of writing was still unknown, its foundations were being laid in the form of ideographic representations. The tombs of Susa, which belong to the 'Ubaid period, have yielded a ceremonial funerary pottery with black painted decoration on a greenish-yellow ground. The paintings must represent the outcome of prolonged effort, and their development suggests links with a far distant past. The principal motifs are drawn from animal subjects and the artist's efforts to reproduce them have finally led him to treat them geometrically. This is proved by the fact that among random examples every intermediate stage can be found.

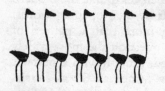 Take for example a frieze of water birds. In the first stage the feet are left out and the necks extended, so that they look like a line of quavers in modern musical notation. In the next stage, the artist discards the body and leaves nothing but a series of vertical lines (the neck) surmounted by a small pothook (the beak).

---

* Evidence now exists that the use of metal, though uncommon, was known at this period. [Translator's note.]

Ibexes, too, are attenuated to the point where they are merely two conjoined triangles, with head and tail relegated to two small excrescences. The horns are, however, disproportionately enlarged into an enormous circle on the animal's head, quite often containing a smaller circle or a square which in turn encloses a chequered design, a series of wavy lines or a leafy branch. The meaning of this decoration is given by the purpose of the pottery in question, which was intended to hold the dead man's food and drink in the after life. Just as both in their earliest tombs and later in their *mastabas* the Egyptians would paint scenes from the dead man's life so that he might relive them and be nourished by his harvests, the inhabitants of Susa, whose tombs were dug straight in the ground and therefore afforded no wall surfaces capable of decoration, instead painted their vase surfaces with a brief summary of these scenes. By this means they believed that the dead would be enabled to feed on the water birds which they had hunted and taken (their capture being assured by the process of painting them on their pottery—see p. 164): they would be able to hunt the ibexes and catch them in the undergrowth (the branch inside the circle of the horns), on the open plain (the chequered pattern), or at the watering place (the square with the wavy lines, the earliest way of representing water, employed by both Egyptians and Mesopotamians). This may not yet be a script, but it is at least the preliminary stage, where painting is used to convey ideas by means of pictures. There seems to be some analogy with the Chinese 'literary painting'. Considered in isolation, this may not appear to be very expressive, with its stream, its flowering tree, its clouds and one or two water birds. But by convention each component feature carries its own deeper significance, which leads the beholder far beyond the surface of what he sees. The species of the trees, for example, may stand for the spring, the way the clouds are drawn may convey the passing of the storm, the birds, the time of day: a whole world is evoked from behind the formal exterior, a universe is re-created by the imagination. The painter has done no more than hint at it.

Moreover, this concept of painting as preliminary to writing fits perfectly with what we can learn from the contemporary archaic monuments, which display the same peculiarities as do the 'written' signs. Thus in both cases the thumb is shown as disproportionately long and is turned backwards (cf. the so-called 'circular base' monument in the Louvre), the foot is exaggeratedly arched and the toes are upturned (engraved shell plaques discovered at Kish): while a sheepfold, whether carved or painted, displays the same bell-shaped silhouette, since it is seen from the short side containing the entrance, and surmounted by its top knot of the reeds which formed the central post.

In the succeeding period we find writing in the civilization known as that of Uruk (approximately 3400–3200 B.C.), contemporary with the use of seals and of metals. In its earliest phase the script is nothing more than an accounting device, which makes certain marks, to show the number involved, beside the objects, the drawing of which is greatly simplified; in a word, true pictography. While some of the objects can be very easily recognized, others present a much more difficult problem, and this can easily be understood since each object requires a separate sign, so that, for example, a number of different liquids would each require some device such as an easily distinguishable type of vessel. In this period 620 tablets have yielded a total of 891 different signs.

The succeeding period is known by the name of Jamdat-Nasr. It lasted until about 3000 B.C. and is distinguished only by the appearance of a new type of pottery, otherwise merely representing the normal development of the preceding epoch. The process of multiplying signs came to a halt and the summary list numbers a mere 437. The succeeding period, known as the Early Dynastic period, saw a selective process at work, and though the scribes did not actually reduce the total number of signs, some were bound to be infrequently used. Later, however, the point was reached where a knowledge of about 300 signs was sufficient to enable a normal text to be read: a number which, though large, marked a considerable reduction on the 900 of the Uruk period.

We do not know the principles according to which the Mesopotamians classified their syllabary, but it seems clear that each sign had its own name which might sometimes be one of its meanings, though more frequently the name referred to some characteristic of the sign itself. For example the sign *mu* consists of an horizontal wedge followed by a group of four small strokes, while the sign *zer* is identical except that it ends with three strokes, and was known as 'unfinished mu'.

From Pictography to Syllabic Writing

This alteration was considerably helped by a fundamental change in writing. Originally, as we have said, a sign stood for an object; but there was no simple way of rendering verbs, adjectives, pronouns or declensions, and no possibility of so doing without some general agreement among the scribes, who could attach other secondary meanings to certain signs. If we imagine, for example, that modern writing consisted of pictures of particular objects, and a picture of a horse was to be read as 'horse', the picture could none the less also convey the ideas of speed, of movement, of travel, and of the distance which travel might involve. These ideas would, however, not present themselves directly, nor be immediately conveyed by the picture of a horse, whose primary meaning would be the plain concept 'horse'. Everything would depend upon the acceptance of the other meanings which the signs could convey, and this immediately removes writing from being within everyone's capacity and converts it into a privilege of a single class, the scribes.

But this by itself does not go far enough, for writing in this sense is merely a vocabulary of expressions and ideas which cannot be used: and this is the point at which the pictographic changes to the syllabic. To us, used as we are to words which can be broken down into syllables and further into letters, the process seems natural, but the discovery was not one which could be made instantaneously. When once the principle was grasped, the scribes had the idea of giving each sign the value of the first syllable of the word which it represented. The sign for 'horse', for example, would have the value 'hor'. But the signs for other words also beginning with 'hor'—for example 'hornet' or 'horizon'—would have the same value.

Consequently at this stage a single character or sign could have several meanings, while conversely one meaning might be conveyed by a number of signs. Thus the whole system had passed into the field of the experts, and had become a highly scientific technique, too complex to be comprehended by the ordinary man.

The situation could indeed have been saved had the syllables been broken down into their component letters. This step was actually taken by the Egyptians, but, since they did not at the same time discard the remainder of the system, which was by then superfluous, they merely succeeded in adding a further complication to their script. The Mesopotamians, however, for their part never got beyond the stage of isolating the vowels, with the result that in the Mesopotamian script identical signs might sometimes stand for objects or ideas, sometimes for syllables, and sometimes even for letters: while conversely each sign might have a number of meanings or values in terms of objects, syllables, or letters, and might often duplicate the values of other signs.

So much for what the signs might mean: but we must realize that they did not retain their primitive form. We discussed the actual mechanics of writing in the passage dealing with the schools for scribes. The scribe soon came to realize (and it can easily be verified) that any attempt to draw an object on a surface of fresh clay with a stylus must be inaccurate, since any curved impression deeper than a faint scratch is bound to be accompanied by cracks which blur the outline. The scribe was quick to see that the only way of getting over this difficulty was to press the end of the stylus on the clay: in fact, to print the sign and not to draw it. This meant, however, that curves turned into broken lines: and consequently the script became a linear one and gradually assumed the characteristics of cuneiform. The process was slow and evolved gradually during the whole duration of Mesopotamian writing, the latest specimens which we possess dating from the beginning of the Christian era.

Originally the script was written from top to bottom in parallel columns which read from right to left, but the writer's hand often smudged and rubbed out part of the preceding column. It thus became the normal practice in writing to turn the tablet 90 degrees to the left and to write the signs horizontally. Gradually they came to be read as they were written, i.e., in horizontal lines running from top to bottom of the tablet and completed successively from left to right, with the result that Akkadian and Ethiopian are the only two Semitic languages which are read in the same direction as those of Western Europe. This naturally means that in order to discover the original form of a sign it is necessary to turn the tablet 90 degrees to the right, thus restoring the signs to their original position.

Original pictograph	Pictograph in position of later cuneiform	Early Babylonian	Assyrian	Original or derived meaning
				bird
				fish
				donkey
				ox
				sun day
				grain
				orchard
				to plow to till
				boomerang to throw to throw down
				to stand to go

The origin and development of cuneiform signs

(From Frankfort: *The Birth of Civilization in the Near East* (Williams & Norgate), by permission)

In the course of time, writing, by now truly cuneiform, underwent some further important modifications. During the period before Mesopotamia was divided into two separate kingdoms it is known as Akkadian: when this division did take place, slight variations gradually developed in the Assyrian and Babylonian scripts respectively. Assyrian writing tended to elongate and multiply the horizontal signs, while Babylonian revealed a tendency to keep its signs in the form of chevrons.

The differing force of the impact of Mesopotamian civilization upon the races of Western Asia was matched by the way in which its neighbours borrowed its script. The Hittites as well as the Mitannians adopted it outright, while the Elamites accepted its principles, but created their own script with certain major differences. Later still northern Phoenicia and Achaemenid Persia employed a script which, though cuneiform, was based upon different principles. These variations however belong more properly to the history of the alphabet.

Decipherment

The deciphering of this script was a matter of great difficulty.[7] At the outset no one confronted by an unknown language in an unknown script, could conceive any solution except a bilingual inscription written in a known language as well as the unknown one. This had happened with Egyptian, which had been read with the help of a parallel Greek inscription. Early efforts had done no more than reveal the values of certain signs, when not merely a bilingual, but actually a trilingual inscription was found. Sir Henry Rawlinson, during one of his expeditions, had taken an impression of a huge inscription carved on a rock face on the road between Kermanshah and Hamadan. This proved to be the account by Darius of the hitherto unknown episode of his reconquest of his country and his triumph over his rebellious subjects and pretenders. It was in three versions, in two of which the signs were both complicated and exhibited considerable variety, while in the third they were simpler and recurred frequently. Scholars set to work at once on the third. The discovery of the inscription in Persia suggested Persian as a possibility, while there appeared to be some analogy with the 'Avesta'*

---

* The Avesta are the Persian scriptures, containing the works ascribed to Zoroaster. 'Zend' is the ancient Persian script. [Translator's note.]

and the 'zend' in that language: further, the similarity of certain signs which recurred at the beginning of the inscription, suggested that they might be a royal formulary 'King, son of', the intervening words possibly representing the names of the most celebrated Achaemenid monarchs. The approach to the problem was sound, and after a long series of false starts, the task, however, being simplified by the presence of a sign marking the divisions between words, the text was mastered and identified as ancient Persian. In 1862 F. Spiegel published a grammar with texts, translations and glossaries of the newly discovered language, and at last the scholars had what they wanted, namely an inscription in a known language as a key to one in an unknown.

Of the two remaining inscriptions, one yielded no results, being in the indigenous Elamite language, of Asianic character, very few words of which are still known. But the third was in Akkadian, i.e., the common language of Mesopotamia, which was subdivided into Assyrian and Babylonian. Whereas the simplicity and comparative fewness of the signs used in the first inscription had indicated (as was indeed the case) the use of an alphabet, the third inscription, with its multiplicity of complicated signs, suggested a syllabic script. The decipherers were, however, baffled by the fact that, as they progressed in their task, they came, from time to time, across certain signs which could not be connected with those which preceded or followed them— i.e., ideograms. Despite this, the inscription was ultimately deciphered, except for certain points of detail, while in the course of their labours the translators were struck by the similarities which the language presented to Arabic, to Hebrew, and even to certain other Semitic languages. Moreover, lacking the dictionary which we now possess, for a long time students of Assyrian had to possess a knowledge of the other Semitic languages in order to discover in the Assyrian vocabulary a verbal root which could give them the clue they required. There are still some unknown features in Assyrian, but they can generally be cleared up by reference to their context: if the unknown word is carefully noted, sooner or later it turns up in a passage in which its sense becomes unmistakable.

This decipherment of a language in which the signs might have different values on different occasions, or alternatively sometimes represented a single syllable and sometimes an entire word (ideogram) did not command unquestioning acceptance, and it was considered necessary to put the matter to the proof. What might almost be described as a competition among the exponents of the new science was held under the aegis of the Royal Asiatic Society of London. The participants were confronted with an unedited text (like practically all texts at that date) and each 'competitor' worked on his own. When the translations were finally compared, they were found to be virtually identical except for quite minor variations.

This was the beginning of a steady stream of translations, but it was not long before the translators found themselves faced with texts in another language. Without a bilingual inscription, Assyriology could not have advanced, for it has since become clear that no true insight into Mesopotamian civilization is possible without a profound knowledge of the language and of those who spoke it. As it was, however, there was no lack of bilingual inscriptions, ranging from dictionaries to inscriptions in alternate lines. The unknown language was Sumerian, the tongue spoken by the peoples who had developed their own civilization in Lower Mesopotamia, which the Semites later borrowed.

Sumerian was an entirely different language, Asianic in character. Some dialects which, though differing from it, were founded on the same principles, are still to be found in the Caucasus. Faced by the fundamental dissimilarities between Akkadian and Sumerian, the Mesopotamians continually compiled more and more lists of concordances with the words in parallel columns, and these formed the foundation of modern knowledge of the language. The Akkadians, who were always conscious of the full extent of their debt to the Sumerians, did not show themselves ungrateful, for even after they had gradually absorbed the Sumerians and reduced them to political insignificance, they still carefully preserved the legacy they had received from them: religion, laws, artistic principles, script and even language, which became the 'sacred' language, like Latin in Catholic countries to-day.

Sumerian, once mastered, was the key to the marked complexity of Assyrian and Babylonian writings, for the Sumerians had already done what the Akkadians did later. Their written signs had the value both of words and of syllables borrowed from those words: but since the two languages were different, words and syllables were read differently. To illustrate the point, let us turn back to our imaginary pictographic script. If we saw a picture of a horse, we would read it as 'horse': but if, for example, our script had been borrowed by the French, they would read the same sign as 'cheval'. There is no need to labour the point, for it will be evident that some signs may well have a number of values, Semitic as well as Sumerian. Anyone, however, who may be tempted to enter this field may feel reassured if we hasten to add that many of these values are rare, and that often one finds on an average not more than three or four values for each sign.

Cryptographic Writing

So complicated a method of writing is in itself a matter for some surprise: but the Akkadian scribes carried it to a still higher pitch in their use of cryptography. This type of writing, which para-doxically employs abstruse ingenuity in a deliberate attempt to discourage those very persons who are really intended to read it, was already practised in Egypt where, as we have already mentioned, Monsieur E. Drioton has made a special study of it.[8] There are many different types of cryptography and many different circumstances to which they might be applied: but one of the most typical is what may be termed 'funerary cryptography'. The Egyptians, who shared with the Mesopotamians the belief that to say a thing was immediately equivalent to doing or creating it, used to inscribe on the tombs of their dead the particulars of the choice offerings which they wished them to receive, and since anyone could make this list a reality by merely reading it, passers by were adjured to do so and thus produce the desired result. Since this wish was expressed in identical terms on every funerary list it became a pure formality and attracted no particular attention. To correct this state of affairs, someone had the idea of wording the funerary inscription in unfamiliar terms—i.e., of employing cryptography—and of giving the letters unaccustomed values, so that a passer who glanced even casually at the monument would be struck by its peculiarity. Intrigued by this, he would read it without understanding it, and might sometimes repeat it: but in any event the inscription would have been read, and the dead would then be satisfied.

This was one use for cryptography: but the most common was

for writing something to be read only by the initiated, such as the formula, which we shall shortly mention (pp. 231–2) for manufacturing different kinds of glass.[9] Every type of work which required particular qualifications and knowledge of some formula became, in virtue of that fact, to some extent secret, and precautions were necessary to ensure that it should not be accessible to all and sundry. Thus, in the particular case of this glass, the scribe had given the signs he used in the written formula a largely arbitrary value, and, for example, instead of writing *a-ba-an* (stone) he wrote *ha-bar-an*, which would be meaningless to anyone who did not possess the key to this particular cypher. Babylonian and Assyrian writing is full, not only of these deliberate attempts to mislead, but also of cases where a hurried and careless scribe (as many were) has mistaken one sign for another. It is, for example, all too common on tablets of accounts, to find that the individual numbers and the totals do not agree. Modern Assyriologists have, in certain cases, managed to persuade themselves that where a sign appears to have an unusual value, this should be added to the accepted meanings: but so beguiling has this pursuit been, that some of them have carried their researches to the point where they have often invented new values for what were in fact merely errors on the part of the scribe. If, for example, we see the word 'platter' spelt 'plater', the explanation is not that in certain circumstances one 't' can be left out, but simply that the writer could not spell properly. As a general principle, no Assyrian sign of which only a single example is known ought to be accepted as authentic, and every new value resulting from the use of a sign which closely resembles what might be expected there ought on *a priori* grounds to be regarded as suspect.

The Library of Ashurbanipal

The scribes must therefore obviously have had to devote much time to mastering this mass of signs, rather as, nearer our own day, the mandarins of China had to do. Obviously, too, writing was an attainment possessed by few, which made the scribe a vital element alike in the intellectual and commercial life of the community. So, when for example, we find King Ashurbanipal boasting of his complete knowledge of cuneiform, it is fair to say that he stands self-convicted of exaggeration: he could never have found the time for it.

Yet, despite this, a certain genuine taste for literature un-
deniably made this monarch, with all his faults of ostentation,
capricious cruelty, ferocity and wanton destructiveness on his
military campaigns, anxious to preserve all the learning of his
age: and it was this that led him to build in his palace at Nineveh
a library which bears his name. He was admittedly not the only
king to have conceived the idea of forming a collection of tablets
which should embrace all branches of learning: many had essayed
the task before him, notably Sargon II, the founder of the dynasty,
but it was Ashurbanipal's achievement to complete the task
successfully, and to widen its scope without precedent. The
library, removed to London, forms one of the principal treasures
of the British Museum.

We need not repeat our description of the tablets and of how
the 'volumes' of a lengthy work were numbered, and we need
add only that the ancient world, like the modern, knew the type
of man who cannot resist enriching his own library at someone
else's expense. Such precautions as were possible were taken,
notably by putting the books under the protection of the gods,
and certain pre-early-Assyrian tablets carry a curse on anyone
who treated books carelessly, did not put them back in their
'case', or stole them.

It is fascinating to speculate on what we should have seen if
by chance we had been learned enough to make good use of the
library of Ashurbanipal and lucky enough to be allowed to enter
it. A list of its contents would be little less than an abbreviated
literary history of this outstandingly brilliant period of the
Sargonid dynasty. Like the preceding eras, however, its main
achievement was to bring to flower potentialities already latent:
it was careful not to introduce revolutionary changes.

Assyrian and Babylonian Literature

Apart from the scribes, who in any event formed only a small
element in the population, most of even the well-to-do Mesopotamians were unable to read or write, though they were in this
less open to criticism than, for example, the ruling classes of the
Middle Ages, since the cuneiform script in itself represented an
obstacle which could only be surmounted by long years of study.
They were thus, when absolutely driven to writing or reading
something, forced to use the public scribe and the public story

teller, who, like his latter-day equivalent in the East, must have gathered around him in public places a whole circle of hearers anxious to learn the high deeds of the national heroes. The supreme character, whose adventures could satisfy almost every audience, was Gilgamesh, legendary king of the city of Uruk, a man of prodigious exploits.

The taste for legendary tales of national epics has not abated in the East to-day. I had the opportunity of seeing this in practice during my excavations in the Persian plain, in the Nihavend district. The officer of the Antiquities Service attached to my expedition was an educated man, who carried in his luggage the stories of Shah-nama, the 'Book of Kings' of the poet Firdausi, of whom Iran is justly proud. Every evening, at the request of the inhabitants and workers of the village, this officer would read aloud extracts from the Shah-nama stories, to which the audience listened spellbound. I could not help wondering whether, in the evenings at harvest time, French peasants would listen with equal interest to a reading of 'La Chanson de Roland'. In any event, whether poems like the Gilgamesh epic were recited in public or not, their texts were in the library where we first learned of their existence.

Religious Literature. The Poem of the Creation

Pride of place goes to religious literature, not only because of the importance which was attached to the worship of the gods in Mesopotamian life, but also because it is both the commonest and most extensive, forming in practice the bulk of such Mesopotamian literature as we possess.

Its masterpiece is the story of the Creation,[10] which has for us the incalculable advantage of representing official Mesopotamian dogma during the late Assyrian period. This does not mean that it was the only dogma current, for in the course of time a number of religious centres established their own sets of beliefs: but our knowledge of them is fragmentary, and they are less representative of contemporary thought than the example we have from Ashurbanipal's library. The poem is often known as the *Enuma Elish* ('When in Heaven . . .') from the two opening words on the first of its seven tablets. The story, like others of extreme antiquity of which we possess only fragments, tells us that in the beginning there was nothing but Chaos, a waste of waters, with

Apsu (sweet water) and Tiamat (salt water); a time when 'the heavens above were yet unnamed and no dwelling beneath was called with a name—none of the gods had been named.'* Then the principles of nature began to be defined and Lakhmu and his spouse Lakhamu, of whom we know nothing, were born of the original progenitors. Lakhmu and Lakhamu represent merely one stage in the still very incomplete process of the organization of the world. Soon they have children, first Mummu and then Anshar and Kishar, comprising the whole of heaven and earth, and finally the three divinities who stand at the summit of the Babylonian Pantheon: Anu the god of the heavens, Enlil the lord of the air (soon also to become the lord of earth as well) and Ea, the god of the waters and of the abyss which surrounds the world, and the offspring of Anu. For reasons and in ways which we do not know, the poem tells us that the three gods and their offspring became the objects of the most bitter hatred to Apsu and Tiamat (possibly because they represented order as opposed to primeval chaos), both of whom planned to rid themselves of their offspring, though the initiative came from Apsu and Mummu, since at first Tiamat recoiled from any such design. The younger gods, however, were warned in time and took counter-measures. Thanks to his magical powers, Ea over-powered Apsu and Mummu, killing the former and imprisoning the latter. Tiamat's rage knew no bounds, and she gave birth to eleven terrible monsters with which finally to subdue her adversaries. One of these monsters was Kingu, who became her husband and was destined to be the leader. But during this long time a son, Marduk, was born to Ea. Marduk (who plays a rôle in Babylonian mythology identical with that of Ashur in Assyrian) was a prodigy from the day of his birth: 'the one wise in wisdom, the most learned of the gods, in the midst of the holy Apsu, Marduk was born. His frame was enormous, the glance of his eyes flashing. His birth was the birth of a man: from the first day he could beget children. His measurements . . . were not fitted for human understanding, difficult to survey. Four were his eyes, four were his ears . . .'

While Tiamat was making her preparations, Marduk had fully grown: but although Ea's magical powers had sufficed to over-come Apsu, neither he nor Anu proved able to confront Tiamat.

---

* i.e., brought into being. [Translator's note.]

Then all the gods, save Tiamat and the army of Kingu, joined forces against her and her followers: they met together at a banquet to concert their defence, and they drank to put themselves in good heart. 'The taste of the sweet drink changed their cares . . . their bodies were filled to overflowing, they made much merry music . . .' Marduk accepts their suggestion that he should be their champion, but, no less prudent than his father, he lays down his own terms: he is to have unquestioned authority over the gods and no one may disobey his decisions (i.e., he has power to fix destinies). The gods accept his conditions, and each gives him the weapon from which he draws his strength. This was the occasion of the trial of the garment (p. 170) in order to prove Marduk's powers.

Before coming to grips, the two adversaries hurl insults at each other. Marduk prepares his weapons, which are partly material and partly forces of nature—the four winds, the thunderbolt, and the tempest. The magic weapons of Tiamat are of no avail and Marduk casts his net over her: when she opens her mouth to belch forth flames, Marduk seizes his chance to launch one of the four winds and stabs the monster's body, swollen and distended by the wind within it. Then Marduk chants a song of victory over the corpse of his vanquished foe: he cuts her body in two, like a 'shell fish' (oyster); from one half he makes the sky and from the other the earth. In the sky he fixes the realms of the trinity of great gods. Kingu had been taken prisoner at the very outset, and Marduk had recaptured from him the tablets of destiny which he had in his possession.

At this point in the story there is a digression, and on the pretext of describing the order which Marduk had imposed upon the heavens, the fifth tablet, which is, most unfortunately, partly destroyed, contained an account of the astronomical knowledge of the period.

After this digression the story is taken up again. Marduk proposes to create a being to be called 'man' whose duty it shall be to serve the gods while 'they shall be at rest'. Man is duly created, but the process demands blood, and this is provided by Kingu, who is put to death. Then Marduk divides the gods into two communities, of the sky and of the underworld respectively.

In their gratitude the gods offer him the Esagila, or temple of Babylon, and each, in bestowing some title upon him, endows it

Marduk fighting Tiamat

with reality by virtue of uttering it. In the beginning Marduk had been armed with power in order to go forth to battle, but, now that he has conquered, he still wields this power and the gods, as they had promised him, strip themselves of their own prerogatives.

There are other versions of the Creation story, but the fragments of them which we possess, though incomplete and disconnected, do not reveal any substantial differences from the *Enuma Elish* as we know it.[11]

The poem can be properly described as the Authorized Version of neo-Babylonian religion, for it answers all the questions which mankind can ask about his own origin and his earthly condition; but most conveniently the answer to every problem rests with Marduk. The poem of the Creation was recited repeatedly at the New Year's feast, which was associated with an ancient tradition borrowed from a nature religion.

The Flood

The tradition of a flood was a live one in Mesopotamia, and like everything else it demanded an explanation.[12] Oddly enough it never appears to have been edited and re-written, and Marduk plays no part in it: but, instead of standing on its own, it was interpolated in the poem of Gilgamesh in the guise of a story told by Uta-Napishtim to his visitor, to explain how he himself and his wife had become immortal. The most complete version of the story occupies tablet No. 11 of the Gilgamesh poem, but there are other fragments which suggest that at some period there existed a whole flood-cycle of poems.

The town of Shuruppak on the Euphrates (the modern Fara) was already old when the gods resolved to cover the earth with a flood. Ea was present at their council, and determined to warn Uta-Napishtim, who was under his protection; so he drew near his hut of branches and dried mud and called out softly 'Wall, wall, hearken to me! Man of Shuruppak, build a ship: forsake wealth, save thy life, bring all seed of life in the ship . . . the dimensions thereof shall be measured.' (Curiously enough the next sentence advised him to store his riches inside.) Ea told him how large the boat should be, but, before beginning the work, Uta-Napishtim asked the god what reply he should give if he were asked about the work he was going to do. He was told to say that Enlil was hostile to him and that he wished to live in the domain ruled by Ea. In order to allay the suspicions of the inhabitants, Enlil would cause *kukku* and *kibtu* to rain down upon them—a most elaborate pun (see p. 168) for *kukku* means both 'the sound of corn being ground' and 'misfortune' while *kibtu* means 'corn' and 'sorrow'. The vicissitudes of the construction are briefly described, and the dimensions as recorded suggest an enormous roofed box, divided internally both horizontally and vertically. The hull was waterproofed with a coating of bitumen; a feast was held to reward the workmen, and Uta-Napishtim embarked his possessions and his family, following himself and closing the door as soon as the rain began to fall. The downpour was torrential, thunder roared, lightning flashed, and the clouds caused thick darkness to fall. 'In the heavens', says the poem, 'the gods were terrified at the cyclone: they shrank back and went up into the heaven of Anu: they crouched like a dog and cowered by the wall. The Goddess Ishtar cried out like a woman in travail, "May that former day be turned into mud because I commanded evil among the company of the gods! How could I command . . . the destruction of my peoples? Did I of myself bring forth my people, that they might fill the sea like little fishes?"' For six days and six nights the wind and tempest raged. When all was quiet, Uta-Napishtim opened the window and saw that the vessel had come to rest on an island which was in reality Mount Niṣir. For six days he stayed there without moving. Then he sent forth first a dove and then a swallow, both of which returned to the vessel. Finally he sent forth a crow, which did not return, and then he released the animals and offered a sacrifice on the top of the mountain.

The poem continues: 'The gods smelt the sweet savour: like flies they gathered together over him that sacrificed.' At this point Ishtar intervened to say that all the gods should take their share of the sacrifice except for Enlil who had recklessly unleashed the flood. Here Enlil himself arrived and on seeing the vessel complained that someone must have escaped. Ninurta suggested that only Ea could have warned those who had escaped, and Ea, whose part in the story we already know, replied 'As for me, I have not revealed the secret of the great gods to Uta-Napishtim: I made him see a vision: thus he heard the secret of the gods.' Then Enlil ordained that Uta-Napishtim and his wife should be immortal and should dwell far away at the mouth of the rivers.

What strikes the reader is the vivid portrayal of the character of the gods, who are endowed with the attributes of primitive man, and the frankness of the description of their alarm and their anger and of the explanations of Ea.

The idea of a flood was deeply embedded in the consciousness of the whole of the ancient world, and a variety of stories about it are preserved in different countries. It is generally believed that those current in Mesopotamia owed their origin to unusually severe flooding by the two great rivers, while J. de Morgan, a geological expert, has suggested that they may enshrine a memory of the floods at the end of the last ice-age, dated to about 8000 B.C., which must have been on such a scale as to leave an indelible memory wherever they were experienced.

The differing phases of the religion which developed over long periods of time and was centred upon particular shrines, are represented by descriptive poem-cycles, like the *Enuma Elish*, which explain the leading part played by one or other of the gods. From the temple of Nippur where Enlil (Bel the Ancient) and his spouse Ninlil were worshipped during the period when Anu had lost his importance and before Enlil had yielded to Bel Marduk, we have a creation-story in which the gods taking part are Anu, Enlil and the goddess Ninmah. They are said to be responsible for the existence on earth of the human beings known as 'black heads', an epithet of which the precise meaning has not been finally established. It may refer to the colour of the hair of the Sumerians, or possibly to their bronzed complexions. If either of these explanations were correct, they would suggest that the Sumerians, whom some scholars believe to have come from an undefined but hilly if not actually mountainous region, must have been in contact with fair-haired or fair-skinned peoples: for otherwise their own colouring would have seemed perfectly normal and unremarkable.

The Myths of Zu and the Dragon Labbu

Both these myths belong to the Nippur cycle. The first is about the birdman Zu, a natural pilferer, who takes advantage of the fact that Enlil is at his toilet, 'that he is washing himself with pure water, that he has left his throne and laid down his tiara', the emblem of his power, in order to gain possession of the tablets of destiny of which Enlil was the guardian and so to usurp his powers. The stratagem, however, was unsuccessful, for the gods took common action and decided to pursue the thief. It is interesting to observe the limitations of the authors of these myths in finding motives for action: once they have found an effective one they repeat it. In this myth, as in that of *Enuma Elish*, the gods keep out of the way of Zu and the forces of his followers: nevertheless it is a god (who must be a king with the attributes of divinity), Lugalbanda, who resolves to capture Zu at a feast to which he invites him together with his wife and his son. We find this situation repeated in the Hittite myth of the great serpent Illuyankas; rather than venture to deliver a direct attack, the god charged with the task of revenge invites him to a feast and there makes him drunk and overpowers him. We possess some cylinder seals which show a bird-man, who probably represents Zu, being led before a god who is seated on a throne and delivering judgment. A later Babylonian version of his story made Marduk the conqueror of Zu, and the god in consequence received the title of 'the breaker of the skull of the bird Zu'.

The myth of the dragon Labbu tells how the gods were seized with terror when the god Enlil drew in the sky the likeness of a dragon, which came to life. In this myth once again we find that only one of the gods dared to confront the animal: he slew it, and the blood ran for many years. Not only is the plot of the story familiar, but it casts an interesting light on the process of the creation of a living creature. The creating god mentally defines the nature-to-be of his creation: when it has taken final shape in his imagination and he has given it a name, he draws its shape, whereby it acquires almost complete life. The Gilgamesh epic contains a similar process of creation. When the goddess Aruru wishes to create Enkidu she first of all plans him in her mind and then outlines his general shape on the ground in a lump of clay which she later animates.

The Poem Called The Fall

To the Enlil cycle belonged a further very curious legend which S. Langdon, its first translator, mistakenly regarded as a story of the fall of man. However, although the poem is full of obscurity, it can be described in general terms. Enlil has intercourse with Ninlil and another goddess and many offspring result from their unions, while their earthly consequences are to produce rain or flood, fertility in the soil, and fruitfulness in human families and flocks. It is, in fact, one of the commonest of myths, which provides yet another admirable example of an extremely ancient belief dating from an age in possession of a religion which was already in process of change at the dawn of history.

The Legend of Ninurta

A peculiar feature attaches to a legend about Ninurta the son of Enlil, which is related to the Nippur cycle. In the poem, which concerns the struggle waged by the god against his enemies, some kinds of stones are said to have fought for him, and others against him. Before the combat they had been nameless, but after his victory Ninurta undertook to endow them with names (i.e., to confirm their individual existence) and with well defined and distinctive qualities. In gratitude for the services received from the stones which had fought on his side, he made them the highly prized ones—marble, lapis lazuli, alabaster and rock crystal —employed in decorating palaces and temples, while the stones which had fought against him became by contrast the common building stone, or that used for door sills and consequently trodden under foot: the dull, the lustreless and the unregarded. The story invites two comments. Firstly it affords one more piece of evidence of the fundamental Mesopotamian sense of order underlying the universe, in which nothing can exist irrationally: and secondly it shows how ill-defined in Mesopotamian eyes were the boundaries between the different categories of physical existence.

The Exaltation of Ishtar

Long as the period of Anu's supremacy may have been, it coincided with the prehistoric, and also no doubt with the earliest historical periods, and we therefore possess very little direct evidence of it. One such piece of evidence, however, may very well be the result of a desperate effort on the part of the priesthood at Uruk, the centre of Anu-worship, to counter the growing influence of the newer gods and must date from a period in which the cult of Anu was on the decline. The story in question deals with how Anu shared his crown with the goddess Ishtar, with whom he had long been in love. In gratitude for the favours which she had granted him he desired to raise her to equality with himself, and he took the advice of the gods on the propriety of such a step. The divine 'family conclave' without a dissenting voice suggested that he should regularize her position, and, fortified by this general approval, he did so, ordaining that her name after marriage should be Antu, the feminine form of Anu, just as Ninlil is the feminine form of Enlil. After she was thus exalted Ishtar (the Sumerian Innini) occupied a place of high importance in the heavens where Anu already dwelt: and she was identified with the planet Venus.

The Realm of the Nether Regions

The nether regions, no less than the heavens, are at the root of certain myths, one of which formed part of the cuneiform tablets discovered at Tell-el-Amarna in Upper Egypt. Taken in conjunction with the translations of certain poems, notably the Gilgamesh epic, which were discovered in Hittite territory, this affords proof of the widespread popularity of Babylonian literature throughout the whole of the ancient world. The story in question tells how Nergal was connected with the lordship of Hell, whose queen was Ereshkigal, the sister of Ishtar. It seems that, though both queen and goddess, she was the first of the prisoners of the *arallû*, the name given to the nether regions which were also known as 'the vast land' or 'land of no return'. This is suggested by the fact that when the gods all wished to assemble for a feast they sent her a message that, since she herself could not come, she should send a messenger who could bring her back her share of the banquet. Accordingly she sent on her behalf Namtar (Destiny), demon of pestilence. When Namtar made his appearance among the gods, all rose to their feet in honour of his mistress, with the single exception of the god Nergal. On his return to Hell, Namtar complained bitterly of this and Ereshkigal sent him back once again, with the demand that Nergal should be given over to her to be put to death. On Namtar's second appearance among the gods Nergal was no longer there, and Namtar could therefore not perform his task; but the gods warned Nergal, who took the initiative. With the help of an escort of demons he made his way to Hell, posted guards at every door through which he would have to pass in making good his escape, attacked Ereshkigal, seized her by her hair, dragged her from her throne, and made as if to put her to death. All her arrogance at once vanished: she implored her conqueror to spare her life, and offered to marry him and to make him her royal consort. This duly took place, and thus Nergal, who seems hitherto to have been quite unendowed, was duly provided for. We shall see in the Gilgamesh epic that Ishtar, the sister of Ereshkigal, also offers to share her power and her wealth with the hero whom she passionately desires.

The Descent of Ishtar into the Nether Regions

The nether regions are also the scene of the well-known legend of Ishtar and her lover Tammuz, which seems to be a conflation of two earlier, and quite distinct, myths. One of these concerned Dumuzi-Tammuz, a corn-deity who died each year and then came to life again, or, in another version which omitted the god's death, divided his life between the company of the two goddesses, spending half underground while nature passes the winter in sleep, and the other half, beginning in the spring, on earth. This myth received an accretion of the myth of the descent of Ishtar to the nether regions. The original version gave no reasons for this journey and the purpose of bringing Tammuz to the upper world is only explicitly mentioned in a late period. The version that we now have runs as follows.

Without any reference to Tammuz, Ishtar determines to descend to the nether regions. On her arrival there she has to parley with the keeper of the gate. Although Ereshkigal is Ishtar's sister, she is filled with joy at the thought of capturing such a prize, and orders her to be admitted. At each of the seven doors of hell through which she must pass the keeper of the gate forces Ishtar to remove part of her apparel: first her crown, and then her earrings, her necklaces, her breastband of precious metal, her belt made of charms of 'stones of childbirth', the bracelets from her wrists and her ankles, and finally her 'garment of modesty'. Thus Ishtar appears naked in the presence of the queen of the nether regions, and overcome with rage, 'without a moment's thought, she attacked her'. In revenge, Ereshkigal bids her minister Namtar to unleash upon Ishtar a multitude of diseases, like a pack of hounds.

During these events in the underworld everything on earth is withering away. Trees and plants will not turn green, and animals and human beings alike are sterile. The gods in their consternation seek to free the goddess, and Ea creates an individual destined to be sacrificed and then to go in search of Ereshkigal and to ask her to give him some water from a particular water skin, from which, no doubt, only the gods might drink. 'When the goddess Ereshkigal heard these words, she struck her thigh, she gnawed her fingers.'

She curses the messenger, and tells him that he shall receive no other food and drink than 'the scraps from the gutter and the water from the conduits of the town'. Finally, no doubt under the compulsion of the messenger's demands, the exact significance of which escapes us, she pours the life-restoring water on Ishtar, and has her led back through the seven gates (reminiscent of Dante's seven circles of hell), at each of which her garments and her jewels are restored to her.

Like many others, the poem contains the stock phrases which are always repeated in similar contexts. The gods, who are almost morbidly ill-tempered, strike their thighs and gnaw their fingers, and they are incapable of gathering together without drinking, often to excess. The curse uttered against the messenger of the gods is identical with that against the temple harlot in the Gilgamesh epic. The general picture which we get of the Meso-potamian Olympus is a lamentable one. The gods are violent, gluttonous, uncontrolled, faithless and vindictive; they are an epitome of the primitive people from whose imaginations they sprang. As we have already said, a certain degree of development in their characters can be observed with the passing of the centuries, but it is useful to remember that they give us a true picture of the average man in the civilization of the time.

The Gilgamesh Epic

The heroic poem with which a reciter could be most certain of commanding his audience's attention was the story of Gilgamesh (Pl. XIX). The hero was King of Uruk in remotest antiquity: he had built the city with its palaces and temples, its gates and its encircling walls, and this achievement, of which he was parti-cularly proud, was eventually to console him for the unsuccessful end of his adventures. He was a good ruler, but his yoke lay heavy on his people, and especially on their wives and daughters: and prayers were universally offered to Aruru, the goddess of fertility, for the creation of a creature to whom he could devote himself and who might thus divert his attention from his subjects. Aruru meditated the creature to which she was going to give life, and then, casting a lump of clay upon the ground, she shaped and animated it. This was the origin of Enkidu the savage, wholly ignorant of civilization, whose body was shaggy, and whose head was covered with hair like a woman's. He ate grass like a deer and slaked his thirst at water holes. He was in many respects an animal and Gilgamesh needed the full strength of the divine element in his being (he was two-thirds divine, being the son of the goddess Nin-Sun, and one-third human) to control him.

But there was in Enkidu an element of something beyond the merely animal, for he delivered captured beasts from the snares of the hunters, who, to rid themselves of him, brought him a harlot from the temple of Ishtar, who in her turn introduced him to civilization in the obvious manner for no less than six days and seven nights. His hair was cut, his body shaved, and he was anointed with oil: but he still knew nothing of bread, nor of human food and drink: and when he tasted them, he drank the fermented liquor seven times and then seven times more, and the usual drunken scene ensued. Finally the temple harlot brought Enkidu to Gilgamesh who had received warning of what was impending in confused dreams interpreted to him by his mother. Their first meeting led to violence, for they came to blows over a goddess who wished to form a union with Gilgamesh. Victory went to the more civilized contestant; Enkidu acknowledged defeat and became Gilgamesh's friend, and the pair set out on a series of adventures reminiscent of those of Hercules, but destined to be short-lived.

The first expedition was to the land of cedar trees (Amanus), there to fight the giant Humbaba, who, for reasons we do not know, was a deadly enemy of Shamash. The story probably contains an echo of the age-old attempts on the part of Mesopotamia no less than Egypt to obtain the wood which her own soil could not provide. A complete section of the poem is devoted to the preparations which the expedition entailed. The weapons which the two friends had made for themselves, in size and weight alike, were fit for giants. The elders of Uruk tried to dissuade them from undertaking this expedition, which concealed unsuspected dangers: but Gilgamesh retorted in terms which sound strange to us, but which were usual enough in Mesopotamia, that 'he wishes to make for himself a name'. His mother, the goddess Nin-Sun, was equally anxious, and she implored the betrothed of the sun to watch over her son.

The description of the cedar forest might have afforded an excuse for several pages of fine writing, and we can only speculate on whether the poet had never been there himself, or whether it is merely an expression of the insensitiveness to natural beauty characteristic of all Akkadian literature. In any case, the forest itself is a place of terror, and the forest glades through which Humbaba stalks are well tended. The giant himself is a fire-breathing monster and we are reminded of the forests of the Taurus and the volcano of Mt. Argeus,* which may still have been active at that date.

The fight follows what might be called the prescribed pattern. Gilgamesh reduces Humbaba to impotence by the device of launching eight hurricanes at him, and while he is held unable to move in the midst of this whirlwind, and despite his pleas for mercy, he cuts off his head.

On his triumphant return from this expedition, the goddess Ishtar, who lives in her earthly temple with her retinue of sacred harlots, meets Gilgamesh crowned and freshly attired as he leaves his palace. She falls in love with him and in order to seduce him she seeks to dazzle him with a vision of the future: he shall have a chariot of lapis lazuli and gold, with golden wheels and a front board decorated with precious stones: when he goes into the temple, all shall prostrate themselves before him: in brief, she offers to make him divine. Gilgamesh refuses with insulting coarseness, and indeed the whole passage is curiously incongruous with what we know of his character as the terror of all the women in the town. He reminds the goddess of her many lovers and their fates: of Tammuz and his death, of the pied bird whose wings she has broken, of the lion, of the stallion, of a herdsman, and a gardener who were changed into animals—'And me also', says Gilgamesh, 'after you have loved me, you will treat as you have treated them'.

This bitterly angers Ishtar, who ascends into heaven to demand the death of Gilgamesh from her father Anu, who, like Aruru, and indeed like most of the gods as portrayed in these poems, takes no direct action, but creates a heavenly bull which even

* Now known as Erjas Daǧ. [Translator's note.]

hundreds of men could not control. Gilgamesh, however, succeeds in subduing it and Ishtar, who has watched the struggle from the top of the temple terrace, curses him. Enkidu retorts by tearing off one of the bull's limbs and hurling it at Ishtar's head, crying out 'If I lay hold on you, I will tie its entrails round your neck.'

Ishtar and her attendants thereupon utter a lamentation for the death of the bull, while Gilgamesh has a vessel for the oil used in the sacred anointing made from the bull's horns. During the following night in a dream (which the inhabitant of Mesopotamia would regard as equivalent to reality) Enkidu sees the gods in council, where Enlil, despite the protests of Shamash, condemns Enkidu(!) to death for having slain Humbaba and the bull, though in each case Gilgamesh had actually been responsible. The punishment begins forthwith, and Enkidu, prostrated with fever, laments his short and brutish life and curses the temple harlot who introduced him to civilization (another sign of the pessimism we shall soon meet again). Shamash upbraids him for his ingratitude but, since the curse has been uttered in due form, he accepts his obligation to give effect to it and changes the temple harlot into a bitch.

Enkidu finally dies, and Gilgamesh's lament recalls their exploits in these words, 'We captured and laid low the heavenly bull, we slew Humbaba who dwelt in the forest of cedars. What is this sleep that now hath seized thee? Thou art become dull and thou hearest me no more.'

Panic-stricken at the thought that one day he too must die, he bethinks himself of a distant ancestor, Uta-Napishtim ('day of life'), and how he alone of mankind escaped from the flood, and now dwells with his wife at the world's end: and he plans to go to him and ask him how he may attain eternal life.

First he comes to Mount Mashu, where the sun rests each night, and which is guarded by huge scorpion-men. After satisfying themselves that Gilgamesh is more than half divine, they describe to him the shadowy road to the end of which he must travel. He does so, and comes to a tree 'beautiful to behold', whose fruit is of lapis lazuli. They are black grapes, for we are now in Syria. The hero travels on, and near the sea he meets a woman called Siduri: she is described as 'tavern keeper' (p. 73), but a more accurate description would probably be 'wine producer', for this is a recognisable allusion to the wine trade which was already being carried on with the coast. When Siduri learns of Gilgamesh's fears, she expressly dashes his hopes. 'Thou shalt never find the life that thou seekest'; for it is the portion of the gods, and death is the lot of mankind; she advises him to enjoy himself while he may and to make merry while he awaits the day of his death. Despite this, she tells him where he can find the boatman of Uta-Napishtim, for by now he is near his goal: this boatman is called Ur-Shanabi ('servant of two-thirds', or of Ea, sometimes known by this name. We know that the gods were ranked in a kind of numerical hierarchy, based upon Anu, whose number was the fundamental Mesopotamian unit of 60. Ea's number was 40, and so he was 'two-thirds' of Anu).

The boatman is shrewd: in order to convey his passenger to his master, he must cross the waters of death, a single drop of which means certain destruction. He makes Gilgamesh help him to cut long poles, and plans to propel the boat like a punt, abandoning each pole as soon as it has been used to move the boat. So long is the crossing of the waters of death that they use no fewer than 120 poles. When Gilgamesh finally reaches Uta-Napishtim, he immediately declares the purpose of his journey and asks him how he contrived to escape from the flood. This section of the poem forms a separate episode and the Uta-Napishtim story described earlier (p. 194) has no organic connection with the main action. Uta-Napishtim is as discouraging to Gilgamesh as everyone else has been. How, he asks, can Gilgamesh really hope that a special gathering of the gods will be summoned for the sole purpose of decreeing him eternal life? He is only a weak mortal: and to prove it, Uta-Napishtim bids him sit down and stay awake for six days and seven nights. As soon as Gilgamesh sits down he falls asleep, and when he wakes up Uta-Napishtim gives him provisions for his journey, and a new set of magical clothes, which will always stay new. At the last moment, however, Uta-Napishtim, at his wife's instigation, reveals to Gilgamesh that a thorny plant, which restores youth, lies hidden in the depths of the water. Gilgamesh ties stones to his feet, like a pearl diver, and sinks to the water's bed. He gashes his hands, but he succeeds in pulling up the plant and bringing it triumphantly to the surface. 'This plant', he cries, 'is called "old man restored to youth"': I will eat thereof, and will regain my own youth.' On his homeward journey the hero wishes to bathe in a spring of fresh water: but while he is doing so a serpent, drawn to the spot by the scent of the plant, steals it from him, just as Enlil while bathing had allowed himself to be robbed of the tablets of destiny. (This is why the serpent, changing its skin each year, always looks young.) Gilgamesh weeps bitterly: he returns to Uruk with the boatman of Uta-Napishtim, where he finds some measure of consolation in showing him the walls of the town and pointing out to him the completion of the work.

But the story is not yet finished. Gilgamesh desires at least to learn from Enkidu what it is like in the nether regions. Enkidu appears to him in a dream, and offers him the chance of coming and joining him, but Gilgamesh, it seems quite arbitrarily, does the exact opposite of what his friend has suggested; Gilgamesh can only call Enkidu back to earth, since he himself has forfeited his chance of descending to the realm of the dead. He asks Enlil, but it is not within his jurisdiction: Enlil asks Sin; he in turn asks Ea, who, more sensibly, puts the request to Nergal, the ruler of the nether regions, who grants permission for Enkidu's spirit to return to earth for a few moments. The poem follows the pattern common to all primitive stories, whereby the author unvaryingly puts the same phrases, word for word, into the mouth of each of the gods as they successively make their plea.

The tale is almost told. Gilgamesh questions his friend insistently, but Enkidu is reluctant to answer, so harrowing is the truth. The dead are ranged in different groups: those who died in battle have the support of their own kindred, but the man who has been left unburied or who has no one to bring him funeral offerings, must roam in search of food: his only sustenance is the scraps thrown into the streets.

So this epic ends on a note as sad as that of the close of the flood story. It enjoyed very considerable popularity, and fragments of it, in translation, have been discovered in the countries bordering on Mesopotamia. Some of Gilgamesh's exploits, notably those in which he subdues monsters, are depicted in art throughout the whole of the Near East: the hero is shown as under attack on either side by two lions or bulls, which he is thrusting back and holding at his mercy.

Gilgamesh in Art

The Gilgamesh motif is found in the very earliest historical period, in Egypt, carved on the ivory handle of a shaped flint knife, and in varying forms it persists throughout the centuries, finally reaching Europe at the time of the barbarian invasions, when it becomes a decorative feature of Merovingian belt buckles. It can be seen again on the Byzantine or Sassanian silks which were so greatly prized in the West as church ornaments or as sudaria for the relics of the saints: and yet again on capitals of the Romanesque period whose art reveals so many affinities with that of the ancient East. In this last context, however, the Gilgamesh motif must be distinguished from the similar theme of Daniel in the lions' den with his hands uplifted in prayer, whereas Gilgamesh is grasping the beasts by the throat. The grouping of the figures in the Gilgamesh scene has sometimes markedly influenced the treatment of Daniel, notably where Gilgamesh is shown lifting the bull by his tail or by a hind foot, and treading its neck beneath his heel. Daniel is sometimes also represented with lions apparently hanging head downwards on either side of him: but Daniel's hands are open and lifted up to heaven, while the lions are licking his feet.

The Myths of Adapa and Etana

To the group of heroic poems which, like the Gilgamesh epic, seek to convey a moral lesson, belongs the story of Ea's son, Adapa, the fisherman who each day supplied the temple sanctuary with fish. Once when he was fishing in the bay, a sudden squall of the south wind capsized his boat. In a passion Adapa cursed the south wind with the words 'I will break thy wings', which was no sooner said than done. After seven days the god Anu observed that the wind was not blowing, and on asking the reason was told 'Adapa, son of Ea, has broken the wings of the south wind'. Anu summons Adapa to appear for judgment before his throne. The charge against Adapa is a grave one, and Ea counsels him how to extricate himself, telling him that, since Anu presumably intends to poison him, Adapa should not accept food from him. Further, he tells him the names of the gods whom he is likely to meet on the way, and advises him how to behave towards them. Adapa does as Ea bids him, and makes his appearance in mourning. At Anu's gate he meets two fertility gods, Tammuz and Gizzida, whom we meet in other texts sojourning in the nether regions during their annual period of death. To their question 'For whom are you in mourning?' Adapa replies 'For Tammuz and Ningizzida who for us on earth are dead'. Pleased with this answer they admit him. He successfully pleads his case before Anu, who decides to offer him the food of life, but Adapa, who has learned his lesson well, will only accept a garment and oil for anointing. By virtue of his refusal he loses his chance of immortality.

This is yet another example of the inconsistencies in the character of Ea, whose prognostications, though he is lord of knowledge, come disastrously to grief. The author in his stories has no hesitation in displaying the gods as endowed with human frailties, and we are left with the impression that this was how they were regarded: powerful, perhaps, but with well defined limits to their power.

The Etana poem belongs to the same group. The hero, anxious to ease his wife's labour, begs the god Shamash to grant him 'the stone of childbirth', which we have already met on Ishtar's belt during her descent into hell. Shamash advises Etana to go to the mountain, where he will find the help which he requires. He does so, and encounters a serpent and an eagle which have joined forces in search of prey. The eagle however had broken his side of the compact, and, disregarding the warnings of one of the eaglets, had eaten the young of the serpent which, following the advice of Shamash, coils up in the carcass of a dead bull and, when the eagle comes to tear it to pieces, grasps the bird and, despite its promises, cuts off its wings and claws and leaves it to die of hunger.

At this point Etana appears on the scene. He gives the eagle food and, when it is cured, it offers to take him to heaven to get from Ishtar the talisman of childbirth which he desires. They rise into the sky; the earth grows smaller and smaller before Etana's eyes: but Ishtar's dwelling, towering even above the heaven of Anu where the symbols of royalty are kept by the god, proves to be beyond their reach. Eagle and man fall back to earth. Man cannot rival the gods.

Moral Stories. 'The Righteous Sufferer.' 'Babylonian Wisdom'

The most famous of the moral tales is the poem called 'The

Righteous Sufferer', which begins with the words 'I will sing of the lord of wisdom'. Fundamentally this is based upon a very ancient poem which is pessimistic in character. The Righteous Man has been laid low by illness: the gravity and variety of his symptoms have baffled the knowledge of the diviners and the exorcists alike, and his prayers have brought him no relief. He cries out 'My god hath not turned his face towards me, my goddess hath not even raised up my head: the exorcist hath not delivered me by his rites from the divine wrath'. He makes his vain confession. 'Prayer hath ever been my care, sacrifice hath been my rule, the day of the procession of the goddess have I held dear: I have delighted in worshipping the king, and his music hath been my joy.'

All men shun him because he has lost all his possessions and because such misfortune must be proof of sin. At this point the Righteous Man finds himself blameless, and concludes, 'What man esteems his good is perhaps what the gods regard as evil.'

Originally the poem ended on this note of melancholy, but during the great religious reformation of the first dynasty of Babylon its character was radically changed. The priesthood thought it politic to add a second section in which the Righteous Man recovers his health, his possessions, and the esteem of his fellow men, because Marduk has taken pity upon him: and the poem ends with the words 'Marduk can give life even in the grave, and his spouse Şarpanit can save even from the abyss of death.'

The poem raises a problem. Should we see a hidden reference to mysteries and a ceremony of initiation when the Righteous Man, mentioning the different gates of Esagila, says that he has proved the truth of each of the names of these gates? 'In the gate of the ceasing of lamentation my lamentation hath ceased: in the gate of prodigies my signs became brilliant' and so forth. This might appear to be a reference to initiation into mysteries somehow related to the names of the gates. It is, no doubt, simply an assertion of the effectiveness of the 'good name' of the various gates which, we must remember, by mere virtue of their titles were regarded as potentially creating the qualities to which these titles referred. Thus it is only natural that, as he passes through these gates, the Righteous Man should see his nature transformed. When Marduk goes in the procession on the feast of Akitu,* he

* The New Year Festival. [Translator's note.]

is hailed by a new name each time that he reaches a new place. It is in this sense, but not in the commonly accepted meaning of the term, that we may see a reference to initiation.

To this group of 'pessimist' literature belong the sayings collected under the title of 'the Wisdom of Babylon', and published by S. Langdon (p. 270). They take the form of dialogue between a master (no doubt in the primitive version the king) and his slaves, and deal with problems of everyday life. Their conclusions frequently contradict those which modern opinion would reach.

Lyric Poetry. Some Hymns

This type of poetry forms a sufficiently distinct section among the group of invocations to the gods which accompanied religious ceremonies, comprising hymns, sometimes of considerable spirit and vigour, addressed to some divinity, to stand out from the great mass of monotonous and unvarying eulogies on which most of the invocations were based.

The eulogy of the river rehearses the creative power of water and the part it plays in trial by ordeal; the eulogy of fire, its power of refining metals. The hymn to Shamash presents him in the rôle of supreme judge, towards whom the whole universe turns, delivering his righteous judgments in heaven and earth alike.

A wide range of epithets is applied to Sin, the moon-god. He is described as a young bull perfect in every part: his beard is said to be of lapis lazuli (cf. the blue-black tint of hair and beard among Mesopotamian men): his orb is a gigantic self-propagating fruit. The god's horns are taken to be a reference to the crescent moon, though they are also sometimes regarded as the boat in which he skims through the midst of the heavens.

Invocations are addressed to Ishtar in her various manifestations, among them as the planet in which she represents both Ishtar of the evening and Ishtar of the morning, in a well-marked rhythm, which runs through the verses and in which some of her attributes are repeated in a kind of refrain. The verse of praise is followed by one expressing the griefs of the faithful. 'My heart takes flight, it soars like the bird in the skies, yea, like a dove: I lament each day.' The hymn closes with a further repetition of the goddess' qualities: she brings to fruition the pro-

phecies of her father Sin and her brother Shamash, and it ends—
'I am Ishtar'.

Some of the hymns have a very distinctive character, and one of
them opens in a manner reminiscent of a Pindaric ode 'I will
sing the glory of Bel-ili! Friend, give ear to me! Warrior, hearken
to me! To sing the praises of Bel-ili is better than honey and wine,
yea, better than the best of pure butter!'

The Fables

The Fable, for which Babrius* is given credit, originated in
the East, and was employed by the Mesopotamians. This was
perfectly natural, for the myths contained thousands of examples
of animals talking and thinking like human beings, and it was
logical to turn them into the characters of moral fables which,
though more limited in scope than the Etana legend, were used
to convey particular lessons. Further, art was at home among its
half animal, half human creations, and this had resulted in the
portrayal of scenes in which the leading actors were purely animal.
The very early cylinder seals from Susa show lions, bulls and
cows in human attitudes such as marching, casting lots or steering
a boat. 'Animal orchestras', so commonly reproduced since their
invention, are found as early as the Tombs at Ur, including the
ass blowing a flute, a theme employed by later writers of fables.

Another branch of the art, if we may so call it, flourished in
Egypt, though it has not hitherto been identified in Mesopotamia.
This was the short, adventure story, not to be confused with
mythical tales, though the latter owed much to it. The most
highly polished examples, however, are found in Egypt, like the
tale of the Two Brothers and the adventures of the Egyptian
Sinuhe, who settled in Syria at the time of the Middle Empire.

Unfortunately the text of the fables which we possess has been
seriously mutilated in the course of time. But despite the lacunae
we can see the horse and the ox disputing their respective merits
and their comparative usefulness, and the tamarisk and the date
palm boasting of their qualities in rivalry, the latter having the
best of the argument, with its leaves, wood, sap and fruit all
staple elements in the economy. Further, scenes like those depicting animals apparently carrying the preparations for a banquet,

---

* According to Liddell & Scott, Greek Lexicon, Babrius, Fabularum Scriptor,
floruit c. 50 B.C.? [Translator's note.]

engraved on an ivory plaque which once decorated the front of
a harp from the royal tombs of Ur, are probably related to this
type of literature.

The Treatment of History

During the reign of the late-Assyrian dynasty, and the neo-
Babylonian Empire, the mode assumed its definitive shape. The
inscriptions which from the beginnings of history had recorded
the king's mighty deeds were succeeded by a variety of narrative
forms which in time became standardized. This enables us to
draw certain provisional conclusions about these narratives, the
style of their composition and the Mesopotamian sense of history.

The Annals record the outstanding events of the reign in historical sequence. In Assyria pride of place is given to military
campaigns, as war was Assyria's staple industry, while in Babylonia first place was given to lists of buildings. We can watch the
growth of the Assyrian Empire as the result of each successive
campaign. The motives involved by way of justification are, as
we have already said, the order of the god Ashur (i.e., the claim
of a holy war), or some failure to pay due respect to the king of
Assyria, which might take the form of disregard of treaty provisions, or negligence in diplomatic relations. The account of the
campaign describes the chosen route, the tale of victories won,
and the monarch's return to his capital, laden with booty.

A second, and less common, type of inscription, known as the
'display inscription', describes the different stages of the conquest
of a particular area, and the third, which is extremely rare, is an
account of a campaign submitted by the king to the divinity
dwelling in one of his temples. In this type the king is careful to
remember that he is the god's deputy, and he gives him an account
of his actions while at the same time offering him thanks (pp. 149–
154).

While these three types of text preserve the memory of the
kingdom responsible for writing them, they take no account of
contemporary history. The Babylonians, however, essayed this
task in the Babylonian Chronicle, and have left a record of the
outstanding events in Babylonia and Assyria for the period
745–668 B.C.

When the inhabitants of Mesopotamia of the mid-second
millennium B.C. wanted to escape from contemporary events and

survey the past, they had at their command the historical records of earlier periods, though in many respects incomplete, as well as dynastic lists. Any attempt to carry these researches too far back involved the risk that the knowledge of the very early periods possessed by the scribes was unreliable: there are frequent discrepancies in the lists which we possess, and, without taking account of the internal discrepancies within each group, two traditions are perceptible, Babylonian on the one hand, Assyrian on the other. These lists are, in fact, a kind of dynastic memoranda, placed in chronological sequence, although sometimes two dynasties were ruling simultaneously in two different centres, or one might emerge before the other had vanished from the scene. In the past fifty years the number of discoveries of this nature has multiplied enormously: and the new discoveries have enabled us (p. 14) to correct the former system of chronology, based on the limited range of documents which had formed the foundation of a fairly stable (though inaccurate) chronology for the country, assuming 4000 B.C. as the officially accepted date for the beginning of history. But the modern habit of attaching significance only to the most recently discovered document, like the claims to recast Middle Eastern chronology every four or five years, without giving time for reflection and a considered judgment on the reliability of the most recently excavated text—these tendencies are to be deplored.

We must accept the fact that the inhabitants of Mesopotamia in antiquity did not regard history in the same light as the modern world, at least intermittently, does so. They were mainly interested in themselves, and were content to leave matters relatively indefinite. They were even more ready than we are to employ large numbers with no point except to convey the general idea of size: we do indeed speak vaguely of 'hundreds' or 'thousands': but not when we are dealing with serious history. For examples we may take, firstly, the astonishing discrepancies in the numbers of prisoners taken by Shalmaneser at the battle of Qarqar; and secondly, the prism of Nabonidus, well preserved and of undisputed reading, in which the scribe has pushed the story back a thousand years in time. There are only two conceivable explanations for such a 'mistake' in an official document, either general indifference or deliberate fraud: and history has no business with either.

Historical Style and Validity

Until the end of our period, historical records were couched in the antique literary style exemplified by the Homeric poems, in which every proper name of a person, a people or a country, is coupled with an inseparable epithet. We find the very phrases used in descriptions of Sargon's campaigns, and even earlier, recurring unchanged in accounts of the last members of the late Assyrian dynasty. This is the consequence of the scribes' system of education, which stocked their memory with ready-made phrases, to be trotted out in a given set of circumstances. True, a few fresh descriptions do make their appearance in the reign of Ashurbanipal, but they are rare features in the generally monotonous record.

Complete historical reliance cannot, in the last resort, be placed on these documents. Not only, as we have seen, were they certainly guilty of exaggerating certain victories, but it is remarkable further that they never mention an Assyrian defeat. Does the Assyrian monarch vainly pursue a defeated enemy? The latter 'like a bird hath gained a retreat where he cannot be reached'. Do the royal armies retreat in battle? They are making a planned withdrawal to the capital. It we want an earlier example, we can find one in the account of the battle of Kadesh between Rameses II and the Hittites, each of whose written records claims it as a victory.

Nevertheless, when due allowance is made for the necessary corrections, the very quantity of the material at our disposal enables us to form a pretty good idea of the policies of the States which were world powers at a time when European consciousness had scarcely begun to stir.

Private Correspondence. Royal Correspondence

The inhabitants of Mesopotamia were indefatigable letter writers, and a great deal of their correspondence—or so we might think—has survived, though we must remember that, since their letters could not be torn up, nothing has been destroyed. It is preponderantly on business, and mainly commercial, matters, and it is extremely uncommon to come across an intimate letter to some absent friend. Since any given letter may deal with a variety of subjects, may switch abruptly from one topic to another, and may suddenly allude to facts in widely varying fields of which we know nothing: all this often complicates the problem of translation. There was a rigid convention governing the opening of a letter. As we saw when we were considering how little scope the cuneiform script gave for individual treatment, no recipient could possibly recognise whom a letter came from merely by looking at it, and so the sender always wrote his name as follows: 'To A from your servant, B': this formula was followed by wishes for the recipient's good health which we nowadays generally put at the end of a letter. Sometimes it was exaggeratedly long-winded but in its simplest and shortest form it ran: 'May [this or that] god grant you life'. Then there followed the substance of the letter, which ended when the writer had nothing more to say. There was no set form of ending. Reproaches or commands from a writer who believes that he has grounds for complaint are freely interspersed with phrases intended to mollify the recipient, such as 'Art thou no longer my brother?' 'Art thou no more my father?'

In the period which we are studying, the most interesting letters are those written by and to the different late-Assyrian kings, which throw light on every facet of Court life and public affairs. There are references to war, and we have already quoted some letters which refer to Sargon's Armenian campaign, and are simply secret reports on the enemy by the king's agents. The monarch also took an interest in day-to-day business, such as transport by boat, the repair of flood damage, and reprimands for neglect of official duty, thus: 'The temple-weavers are neglecting their work', or requests for an audience with the king, 'On the subject of the king's message to me: "later, you shall be granted an audience: in the meantime, if you have something to say to me, put it in writing"; how can I bear to be refused an audience? Towards whom, in future, shall I turn my eyes?'[13]

There are a number of police reports on missing persons, e.g., 'The king hath written "Let him be brought before me." He has been sought in Bir-Halza ,but has not been found, and in his native town, but he was not there. His brother was found there, almost alone. He was arrested and brought before me. I asked him "Where is your brother?" and he replied "I have not seen him." I am sending the brother to my lord . . .'[14]

In the two following letters we see officials taking an oath, and can observe the hierarchical structure of official society, while the second letter stresses the importance attached to this particular ceremony.

(1) 'To the king my lord, from his servant Ishtar-shum-eresh. Health to the king my lord, and may Nabu and Marduk bless him. The scribes, the diviners, the magicians, the doctors, the observers of the flight of birds, the palace officials who dwell in the city have taken an oath to the gods on the sixteenth day of Nisan: now they can take an oath to the king.'[15]

(2) 'To the king my master from his servant Kaptia. Health to the king my master. Regarding the matter of the oaths of Babylon about which the king wrote to me, I was not present, for the king's letter only reached me after I and my brothers had left for the country of Arashi on a tour of inspection, and I could not reach Babylon in time for the taking of the oaths. On my journey I met the great chamberlain of the palace. When he had led me to Uruk in the presence of your gods, I should have been able to receive the oaths sworn to the king my master. But I had not full confidence in these oaths sworn privately, and I thought: "Let the soldiers with their sons, and their wives as well as their gods, swear the oaths which are due to the king: but I will accept them according to the formula laid down in the letter from the king, when the Elders shall come to swear their oaths to the king my lord."'[16]

Finally, here is an astonishing letter from some high official, whose name we do not know, to King Sennacherib, who had reversed the laws governing the succession by nominating his favourite younger son Ashurbanipal to the throne of Assyria, and his elder son to the throne of Babylon.

'What had never been done even in heaven, the king, my lord, hath brought to pass on earth, and hath made us witnesses of it. Thou hast robed one of thy sons in the royal robes and hast named him as ruler of Assyria, and hast named thy elder son to succeed to the throne of Babylon. What the king my lord hath done for his son is not for the good of Assyria. Surely, O King, Ashur hath granted thee power, from the rising to the setting of the sun, and, as touches thy dear children, thy heart may well be content. None the less, the lord my king has conceived an evil plan, and thou hast therein been weak . . .'[17]

Compare this with the following letter from a citizen of Babylon who had come to lay his complaints before the king and had rapidly been dismissed from the royal presence.

'I am as a dead man, I am faint after the sight of the king my master. When I see the countenance of the king my master, I begin again to live, and, though I am still hungered, I am as though refreshed. When last I was granted an audience of the king, I was overcome with fear, and I could not find words to utter . . .'[18]

This terror of royalty is indeed far removed from the other respectful but undaunted reminder of duly established law. We may well feel baffled by the Assyrian court with its strange mixture of servility and frankness towards the person of the king, which is so marked a feature of the ancient East.

The Sciences: the Object of Revelation

The historian Berossus, in his *History* which is entirely lost save for a few fragments, preserves the memory of an early tradition about the beginning of civilization in Mesopotamia. According to this, the primitive inhabitants in their settlements on the lagoons on the Persian Gulf, saw a fabulous creature, called Oannes, half-man and half-fish, rise from the waters. It spent its days among them, instructing them in every branch of knowledge, and each night returned to the depths. Four times a similar vision rose from the waters to complete the work begun by the earlier visitants, and it was generally believed that from this time onwards virtually no invention of note had been made.

The very concept of revealed knowledge renders it not only worthy of respect but also in some degree sacred. The first effect of this is upon its diffusion, for it cannot be broadcast to the world at large, but must be confined to the privileged few deemed worthy to share it. This means first and foremost the priesthood who, in turn, as guardians of this sacred treasure, will bestow it upon those who prove themselves worthy to receive it: namely, the initiates. This conception of initiation is indeed the limiting factor in the process of instruction. In the first place it prevents the publication of matter too secret or too dangerous to expound in books. Thus instruction is bound mostly to be given orally and the 'forbidden' subjects only passed on gradually. We do not, in fact, possess a single textbook which expounds the whole of any branch of learning. The priests were careful to give the world at large only treatises whose deeper significance, beneath their simple exterior, could not be understood without a key. In the texts we are continually confronted by the phrase 'To the initiated, you shall explain . . .'

This prohibition was not universally applied to the reading of a text, but to its interpretation, for as we have already seen to be true of language and numbers, Babylonian thought often sought cover in symbolism. An excellent example of this tendency, to which I have referred and which merits particular attention, is a tablet explaining the significance of the great temple of Bel-Marduk at Babylon. It consists of a series of numbers, recording the dimensions of the courtyards, the terraces and the buildings of the temple Esagila, 'the lofty-headed temple' as it was known by reason of its tall *ziggurat*. But in the midst of his straightforward description, the scribe suddenly introduces the cautionary formula: surprisingly, indeed, since there appears to be no special significance in this list of numbers and dimensions. True enough: but the secret is their meaning, for we know that numbers were often used to conceal some sacred mystery, and comprise a mysterious language with a significance beyond our comprehension. We can recall Sargon building the outer walls of Khorsabad of a length 'of the number of his name': and it is this which must be kept a secret save from the initiated.

Mystery Societies

All this raises the question whether 'mystery' cults existed in Assyria and Babylonia, as they commonly did elsewhere, for example in Greece. The secret was a well-kept one, but there are grounds for thinking that such cults were in being.

In the justly celebrated poem commonly known as 'The Righteous Sufferer' the unfortunate individual whose trials are described is at the last justified by the god Marduk. The man who had descended into the grave returned again to life in Babylon: and each gate of the city gave him a direct experience of the bliss suggested by its name, e.g., the gates of abundance, of the good genie, of peace, of life, of the sun, of the oracles, of the sweeping away of curses, of 'the mouth's inquiry', of the end of lamentations, of lustral purification: and after these experiences he was admitted to the presence of the god Marduk:

he worshipped his consort the goddess Sarpanit: he was admitted to offer them prayers and invocations.

There is evidence that some of the doors of Esagila were in fact known by these names, and the question is therefore whether the text is merely the record of a pilgrimage to a holy place or the description of a ceremony of initiation, in which the believer experienced degrees of bliss in proportion to his progress through the stages of knowledge. The latter explanation is plausible, and we shall return to it later.

We must insist on what we have already said more than once; every feature both of a text and of a religious ritual has an esoteric and symbolical significance. We have already quoted numerous examples of this, and the longer we study Babylonian civilization, the more certain it appears that their thought contained an esoteric element. At the root of everything lies the symbol: and though we may frequently not even suspect its existence, our knowledge allows us to infer it even at the expense of interpretations which might otherwise seem far-fetched. Thus even if there are no positive grounds for reading such a degree of subtlety into this particular question, it was at least something of which the Mesopotamians were perfectly capable. For proof, we have the tablets from which we have already quoted.

The Mesopotamians, who combined a respect for religion, which they shared with other peoples of antiquity, with a power of logical reasoning peculiarly their own, were bound to draw certain conclusions from this concept of revelation. It was not capable of improvement, and various attempts from time to time to do so had, if tradition could be believed, been of little profit. The only thing that mankind could bring to the knowledge revealed by the gods was, in short, a general method of systematizing it. The naturistic and ultra-polytheistic character of Babylonian religion emphasized universal belief in this revelation. In a monotheistic religion in which everything is the creation of a single divinity, belief demands a certain self-consciousness in order to thank God for all that is good in life: and this belief was bound to be even stronger for each individual Babylonian for whom nothing, whether natural or invented, lacked its appropriate god. Barley was the pure goddess Nidaba: the vine brought immediately into his mind the goddess Geshtin-anna, 'the heavenly vine'. The inhabitants of the town of Umma had but to look at their fields and gardens to be reminded of their god Shara, the written form of whose name was the ideogram for greenery. It was, in short, a kind of reference of myths to an historical basis, but carried only to the point where the gods themselves were the inventors, and had not as yet made over their powers to the select band of initiates. Each improvement is the result not of personal effort and inquiry, but of a fresh benefaction bestowed on man by one of the gods of the inexhaustible Babylonian pantheon.

This is why the modern division of thought and learning into arts, natural sciences and applied sciences was entirely alien to the Babylonian imagination, which regarded all branches of science as equal in importance, and, because of their origin, as all equally exact. We shall ourselves do well to realize that our own modern division can no longer claim precision, and that we may one day have to alter it, for the 'truths' of physics, chemistry and mathematics are staggering under the impact of recent discoveries. The Babylonians, untroubled by doubt, could not see, as we can, the process of the evolution of knowledge, though in their case it was admittedly slower. In forming our judgments on primitive societies we must be careful not to blame them unfairly for their apparent stagnation. Mere thought, by itself, does not create progress; it requires both skill in performance and experiment, which at each step forward make possible the exploitation of new horizons, whose potentialities extend ever ahead and yield an endless rhythm of new results. Discovery can be made only in a climate of opinion favourable to the discoverer. The history of science proves that almost every generation has encountered those who have trodden the same ground before them: but for want of recognition by contemporary society, or for want of the necessary equipment, the actual process of discovery was retarded.

With these diverse conditions in mind, we will, in the interests of simplicity, consider the sciences under their familiar names: mathematics and its applications, astronomy, the physical sciences and chemistry.

Mathematics

In our account of Babylonian mathematics we can rely with confidence on the thorough studies of the subject by F. Thureau-Dangin, the results of which have been published in several volumes.

The ingenious sexagesimal system of numeration, based upon the number 60, or upon a multiple or a factor of 60, was employed alike by the Arabs and the Greeks, and is still used in Western Europe for the mathematical measurement of arcs and angles and for divisions of time. It was regularly used by the Babylonians and, before them, by the Sumerians. It has been asked what advantage was to be found in this system, which has, moreover, left its mark upon modern numeration, e.g., when we speak of the dozen or the gross, or talk of 'several dozen' meaning no more than 'a large number' as an alternative to using 'hundreds' or 'thousands', e.g., 'I will give you a hundred (a dozen) guesses.'

We may grant that the fact that the number 60 is the lowest number containing the largest number of factors, accounts for its being used to divide the year into days, as the unit for expressing the number of degrees, and to divide the circle into six segments.

The system was probably first used in connection with numeration, and was only at a later stage applied to the science of measurement.

We know that the Sumerians counted in units from 1 to 10, which is of course the natural process, since the fingers provide the obvious digits. Instead, however, of continuing with the progression from 10 to 100, they stopped at 60 and, starting from that fundamental, began to graft a system based upon the unit of 60 (or upon its factors, 6 or 12) on to the decimal system. The progression of the decimal and the Sumerian systems can be expressed in two parallel columns, as follows :—

Decimal	*Sumerian* (Sexagesimal)
1	1
10	10
10 × 10	10 × 6
(10 × 10) × 10	(10 × 6) × 10
(10 × 10 × 10) × 10	(10 × 6 × 10) × 6

The system of measurement employed by the Sumerians was only in part sexagesimal. The table of weights, for example, was based on the arbitrary concept of the 'load' which could be carried by a man or an animal, while conventional values following the sexagesimal system were assigned to smaller weights, like the *mina*, which was one-sixtieth part of a 'load', or the *talent*, a multiple of the *mina* (equivalent to the 'load' itself) and its sub-divisions.

We owe to the Sumerians the concept of subdividing the day, which they regarded as beginning at sunset, into twelve 'double hours', each of these being subdivided into thirty parts. The astronomer Kidinnu (Greek 'Kidenas') laid it down that a day should begin at midnight, a measure causing less error than a reckoning to sunset. This division of the day into 360 parts was applied to the circle. The ecliptic was divided into segments of twelve double hours. In the end the Zodiac, in which each sign covers one-twelfth of the full circle, or 30 degrees, resulted from this conception. This division, which dates from the close of the Achaemenid period, enlarged the scope of astrology, which was only fully grasped when the implications of the precession of the equinoxes were realized. The interest of the Sumerian system, despite its disadvantages in deriving partly from a decimal and partly from a duodecimal system, lay in the fact that the size of a number was not absolute but relative, and was expressed by its position.* It joined a series of fractions in declining powers of 60 to a series of integers in rising powers of 60. This made it an extremely flexible instrument for the purpose of calculation. By only partially adopting this system, the Greeks deprived them-selves of this advantage, and so to some extent did the Hindus, since they only took over the part which related to the integers; while when at last the system was introduced to Western Europe by the Arabs, the world had to wait until the sixteenth century A.D. for a full realization of the advantages of a series of numbers in declining powers.

We possess a number of important collections of Babylonian problems, which demonstrate that they were able to calculate the exact volume of a pyramid and of a truncated cone. They regularly employed an approximation (3) to π. They did not measure the size of angles from the horizontal plane, but by the size of the deviation from the vertical. They regarded two-dimen-sional figures as standing in the vertical plane (just as we speak of the 'base' of a triangle), but they saw them, so to speak, inverted and accordingly described them in terms of the shapes which

---

* There was no visible sign of the digit, which had to be deduced from the con-text. [Translator's note.]

they suggested: thus a triangle was a 'nail's head' and a trapezoid was an 'ox's head'.

While Babylonian geometry was content to satisfy the requirements of everyday life, algebra, the development of which was very greatly assisted by the methods of calculation which the Babylonians had perfected, advanced with giant strides, and considering the period represents an astonishing achievement. Thureau-Dangin, indeed, in face of the mastery of quadratics displayed by the Babylonians, believes that beyond doubt it must have had a history stretching into the distant past and that 'it must have been a legacy from the Sumerians'.

Collections of Problems

The surviving collections take different forms. Sometimes they merely state the problem: sometimes they state the answer as well: sometimes they state the problem and the steps required for discovering the solution, the actual process of calculation being left to the student: and sometimes they state the problem, the method of working it out and the answer. Examples of the two latter types demonstrate perfectly that arithmetical tables must have been applied: but there is no theoretical explanation of the successive operations employed. We will quote an example of one problem of each type: for clarity the Babylonian terms are replaced by others with which we are familiar.

(1) A rectangle. I have multiplied the length by the breadth and have thus obtained the area. I added the length and the breadth and the sum is equal to the area. I added the length, the breadth and the area, and the total sum of all three is nine. What are the dimensions?[19]

(2) I have added the area of four squares and the sum is 1 minute* 30 seconds. The sum of their sides is 2 minutes and 20 seconds. What are the sides of the four squares?[20]

Answer.—The first is 50 *ninda*†, the second 40, the third 30 and the fourth 20.

---

* In these problems the signs for 'minutes' and 'seconds' are here used to indicate fractions in successive powers of 60. Thus 1′ 30″ (one minute thirty seconds) $= \frac{1}{60} + \frac{30}{60 \times 60}$. For an explanation of Problem (3) see Appendix A. [Translator's note.]

† *Ninda* could be either a measure of length or a square measure. [Translator's note.]

(3) A stone of unknown weight. I have subtracted $\frac{1}{7}$ of its weight and $\frac{1}{3}$ shekel and 15 grains. I restored $\frac{1}{11}$ of the amount subtracted *plus* $\frac{5}{6}$ shekel, thus restoring the stone to its original weight. What was that weight?[21]

Answer.—I write down, 7, 11, 25 seconds and 50 seconds. I subtract 1 from 7 (= 6) and I add 1 to 11 (= 12). I multiply the remainder by 50 seconds. I add, and from the total I subtract 25 seconds. I multiply the remainder by 7. This gives me the original weight of my stone.

(4) A field. I have squared the difference between the breadth and the length. I have subtracted 8 minutes 20 seconds from the area. The side is 10 units longer than the front.

Method of solution.—Square 10. 1 minute 40 seconds + 8 minutes 20 seconds = 10 minutes. $\frac{10}{2} = 5$, and $5^2 = 25$. 10 minutes + 25 seconds = 10 minutes 25 seconds, which is the square of 25 seconds. Add 5 seconds = 30 seconds = the side. Subtract 5 seconds = 20 seconds = the width.[22]

Along with these very extensive collections of problems, in order to simplify calculation, the Sumerians had drawn up tables of the steps required in the different operations. These tables were needed because the various units of measurement of area and of volume were derived from the 'finger' and the 'cubit' respectively, just as in modern Europe measurements are based upon the metre.

Although all this is essentially empirical rather than theoretical, and although Rey has gone so far as to describe it as a method of perpetual trial and error, only the successful results of which have been preserved, it is undeniable that Babylonian mathematics remain 'unique in the ancient world and far superior to everything which has been bequeathed to us by antiquity'.

Geography. Cartography

We do not possess any clear statement of the Assyrian conception of the earth, and we must deduce it as best we may from the numerous documents which refer to the subject. The Assyrians were convinced that the earth was not a sphere but a circular disc bounded at its circumference by a rim of mountains on which the sky rested like a dish cover. There were two outlets in the mountain, one for the rising and one for the setting sun, but the question of the path which its orb followed during the night—whether it followed a circular course in the thickness of half the rim of mountain or whether it passed underground beneath the disc of the earth—was never clearly established. The earth was, however, believed to float upon the waters of the abyss, the counterpart of the 'stream of bitter water' which encircled it, though this fact was apparently no impediment either to the presence of sweet waters underground, which fed the springs and the rivers, or to the existence of the nether regions beneath the earth's surface. The whole Sumerian and Akkadian notion of the earth was indeed extremely hazy, and we can only conclude that the men of learning, in the person of the priests, who had devoted themselves unsparingly to constructing divine genealogies and to establishing order in the pantheon, had never turned their attention to the problems of defining an internally self-consistent cosmography.

It is clear from the numerous documents relating to the sales of estates, fields and houses that the Mesopotamians possessed a sufficient degree of mathematical knowledge to tackle problems of surveying, and they also knew how to draw accurately proportioned plans of their cities. Direct evidence for this exists in the shape of a cuneiform tablet which shows the general ground plan of the city of Nippur, and proved to coincide remarkably closely with the plans drawn by the American expedition during their excavation of the city.

It has been observed that Assyrian and Babylonian monuments, unlike those of western Europe, are not orientated towards the four cardinal points of the compass, but to intermediate points, i.e., north-west, instead of north, and south-east instead of south. This is believed to be connected with the direction of the prevailing winds in Mesopotamia.

There is a tablet of the Persian period which represents a skeleton map of the earth's surface as the Babylonians conceived it. At the centre of the terrestrial disc lies Babylon (like China lying, in Chinese eyes, at the centre of the world): certain towns and canals are marked, then comes the encircling ocean and finally, still farther outside, the most distant regions are indicated by triangles. It is interesting to see that the northern triangle carries a note 'Country where the sun is never seen'. The polar night must evidently have been known, at least by hearsay.

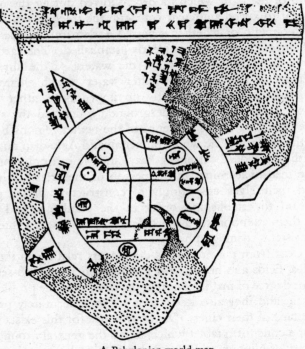

A Babylonian world map
(*From Chiera: 'They wrote on clay',
by permission of the Cambridge University Press*)

Some tablets are regular itineraries, giving the distances between one town and another and the time required for the journey. They afford yet further proof, if any were required, of the development of commerce and the frequency with which journeys were made through the different countries of the Empire and the adjacent territories.

The Calendar. Astronomy

The Mesopotamians regarded astronomy as a means rather than an end, its principal use being to act as a guide for the purposes of astrology (which we shall discuss later) and to make it possible to fix the calendar. It was in about 1100 B.C. that the Assyrians, who had themselves taken the calendar over from the Babylonians, adopted it in the form which we find in use in the late Assyrian period. This 'luni-solar' calendar comprised twelve months of thirty days apiece, namely (beginning at the start of the Babylonian year) Nisan (March/April) Iyyar (April/May) Siwan (May/June) Tammuz (June/July) Ab (July/August) Elul (August/September) Tisri (September/October) Marcheswan (October/November) Kislef (November/December) Tebet (December/January) Sebat (January/February) and Adar (February/March).

Since the cycle of twelve months contained only 360 days, an intercalary month was interposed at regular intervals either half way through or at the end of the year. This was called by the name of the immediately preceding month, i.e., second Elul or second Adar. In practice, however, this calendar proved to have unsuspected defects. Thus the observations upon which the announcement of the beginning of a new month was based might be prevented by bad weather, and it might therefore be postponed for one or two days. The beginning of a new month was decreed by the king, and consequently reports from the court astronomers, in the form of letters giving the results of their observations, are a prominent feature of official correspondence: e.g.,

'On the twenty-ninth day I made an observation': and according to whether there had been clouds or not, they end 'We saw [or did not see] the moon'. A more detailed letter runs as follows:—

'On the thirtieth day I saw the moon, which was at the elevation of the thirtieth day. At the present time it is at the elevation proper to the second day of the month . . . Thus the king can fix the first day of the month.'[23]

A possible consequence of this kind of time lag was that it might prove necessary to introduce two intercalary months in the same year.

The beginning of the year in the month of Nisan meant that it coincided with the first new moon following the vernal equinox, but the particular importance assumed by Tisri in the religious texts must reflect some memory of a distant time when the year began in the autumn.

The sky was considered to be divided into great zones as the earth was divided into kingdoms. Thus the central zone, running diagonally across the north-south axis, was the way of Anu: above it was the way of Enlil, and below it the way of Ea.

Tables of Fixed Stars

The Assyrians and Babylonians, as far as their primitive resources permitted, had recorded and named the visible stars in
each of these zones.[24] The way of Enlil contained thirty-three,
including the constellations of Cassiopeia, Perseus, Auriga, Cancer,
Leo, Corona Borealis, the Great Bear, Draco, the Little Bear,
Serpens, Lyra, Vega, Dolphinus, Andromeda and the planet
Jupiter.

The way of Anu contained twenty-three, including Aries,
Pisces, the Pleiades, Aldebaran, Sirius, Canis Major, Hydra,
Corvus, Virgo, Libra, and Aquila. A tablet of the Seleucid
period, now in the Louvre, bears a plan of some of these stars—
Corvus, Virgo, Leo, Hydra, etc.—beside the text.

The way of Ea included only fifteen stars, among them being
the Piscis Austrinus, Aquarius, Centaurus, Lupus, Scorpius,
Antares and Sagittarius.

The Mesopotamians distinguished between planets and fixed
stars, comparing the wandering planets with wild goats, and the
fixed stars with tame goats.

Observation combined with calculation had enabled the Mesopotamians to compile tables of the fixed stars together with a
record of the distances between them.[25] These were expressed in
units of time, related to the weight of water escaping from the
clepsydra (a device known to the Babylonians, and used as a
subject on which problems were set) between the passage of the
two stars at the meridian. Thus an entry in the table might read
'Two and a half minas [in weight of water] from Gamtu to the
constellation of Gemini.'*

There was a second method of measuring relative position,
in the form of divisions of the parallel on which the stars were
supposed to lie, expressed in degrees. An entry in the table might
read 'Five degrees at ground level from the constellation of
Gemini to the constellation of the Evening Star.'

Finally there were absolute or 'celestial' measurements, expressed by reference to the absolute *bêru* of 360 degrees, and of a
magnitude of about six and a half miles: and a tablet might thus
say 'There are eighteen thousand *bêru* in the sky, from the constellation of the Evening Star to the solitary Star.'

* See Appendix B on methods of calculating astronomical distances. [Translator's
note.]

These results were all the more creditable since the only instruments available to the Mesopotamians for observing the heavenly bodies were tubes to act as view-finders, the *clepsydra* or water clock, the *gnomon* or sundial and the *polos* consisting of a hollow hemisphere with a needle fixed at the centre, and casting its shadow on the walls which were marked off at intervals.

The astronomers did not confine themselves to waiting for the actual appearance of the moon in order to fix the beginning of the month: they kept the king informed on the parallel phenomena of the stars, sun and moon, on the precise moment of the equinoxes, and on lunar eclipses. We cannot help a feeling of surprise at the interest taken by the king in celestial phenomena: no doubt he was encouraged to do so by his personal astronomers, with astrology as the ultimate end in view. Their reports, indeed, often take the form of a reply to some question which he himself had asked.

Further, in accordance with the practice of trying to incorporate scientific principles as then known in narratives with a religious or an epic flavour, there was one version of the Creation epic which attempted to include the whole corpus of current astronomical knowledge by attributing to Marduk the creation of the heavenly bodies and of their movements. The tablet in question is, however, very largely lost. The most advanced research on the subject of Babylonian astronomy has resulted in the credit for some of the discoveries hitherto attributed to Hipparchus being given to the astronomers known as the Chaldaeans. The real pioneers in this field seem to have been a group of third century B.C. astronomers including Soudines of Chaldaea (who was living at the court of Pergamum in 239 B.C.), Naburianos, of whom we know nothing beyond his name, and Kidinnu (Kidenas in its Greek form), the author of the lunar canons.

Natural Sciences. Botany, Zoology, Mineralogy

The Babylonians were excellent observers and had for a long time been conscious of the wide variety of visible species. The point has been touched on several times in this book. The interesting feature for our present purposes is what appears to have been their purely empirical approach to the problem of classifying different varieties. The garden of Merodach-baladan, for example (p. 48), was arranged in plots in which the plants

were grouped not with any regard for scientific principles but
with reference to their common uses. Similarly a tablet from
Susa records a list of plants which were used in the manufacture
of unguents, all of which carry the ideogram signifying 'scent'.

One of the most surprisingly persistent and universal human
habits is the way that peasants name objects after their resemblance to something familiar. Like ourselves, for example, the
Assyrians had a plant called 'hound's-tongue'. There seems to
be some mysterious compulsion towards the use of such names,
though the plant may have been quite different from that which
we know by that name.

Some plant lists survive in which the names do not seem to be
in any logical sequence, while other lists form a kind of dictionary
with the Sumerian and Akkadian names in parallel columns. A
little thought will show that this is bound to be the case. We
already know that the name of an object confers existence upon
it, but at the same time the knowledge of the name confers power
over the thing itself. Possession of the list of names guarantees
possession of the objects themselves, while their classification,
if the order is not purely arbitrary, represented to the Babylonian
an end in itself.

The boundaries of animal, vegetable and mineral were very ill
defined. Thus hail had the same determinative as stone, and as a
date stone, while what we should regard as grass is frequently
described as shrub and vice versa.

The inhabitants of Babylonia were no less interested in the
observation of animals, and birds and fish too are as accurately
and recognizably depicted on the bas-reliefs as are the contemporary mammals. A list of slightly later than 2000 B.C. which
names the fish that were sold in the market at Larsa, near the
Persian Gulf, and must include fish both from the lagoons and
from the canals, comprises no fewer than eighteen edible varieties. The evidence at our disposal shows that certain species of
animals—such as the long-bearded ram with widely separated
curving horns—have by now disappeared: or confirms that
certain animals were found wild within the borders of Mesopotamia: e.g., the small horse of the steppes (*Equus Przewalskii*)
with a head resembling that of a camel, and a short thick and
stiff mane. The appearance of a humped or Indian ox, on a vase
dating from the earliest historical period, proves that even at this

early date commercial relations existed between the two countries.

The different stones were also listed and classified. Many of them are identifiable, and we have already enumerated the basic industrial minerals during our survey of commerce. Stones, like plants, were sometimes named after some supposed resemblance of shape to part of an animal's body. We possess a Sumerian epic which purports to explain their names, and this affords an excellent example of the way in which, instead of writing the modern type of purely descriptive treatise, the Sumerians summarized the natural properties of objects, and commented upon their names in their didactic poems. As a result of some circumstances which are unknown to us, the great god Ninurta was confronted by an alliance of his enemies. The stones took sides in the matter, some for and some against him. He was victorious: and the latter suffered in consequence. All this must have taken place at an extremely remote period, since the stones were still but scarcely differentiated matter, for the god's immediate concern was to give them a name and to settle their destiny. To those which had been loyal to him he granted beautiful names and the happy fate of becoming the fine textured stones used for the statues and altars of the gods, precious stones for making jewellery, or ornaments for use in worship. But the hostile and defeated stones were condemned to mean uses and to worthlessness. They must become rough paving stones, door sills trodden underfoot, or simply remain as pebbles in the road (p. 198). The Mesopotamians knew a wide range of stones, even—and specially—the beautiful and rare ones of which they made the cylinder seals which everyone carried, like blue spar and lapis lazuli, rock crystal, jasper, cornelian and countless others.

Chemistry

A large section of the science of chemistry, as practised by the Mesopotamians, consisted of its practical application. They were already skilled metal workers, expert in the treatment of mineral substances, in refining metals and in compounding unusual alloys, which they obtained by slight variations in the proportions of the ingredients. For example, the formula for the type of glass known as 'copper-lead' consisted of 60 parts of ordinary glass, 10 of lead, 15 of copper, $\frac{1}{2}$ of saltpetre, and $\frac{1}{2}$ of lime: but if the same ingredients were used in the proportions 60, 10, 14, 1 and 2, the result would be the variety known as 'copper of Akkad'.

Cupellation and successive re-heatings were the processes usually employed in the refining of metals. A text dating from the reign of Nabonidus recounts the various tests to which an ingot of 5 minas (1 pound 1 ounce approx.) of gold from the royal revenues was subjected. At the stage of the first heating in the furnace, the loss was $\frac{2}{3}$ of a mina and 5 shekels, and the residual gold weighed 4 minas and 15 shekels. At the second re-heating, the loss was $\frac{1}{2}$ mina and 2 shekels and the pure gold was reduced to $3\frac{2}{3}$ minas and 3 shekels.

When gold was sent from one sovereign to another, it was quite common for the recipient to complain of the excessive loss which the metal underwent during the refining process. The King of Egypt, which was one of the main suppliers, never made a present of all this gold to his correspondents, and by far the greater part of what he sent consisted of the raw material which was converted into manufactured articles and then sent back again to the Egyptian court. King Burra-buriash of Babylon (approximately fourteenth century B.C.) twice complains to King Amenhotep IV of Egypt about the poor quality of the gold which he has received, and pretends to believe that it must have been adulterated without the Pharaoh's knowledge, since 20 minas when put into the furnace yielded less than 5 minas of pure gold.

Analyses carried out on the various gold objects discovered in the Royal Tombs of Ur (first half of the third millennium B.C.) have revealed remarkably wide variations in purity, ranging between seven and twenty-two carats (from 291 to 910.6 parts in 1,000): while analyses of alloys dating from the reign of Nabonidus give results of 968, 914 and 870 parts in 1,000 respectively.[26]

Artistic Conventions

We have already discussed the picture of the world which the Assyrians had formed, as well as their methods of drawing a plan of a building or an area, and have seen that while the former bore no relation to ours, their method for the latter was precisely the same as that used to-day. But if we are to attempt to pass a fair judgment on their artistic achievement, we must ask how they saw the material world around them and how they attempted to reproduce what they saw, since we cannot fairly judge their performance by modern critical standards. Indeed the mere existence of these standards is a standing temptation to us to regard them, quite falsely, as the only valid ones, and our means of expression as the highest expression of reality. In truth, of course, our assumption that our critical principles alone have validity results from our long familiarity with them as those which have governed the taste of the western world since the supremacy of Greece. We must, however, remember that the duration of this period—about 2000 years—is quite certainly less than that during which both the Far East and (during antiquity) the Near East respectively accepted the authority of their own traditions. Even if it can be claimed that three-dimensional carving makes the smallest demands on convention, it must be conceded that the art of drawing, which has to solve the problem of representing three-dimensional objects in two dimensions, is bound to employ certain technical devices—with a greater or lesser degree of success—or to disregard the third dimension completely. The conventional character of these devices is shown by the fact that different peoples, facing this identical problem, have each resolved it in their own way, and that their acceptance is the result of a long period of apprenticeship, and indeed of a deliberate distortion of the perceptions before this result is possible. Without some such apprenticeship, which is really a process of 'opening the minds' of our receptive faculties, the result for the uneducated is a lack of comprehension: as witness equally the savage who uncomprehendingly turns a drawing over and over in his hands, and our own readiness to condemn novel artistic conventions.

Statuary

We may begin with statuary which, of all the arts practised by the Assyrians, called for the fewest conventions. The subject need not detain us very long, since the inhabitants of Mesopotamia did not greatly like three-dimensional representations of the human body, at any rate on a large scale, if we count the statues of this period which have survived. We must also remember that, quite apart from the limited interest which the Babylonians seemed to take in this form of art, life-size statues required blocks of stone which were harder to come by than the slabs used for bas-reliefs. Further, as we know from inscriptions, the statues of gods or of great persons were often embellished with precious stones which could not be looted without the statues being broken. But it still remains true that the Assyrians were never seriously interested in the human body. Such statues as we do possess are invariably clothed, and the actual form of the body beneath is virtually invisible under the thickness of the sculptured garments: in one case a torso which is believed to be that of the goddess Ishtar, bearing the name of the king Ashur-bel-kala, is a very poor piece of work.

The quality of the sculpture shows a very marked decline since the Gudea statues, over fifteen hundred years earlier than the period of the Sargonid dynasty. The earlier period, like the later, employed conventions, but not of a kind to restrict the efforts of an artist fully conscious of the beauty of his model. An Assyrian statue, in direct contrast, seems—though it did not—to have originated in the bas-relief. A typical example is the statue of Ashurbanipal in the British Museum, in which the third dimension has been deliberately understated and which is, in any case, no larger than a child. Anxiety on the part of the sculptor to create durable work, which could serve as the model's *alter ego* and replace him before the god in the temple, led the sculptor to produce a pilaster-like figure, and to take advantage of the long robe worn by the kings and the gods in order to avoid having to carve the legs. We know from the bas-reliefs that this was technically within his power, but the legs would have been the most fragile feature.

We can, on the other hand, derive pleasure from the skill of the Mesopotamian artist in depicting animals. Here too, however, we are not dealing with large-scale sculpture: the statuettes of animals are clearly superior to those of human beings, which were more common than large-scale statues.

Bas-Reliefs

Discoveries made in recent years have revealed to us a series of frescoes sufficiently extensive to be fully studied, and when we turn from statuary to examine bas-reliefs or painting, we no longer feel that the artist is working under any sense of inhibition, but that we are in the presence of a long-established tradition: the artist has manifestly executed the non-representational elements with such familiarity and unhesitating fluency that we, as spectators, can accept what we see without a sense of revulsion, though the idiom is alien to us.

By way of example, we may examine the works executed during the various reigns of the late Assyrian dynasty. In the time of King Sargon himself, the reliefs are on a large scale, with characters often taller than life size. The details are clear and well spaced, while the landscape in which they are set is only occasionally suggested and is often totally disregarded. There are a few large-scale themes running the length of the panels, but not large numbers of figures. But by the time of the last of the great monarchs at the close of the dynasty, we can see that the artistic conventions have changed as radically as decorative art in France between the great designs of fruits and flowers (a legacy from the preceding century) of the period of Louis XIV, which were gradually refined into the posies of Louis XV and the miniature flowers of Louis XVI. In precisely the same way, by the time of Ashurbanipal, the Assyrian bas-reliefs are divided into sections with the human figures carved on a smaller scale. Moreover we find true battle scenes, wholly unlike similar scenes dating from the reign of Ashurnasirpal, with bodies, chariots, horses and fighters in inextricable confusion among the dead and the wounded. Art had, indeed, reached a point where it must either strike out on a fresh line or atrophy, for traditional formulae had been logically developed to their final conclusion.

In its early period, Assyrian art, which was probably comparatively insensitive to the beauties of nature, put as little emphasis as possible on landscape. It was sufficiently indicated by a few easily identifiable trees, like date palms, dwarf palms and conifers: to suggest the South, the typical thickets of reeds tall enough to give cover even to men on horseback (!): to suggest the North, the vine, whose twisting and branching shoots formed lovely decorative patterns.

The most attractive representation of landscape is unquestionably that of a corner of the game reserve in which the lions belonging to Ashurbanipal were kept. One animal is shown lying down and the other standing in a setting of vine-wreathed trees, while a large flower springs from the ground. The whole composition forms a rural scene of striking charm.

Perspective

This particular scene, however, consists merely of what might be described as a two-dimensional view of a piece of landscape, and it gives no clue to how the Assyrian artist dealt with the problems of perspective. His fundamental principle seems to have been to follow the bidding of the intellect rather than of the eye, and, ignoring the illusion that, with increasing distance, human figures appear to grow smaller, to carve them all on the same scale. The result is that perspective is not applied either to human figures or to features of the landscape. The latter are indeed entirely disregarded and the component features of the design are merely superimposed as it were in mid-air, or alternatively distributed between different levels, the spectator having to follow them from top to bottom, or vice versa, according to whether the action is focused at the top or the bottom of the relief. But although perspective in the modern sense was not employed by the Assyrians and Babylonians, they had one wholly idiosyncratic convention whereby the various characters—gods, kings, courtiers and common people—were portrayed on a diminishing scale in proportion to their rank or importance. The colossal bas-reliefs from Sargon's palace, now in the Louvre, depict Gilgamesh, the Assyrian equivalent of Hercules, struggling with a lion (Pl. XIX). The important figure in the group is the hero himself, and so he is represented on a gigantic scale. The lion is by comparison tiny, and the hero can crush it against his chest and stifle it without the slightest difficulty.

If the scene is a stream or a fishpond with tree-fringed banks, the artist first depicts the stream or the pond and then, as if from some imaginary central standpoint, lays the trees on the banks flat and in profile. Every feature of the design is presented as if from the point of view of a spectator walking and successively standing in front of each feature in turn. The Assyrian artist will not draw a three-quarter view of a building, an angle at which one side would appear to recede, though in reality of the same height as the façade. He would imagine himself standing directly before the building out of sight of the other sides and carve the face he could see.

This approach meant that an artist was, for example, unable to represent in profile the assault and capture of a town by soldiers scaling ladders, since a ladder consists not of a pole but of two uprights with lateral bars. The sculptor would therefore carve the front view of the ladder, and the attackers would consequently appear to be climbing off the ladder altogether, and parallel with one of the uprights (Pl. XX). He could not, as might be supposed, show them standing on the rungs, since by so doing part of the ladder would be concealed, whereas he knew that the ladder was actually complete and must be depicted so. This accounts for the convention, in a representation of an archer drawing a bow, of the part of the bowstring in front of the archer's face being omitted. Confronted by two improbabilities, the artist would choose the lesser.

When we come to the human figure, we find that the head is generally seen in profile and the upper part of the body is seen full face, or occasionally at a slight angle. The pelvis, like the head and the legs, is seen in profile, while the feet are shown one behind the other and in the same plane. The arms are always shown and the artist never makes any attempt at foreshortening, which of all modern conventions was most alien to the Assyrians and has indeed taken many centuries of education to win acceptance. The artist attempted in every detail to observe as closely as possible the principle of depicting things as they actually are. Thus the human eye when seen full face has its own expression and look, and so the artist carves the eye full face in a head drawn in profile. Similarly the Assyrian wore his beard square: but since a beard would not look square on a face seen in profile, the beard would be shown full face though its wearer was in profile (Pl. XIV).

A number of consequent minor conventions have been studied in detail by R. Flavigny. Thus when we are looking at a religious scene, we must look at all the architectural features and the ritual furnishings and visualize the columns and sacred fires, which are shown in line behind the god, as actually on either side of him. If a chariot is depicted approaching at full gallop (which is not common) the four horses are represented in pairs in front of the chariot as if they were tearing it apart, and so the front of the chariot is visible. Often we find a sideways view of a god seated upon a throne, which rests upon two crouching lions. The artist has carved them both separately, one in front of the other.

Finally we may find a worshipper between two identical gods, one facing right, and the other facing left. The probable explanation is that, in the interests of symmetry, the figure of the god has been duplicated, with a representation facing in each direction.

The artist rings the changes upon these conventions with supreme skill, and makes the most of them. If, for example, he is faced with the problem of showing soldiers at work in a camp or a fortress, he either takes us right inside their tents and shows us the interior, or he may draw a ground plan of the outer walls of the fortress, and project the towers outside it, like the trees round the fishpond described above. Then, in the free space left inside, he shows as it were in section the men busy at their cooking (Pl. XXI).

Exceptions to these rules are rare and suggest a few isolated individuals working in advance of their time. One such exception is the representation of the royal stables, in the reign of Ashurbanipal, which is shown three-quarter face. The large figure of an officer is standing at the entrance, while inside—the walls except for the uprights have been removed by the artist, so that what is happening inside is visible—we can see the small figures of horses and grooms.

Another exception comes from Khorsabad; this is a relief of Assyrians hunting birds in a forest (Frontispiece). In the foreground is a beardless hunter, while a second hunter, bearded, and older, though much smaller, is shown at what appears to be some distance. Unless the larger figure, as I have said, is a prince (p. 133), we must regard this relief as representing an attempt at the use of perspective in the modern sense.[27]

The Gallop in Art

The representation of animals possesses its own individual conventions, some of them unavoidable, like that demanded by the attempt to depict horses at the gallop. Until the advent of the cinema, no nation had ever managed precisely to analyze the exact sequence of the movements of a galloping horse, and each nation in antiquity selected and employed its own formula. The Greeks, for example (cf. the Elgin Marbles), represented it as a kind of canter: the Egyptians and the Assyrians thought of a galloping horse as rearing up on its hind legs as though it were about to jump, with the difference that while the Egyptians showed the forelegs bent, the Assyrians showed them extended. Finally Aegean art shows a horse flying through the air with all four feet clear of the ground. A detailed analysis of the movement with the aid of a moving camera shows that none of these conventions caught the actual movement, the Greeks alone getting somewhere nearer the truth. We must regard the extended gait as merely another convention employed by the Assyrians, though one which should occasion no surprise in view of the impossibility of accurate observation.

Another example of pure convention is the treatment of a line of human figures, or of a chariot drawn by several horses, when the spectator is imagined to be looking directly at the object in question. The artist suggests the requisite number of persons or horses, up to about four, by carving one or more lines exactly following the outline of the principal figure. This particular convention is indeed not solely confined to Assyrian art. The same practice is followed when an animal with horns is supposed to be seen so precisely in profile that only a single horn is visible. In these conditions the artist only represents one, and this is no doubt the origin of the myth of the unicorn. Equally, if a lion is charging it is shown in profile; if it is actually attacking its prey, the sculptor represents it with its fore legs extended and one crossed behind the other, in a wholly unrealistic attitude—not even that of the bear when about to smother its prey.

In conclusion we may mention a convention governing the sculptural treatment of the huge monolithic winged bulls which guarded the gates of the palace, flanking the entrance through which the visitor had to pass. It is perfectly logical, since the spectator is always supposed to be directly in front of the object at which he is looking. The visitor would in fact see them alternately facing him and sideways on to him. Thus on the reliefs the flank of the bull is seen in relief, while the forequarters and the head are treated three-dimensionally. Accordingly the artist has given the animal, seen in its two-dimensional aspect, the normal four feet: but to correspond with the three-dimensional forequarters, the artist has repeated the front foot, so that the animal actually has five feet (Pl. IV).

Reduced to words, the device sounds like an impossibly clumsy monstrosity, which could scarcely fail to shock the spectator. But in reality, thanks to the sculptor's skill and to his mastery of the conventions within which he worked, many of those who see it fail to notice it and feel no more sense of incongruity than they do at the curious hybrid conceptions of Assyrian sculpture: the animal-headed men and human-headed animals.

This is due to the admirable proportions and the ease and certainty with which the artist has imposed unity upon the separate
features. We may end by re-emphasizing once again the supreme
skill with which the Assyrians had learned to portray animals. The
lion at the point of death with blood gushing from its mouth, the
lioness with her hindquarters paralysed by an arrow but none the
less dragging herself to challenge the hunter, the lion leaving his
cage: all these are genuine masterpieces of observation.

Like the paintings by which they were later succeeded, the
reliefs were never coloured all over, only certain features, such
as the black beards and some touches of red or blue on the garments or the ornaments, being heightened with colour. This
discrimination in the use of colour seems to have been an accepted
practice at this date in the Near East, for the marble Phoenician
sarcophagi, known as 'anthropoid', since like Egyptian coffins
the heads were modelled in low relief, had the hair and the eyes
alone picked out in colour, the rest being unpainted.

CHAPTER IV

RELIGIOUS LIFE

The Documentary Evidence

AT LEAST so far as the actual practice of worship is concerned, we have access to direct sources of information about the religious life which loomed so large in Babylonia. The countless descriptions of ritual which have been preserved are particularly valuable, not only for the light they cast upon every detail of the ceremonies observed at the various festivals but also because we can thereby infer the practices followed upon other occasions. A statement that certain actions are peculiar to the festivals shows that the others must have been a matter of everyday performance. Indeed, admittedly with some gaps, it would be possible to reconstruct the religious calendar for an entire year.

It is true that we possess no specifically ethical writings on the subject of good and evil; but the necessary knowledge exists in the lists of sins and in the warnings and curses in which particular actions are denounced as abominable to the gods, and it only requires patient analysis in order to extract from these texts the Babylonian idea of good and evil. But whereas modern thought regards these concepts as having some kind of absolute existence, they were long looked upon in Mesopotamian religious thought as consequences of the will of the gods, good being what met with divine approval, and evil with divine displeasure. It was only during the first dynasty of Babylon that abstract conceptions such as *Kittu* (Right) and *Mesharu* (Justice) became accepted features in the Babylonian pantheon. We can hear an echo of the earlier mode of thought in one of the most pathetic fragments of Babylonian literature which we possess, the ancient poem of the 'Righteous Man's Sufferings'. In this work the hero, overwhelmed by misfortune, recounts his past deeds and, finding nothing in them but virtue, concludes, in the profoundest pessimism, by asking whether what man believes to be good may not be evil in the eyes of the gods.

Equally we have no explicit account of the individuality and
character of each of the gods, and once again we have to depend
upon comparative analysis for what we know of their parentage,
their family relationships, the attributes which each enjoyed,
the reasons why they were worshipped and indeed the whole evidence of their true nature. The Babylonian satisfied his desire
to make some permanent record of fundamental religious truths
by the composition of poems of epic character like those of the
'Creation' and the 'Descent of Ishtar to the Nether Regions'. No
doubt when we have studied the whole of this literature we shall
be left with a feeling of depression: we shall conclude that the
religion which it reveals fails to match the memory of one of the
greatest civilizations of antiquity, which endured for close on
three thousand years. Perhaps we need to remind ourselves that
any belief must carry the stamp of the age which fashioned or
received it, and that any element of the sublime which it may
contain becomes perceptible only later in time when thought has
been able to sift the pure metal from the dross. Each succeeding
period forms but a single link in the chain of time, and depends
inescapably upon its predecessor, while in the realm of thought,
centuries must pass, and a fresh mental vocabulary must be
constructed, before the necessary assertion can be made and the
way be opened to realms beyond those of accepted traditions:
just as in the physical world only improved technical skill can
lead to new experiment which will in turn point the way to fresh
discovery. The failure of Babylonian thought to construct a
homogeneous religious system was not due to any fundamental
inherent weakness, but because its level of achievement was
virtually predetermined by its occurrence in time.

Inconsistencies and Contradictions

The most striking features which emerge from any survey of
Babylonian religion are its incohesiveness and its contradictions.
Babylonian belief was polytheistic in character and the pantheon
which it envisaged was for a number of reasons full of paradox
and repetition in the qualities which it ascribed to the gods.
Divinity itself may not have been the result of direct revelation,
but the most important types of applied knowledge were, and it
was accepted that any advance upon what the gods had
granted was merely incidental. This was the principal reason,

implicit if not explicit, why modifications were largely impossible.

Moreover, Mesopotamian religion sprang from a variety of roots and followed the pattern of growth of the country itself. One by one the most ancient Sumerian cities, each of which had enjoyed autonomy during its earlier years, and possessed its own priesthood with its own elaborate traditions, absorbed their neighbours. We must realize that these traditions had a dual aspect. They were on the one hand bound to match the general outlook of the age when they were formed, which imposed a general kind of unity upon them, and on the other to harmonize with the organization and with the particular inclinations and needs of each individual city; which led to important differences of detail. A system of parentage and relationships for the gods like those of mankind were accepted elements in religious thought, and within this framework each priestly authority had worked out its own individual set of beliefs, just as it had selected one particular god as tutelary deity of its city—and generally a different deity from that chosen by the neighbouring towns. As the cities gradually formed larger units, first the different pantheons coalesced and then the Sumerian gods were brought into contact with the gods of the Semitic invasion, with an inevitable process of give and take. The Semites brought their own religious ideas with them and fostered them alongside those which they had assimilated from Sumer; they preserved the Sumerian pantheon, but they rechristened every Sumerian god with a Semitic name, thus (since none were abolished) doubling the total number of deities currently worshipped. The natural consequence of all this was that according to the doctrines of various groups of priests any given deity might on different occasions be regarded as the son of different parents. Perhaps the most striking example of inconsistency is to be found in the way that the names of different pairs of divinities were linked. Ishtar, who was the most highly honoured of all goddesses, was often regarded as the wife of the tutelary deities of the great cities and when the two pantheons were assimilated, numerous gods could claim to be her husband.

The Reforms of the First Dynasty of Babylon

There were bound, as time went on, to be a number of comparatively minor adjustments of which we do not know, but the major reform took place at the period of the first dynasty of

Babylon. The method of approach to the problem was indirect. The ruling house may have reckoned that its formal adoption of the tutelary deity of one of the ancient cities might well anger the other cities as well as appearing to pay a mark of respect to the city whose particular god it was adopting; and it accordingly decided to create new order among the multiplicity of gods who belonged to the pantheon. Marduk, a god who had as far as we know hitherto occupied a comparatively minor position, was selected not merely to be the principal god of the new state but also the principal god of Babylon and Babylonia. In virtue of this position he was placed at the head of the pantheon. By an adroit stroke, the priesthood saw to it that neither the number nor the importance of the older established deities should be impaired: all that happened was simply the selection of one god to supremacy without doing away with any already existent. The same process was carried through in Assyria in respect of its national god Ashur, whose spouse was Ishtar.

Due authority for this revolutionary process, which the Babylonian priesthood regarded as of great importance, was provided by the Creation epic. This, as we already know, depicted the gods as helpless with terror in face of the menaces of Tiamat, or Chaos, and appealing for help to Marduk, voluntarily granting him all their powers in order to ensure his success. There were some schools of religious thought which also regarded him as the creator of the world. However, despite these radical changes, there was no break in the old established tradition of worshipping the other gods, and of making fresh copies of the hymns in their honour, and no sign of any embarrassment at the inconsistencies between the hymns and the new cult. This was no doubt due partly to the vagueness which is a normal feature of Oriental thought and partly to the fundamentally polytheistic character of Babylonian religion.

Primitive 'Nature' Religion and its Development

Before we begin a detailed study of religion in the period of the Sargonid dynasty, we must briefly describe the earliest forms it took, since these left important traces. So far as we can judge, in its very earliest phases, which were already over before the date of the earliest surviving written records, the religion of Mesopotamia was founded upon the worship of the vital forces.

Since man, in the well-known phrase, is the measure of all things, Mesopotamian thought expressed these forces in terms of spirits of generation and reproduction represented by the unit of male and female, as in the human family. This group always contained a third figure in the form of a young male god (the child) who was always a slight embarrassment to the Babylonian theologians, since he possessed the powers and the characteristics of his father, whom he therefore tended to duplicate: and he was regarded as either son or lover of the goddess, according as circumstances demanded, and, sometimes, as both simultaneously. This religion, which was fundamentally 'Asianic' in character and in some respects distinctly resembled primitive Indo-European religions, diluted these vital forces by the creation of divinities with a specific and limited function—divinities of corn and forest, of vine and stream, besides spirits of a lower order, or demons, in an attempt to account for the malign forces of evil.

The next stage came when this archaic Sumerian religion, while preserving its element of nature worship, combined with it various other features explicable only by contact with Semitic religion: contacts dating from before the historical or possibly even before the prehistoric period. Semitic civilization was not materially so far advanced, but while it took over Sumerian civilization in almost its entirety, it possessed enough ideas of its own to alter and enlarge its character from its own resources.

At this period the dominant figure in the pantheon was the god An, converted by the Semites into Anu. An, or Anu, dwelt in heaven (his ideogram is the same as that for 'star'), and possessed almost limitless powers, including those formerly ascribed to the spirits of generation and reproduction. His nearest associates were Enlil (the god of the wind); Enki (the god of the underworld and, later, also the lord of the bottomless waters of the abyss upon which the earth rested): followed by the gods of the heavenly bodies like Enzu the moon god, the lord of knowledge, Utu the sun god and Nergal, the ruler of the nether regions or kingdom of the dead, who were in his charge. Each of these gods also had a wife, the most important being Ishtar, who embraced a wide range of identities under the one name. It must not be imagined that the element of nature worship had wholly vanished: on the contrary we still find the gods Dumuzi, Ningizzida, Shara and Ningirsu, lords respectively of harvests, of the 'wood of life', of green things and of the river floods, together with their wives Baba goddess of health, Nintud goddess of childbirth, Gatumdug the kindly giver of milk, Geshtin-anna the heavenly vine, and Shala the lady of the corn ear. None of these deities was of the first rank of importance like those mentioned previously, but they bear witness to an age already past: this fact is no doubt due to the influence of the Semites, who must have introduced the astral divinities.

Finally there came the third period, which we have already briefly mentioned, which must have seen the introduction into the pantheon of the two great deities who were destined to become what might be called the national gods of Babylonia and Assyria, namely Marduk and Ashur. Except for the inclusion of a few comparatively minor deities during the Kassite domination of Mesopotamia, which lasted for several centuries during the second millennium B.C., religion had assumed the form in which we can study it under the Sargonid dynasty and the neo-Babylonian empire.

The Composition of the Pantheon
The first triad of gods: Anu, Enlil, Ea

If we now proceed to enumerate the main gods in the Babylonian pantheon, it must be understood that it would take a whole book to make a complete list of them. The new documents which are constantly being discovered are continually bringing to our knowledge fresh ones who, though of minor importance, illustrate the astonishing proliferation of divinities which took place in Mesopotamia. It was no doubt under the conflicting pressures of the complexity of the pantheon and fear of the necessary process of elimination that the priesthood attempted at least to achieve some kind of classification and that the great gods were grouped by threes, the first, consisting of Anu, Enlil and Ea, being the sole rulers of the universe.

Anu was the most important divinity during the Sumerian period. His dwelling was in heaven, and there it remained, although in practice other gods were as powerful as he. The Anu-cult was centred on Dêr in Akkad and Uruk in Sumer, where together with his daughter Ishtar he was worshipped, in his temple called the E-anna, the mansion of Anu or of the sky (the same sign—a star—stands both for his name and for his dwelling). Anu, whose cult was gradually rivalled, if not actually surpassed, in importance by that of Ishtar, had another extremely celebrated temple in the 'holy' quarter, called Girsu, of the city of Lagash, and here also, at least from the time of Eannatum, from whose reign dates the Stele of the Vultures, the earliest of the great surviving monuments, Ishtar (known, among other names, in Sumerian as Ninni), was also worshipped as Anu's daughter, her cult soon outstripping in importance that of her father. Until the neo-Sumerian period, and the rise of the dynasty of Babylon, with its introduction of Marduk, Anu was acknowledged as the greatest of the gods, the king before whom the symbols of kingship were laid—sceptre and diadem, staff of commandment and crown, their obvious duplication being a clear reference to the twin kingdoms of Sumer and Akkad, like the two kingdoms of Upper and Lower Egypt. At the door of Anu's heavenly dwelling, the plane of the ecliptic, dwelt two very similar vegetation deities of the nature-cycle, Tammuz and Gizzida (or Ningizzida). However the worship and the titles which alike belonged to Anu were in themselves no impediment to worship of the other gods, for no cult of any single divinity ever excluded that of some other god unless the worshipper deliberately made it do so.

Evidence of Anu's pre-eminence can be found in the way in which he acts as host to all the other gods. The heaven of Anu is where they gather at times of merrymaking and of sorrow, when threatened with the destruction from which Marduk is destined to save them and at the time of the flood which laid waste the shrines where they dwelt upon earth.

The second of the first triad of great gods was Enlil (in Semitic —Bel, meaning 'Lord'), who ruled over the earth. In Sumer his worship was centred upon Nippur, and as early as the early Sumerian period we find a king of Lagash addressing him as 'king of the gods'. The supremacy which he occasionally enjoys is no doubt the reflection of a priestly tradition, for though he bears (together, albeit, with many other deities) the titles of 'the wise' and 'the prudent', he is responsible, in defiance of the wishes of Ishtar and Ea, for ordering the onset of the flood. We can judge how greatly his authority had diminished from the fact that, when Marduk arrived on the scene, he in his turn assumed the name Bel (Bel-Marduk) while Enlil, its former owner, became Bel the Ancient. Enlil's wife was called Belit, the lady, the feminine form of her husband's name.

The third of these three gods was Ea (Enki in Sumerian). He was lord of the ground, or more properly of the world underground, which the Babylonians regarded as the abyss of waters upon which the terrestrial world floated, but not the nether regions, which were ruled over by the god Nergal. Ea's very name, with its meaning of 'house of water', is itself descriptive of his realm. The Babylonians believed that wisdom and knowledge resided in this abyss, which they knew by the name of *apsû*, which is simply the Semitic form of the Sumerian *ab-zu*, meaning 'dwelling of knowledge'. Ea's wife was Damkina, who was not at all prominent, while he himself was the protector of the human race. There are, indeed, certain theological traditions which make him a creator of mankind, according to which he formed man of clay and breathed life into him; he was also known as the divine potter and he was responsible, from his forewarning of the flood, for securing the escape of one pair of human beings. Since he ruled the domain which was the seat of knowledge, he was the protector of every kind of advanced learning—divination, magic and medicine, and he was described as the god whose eyes were bright (with understanding). The holy water used in religious ceremonies was drawn from the wells which belonged to his kingdom and which were themselves connected with the subterranean lake or with the mouths of the two mighty rivers Tigris and Euphrates, which were themselves divinities.

Briefly, then, this first triad of gods between them exercised supremacy over three—air, earth and water—of the four elements, though Anu's sovereignty over the air was not undivided, for the sky was shared by the same three gods, the way of Anu being flanked by the heavens of Enlil and Ea respectively.

The Second Triad: Sin, Shamash and Ishtar

Although in a sense the first triad might be regarded as a logical and self-sufficient unit, there were other divinities who could not possibly be left wholly out of account. This leads us on to the second triad, composed of Sin, the moon god, and his two children, Shamash the sun and Ishtar the planet Venus.

The name Sin is the Semitic form of the Sumerian *En-zu*, meaning the lord of knowledge, a fact which in itself gives a hint of two conflicting concepts, according to one of which knowledge resides in the sky, while in the other it dwells in the waters under the earth. The Mesopotamians were in a minority in making the moon a god and not a goddess, and they ascribed very great importance to him. It was he who governed the passing of the months by his waxing and waning: for the year consisted of lunar months which had, from time to time, to be adjusted in order to harmonize with the passage of the true year. As a consequence the number 30—the number of days in a complete lunar cycle—became a synonym for the god Sin, and it was written with the sign for 'day', enclosing the sign for '30'. The unvarying lunar cycle gave Sin a special connection with order and wisdom. The Mesopotamians envisaged him as a man in the prime of life wearing a long beard of lapis lazuli, while in the crescent moon, which in the latitude of Mesopotamia rises almost parallel to the horizon, with its points upwards, they saw the boat in which he sailed through the heavens.

The second god in this triad was Shamash, the sun (the Sumerian Utu). We may be surprised at his being only the son of the moon god and not supreme in his own right, for we regard the sun as by far the more important of the two. But in the East, by contrast, while the early morning sun, warming the earth and chasing away the shadows where the evil spirits of terror lurk, is a welcome arrival, he is progressively less so as the day wears on and he travels on his course. At his zenith he is no longer the benefactor of mankind, but a murderer parching all growing things, and making a desert of the plain, causing sunstroke and bringing death and suffering. Moreover, at this point, the sun loses his character as Shamash and becomes Nergal the god of the nether regions, whose realms are peopled with the victims of the sufferings which he himself inflicts upon mankind. The fact that Shamash is regarded primarily as a god of justice is an interesting sidelight on the mode of primitive thought which formed this conception of the all-seeing sun, flooding the world with light and dispersing the night which conceals the wrong-doer: attributes most appropriate to a god of justice. It was under his auspices and his protection that the great legislating kings, like Hammurabi, placed their laws, and this monarch's famous 'Code' (now in the Louvre) depicts him in adoration before Shamash.

At what must certainly have been a comparatively late stage in the development of the cult of Shamash, he was regarded as the father of two children, Kittu and Mesharu, 'right' and 'justice', both abstract theological conceptions beyond the intellectual range of primitive thought. His wife was the goddess Aïa.

This second triad is completed by the goddess Ishtar, who may be described as the epitome of Ninharsag, Ninni or Inanna, and indeed a large number of other Sumerian goddesses, all of whom embodied the principles of fertility and reproduction. Her presence as an equal member with the other great gods in such a triad is striking evidence of the strength of the worship of the forces of nature, which was indeed rooted very deeply in primitive societies: for, though the Code of Hammurabi may have granted to women in Babylonia rights which in France, for example, they have only acquired since the beginning of the twentieth century, like giving evidence in a court of law, Semitic society was far less ready than Sumerian society to grant women any true responsibility in the life of the country. The royal consort in 'Asianic' society was a member of the Council, signed acts of state, owned property and had her own household, which she managed through the agency of her personal chamberlain. In Mesopotamia, any considerable period of rule and any genuine exercise of power was an event of such rarity as to be a source of legend, such as that of Semiramis. Moreover, this was not confined to Asianic peoples, for in primitive Greece the women ran the household. This is clear from the story of Nausicaa in the *Odyssey*. When the princess is telling Ulysses how he can get aid from her royal father, she bids him enter the palace where in one of the rooms he will find the king drinking as the gods drink: but Ulysses must not linger with him but go farther and cast himself at her mother's feet, since she will make the final decision.

The fact that Ishtar epitomizes so many different goddesses makes her genealogy most obscure. In different contexts she is variously known as the daughter both of Sin and Anu, and sister both of Shamash and of Ereshkigal, the goddess of the nether regions. A list of her husbands and lovers would fill a book, since under one name or another she is the wife of the 'great god' of almost every city. She represents the blending of two different characters in the person of one goddess: the lady of love and the lady of battles. Nor need we see in this dual conception all the philosophical or poetical explanations which have at various times been advanced, like love as the brother of death, or death as the counterpart of love. In Ishtar the dominating principle of fertility is combined with the character of the lady of battles. But her different aspects are always worshipped under two separate names. Thus at Uruk she is adored as Ishtar of nature worship, while the Ishtar of Halab and of Arbela are both the lady of battles: and the two aspects demand different characters, attributes and symbols. In still later religious systems the double aspect of the forces of nature inherent in Ishtar are plainly visible: as Venus she is the goddess of love and of pleasure, and as Cybele she represents fertility incarnate.

Ninurta, Nusku, Nergal, Adad, Tammuz

We must realize clearly that the first triad (Anu, Enlil and Ea) were, in themselves, practically sufficient to explain the universe, the only missing element being that of fire represented, and then only incidentally, by Shamash in the second triad. Nevertheless the pantheon contained a number of other divinities, subsidiary to the principal members, of narrowly defined functions, whom the priesthood were unable to classify.

The first of these was Ninurta, or Enurta. By the late Assyrian period he had become the god of battles, but he had begun as a nature divinity. In the earliest Sumerian period, when he was the lord of Girsu (Ningirsu), the sacred quarter of Lagash, he was a fertility god, who governed the annual flooding of the rivers without which no green thing could have grown. Formerly his symbol was the plough, but by the Assyrian period this had been replaced by weapons. He represents a conflation of other deities, including Inshushinak the god of Susa and Zababa the god of Kish. The diversity of his ancestry is expressed by his apparent polygamy, and in various contexts he is found as the husband of Baba, of Ninkarrak, and of Gula. These three female divinities embody a diversity of characteristics. Not only do they watch over the health of mankind and cure his sickness, but they can on occasion also bring death upon him. Gula's companion, the dog, was later, in Greek mythology, to become the companion of Aesculapius.

The element of fire was personified by the god known in Sumerian as Gibil, and to the Semites as Nusku. He was the god of flame: his worshippers praised his usefulness as they gave thanks to him, since burnt offerings would not have been possible without his aid.

Running water too was a god, and was specially concerned with the administration of justice, since it had the power to distinguish the innocent from the guilty. It was in fact the embodiment of what the Middle Ages called the Judgment of God, in which the accused was thrown into a river and was proved by the god guilty or innocent according to whether he sank or floated. This method of establishing the truth was enshrined in the Code of Hammurabi.

Nergal, the god of the nether regions, was, comparatively speaking, an upstart. Originally, as we have seen, a deity of the sun, he was the destroyer of life who went in search of a kingdom. He forced his way into 'the land of no return' known as the *arallû*, ruled over by Erishkigal, the sister of Shamash and Ishtar, and offered a certain degree of violence to the queen, who straightway offered to make him her consort.

Adad, the next in this group, who was an important member of the pantheon, was the lord of storms, including not only tempests with thunder and lightning, but also the welcome and kindly rain. He was neither Sumerian nor Semitic in origin, as we know from the early Phoenician legends discovered at Ras Shamra, in which we read that when every other deity in the pantheon had been presented with his own temple, Adad alone was unprovided for: from which we can gather that he was not a member of the original company of gods. In fact he was the greatest god of the Asianic world, believed to dwell on the mountain peaks, armed with thunder and lightning, his animal attribute being the bull, whose bellowing was supposed to resemble the sound of thunder. Adad represented the supreme principle of generation, embodied in a secondary and more specialized form by the divinities of trees, springs and the like.

The wife of Adad was Shala, whose character is sufficiently explained by her epithet 'lady of the ear of grain'. While on the subject of fertility divinities who survived into the Assyrian epoch, we may mention Nidaba or Nisaba, a vegetation goddess particularly associated with the reeds which grew densely in the marshes of the river deltas and in the canals. Because the reed was used to make the instruments for writing on clay, Nidaba became the goddess of numbers and prophecies derived from them. She was in addition the goddess of an extremely useful product: namely the marsh horsetail plants which, when burnt to ashes, produce soda, which in turn when mixed with oil and clay resulted in a kind of substitute for soap.

Last in this group was Tammuz, who endured into the first millennium. He always gave his name to one of the months in the calendar, his festivals persisted, and although in the course of time his worship diminished in importance, the legends about him never died. Finally indeed he came into his own again round the shores of the Mediterranean, when in the Greco-Roman period he was worshipped as Adonis, a name which is simply a variant of the Semitic *Adon*, meaning lord.

Heroes, the offspring of a divine father and a mortal mother, were also worshipped: we are already familiar with Gilgamesh, who was more or less the Assyrian equivalent of Hercules and, like him, performed legendary exploits. He was never so deeply revered later as he had been in the third millennium B.C., but the memory of his mighty deeds was kept green.

Demons

Demon of the south-west wind

Both Assyrian and Babylonian religion were profoundly influenced by a belief in the existence of genies or spirits, both good and bad, by which mankind was perpetually surrounded. There was no settled tradition to explain their parentage. The evil ones were regarded as the children of the ancient and evil gods, whom Marduk had to defeat in order to free his fellow deities from their influence, while the good ones were supposed to be descended from some of the great gods who were still worshipped.

The whole family of divinely descended demons was very unequally divided between good and bad genies. The good genies were exemplified in their visible state by the winged bulls which formed the decoration of the palace gates, or, in their invisible state, were among Ishtar's bodyguard and formed a part of her 'series of numbers'; we know that the gods were ranked in a hierarchy, so that they could be collectively expressed by a series of numerals. In its written form the name of these particular good genies was composed of the sign of the goddess Ishtar inside the sign which meant 'One third (or two thirds) of Ishtar'. Since the goddess' own number was 15, that of the good genies would be 5 (or 10).

The good genies were heavily outnumbered by the bad ones, who were regarded as the children of gods who might themselves be either friendly or hostile to mankind. They were sometimes described as offspring of Bel and sometimes of Anu (though in these cases their mother was believed to be a goddess of the nether regions) and sometimes even of Ea and his wife Damkina, although both these deities were favourable towards mankind, an inconsistency which was got over by describing them as 'spleen of Ea'. These demons, which were envisaged as dreadful deformed monsters, formed several groups. Of these the first, and most commonly encountered, were the evil *utukku*, also known as 'the Seven' though their numbers might on occasion vary. The references to them are quite extraordinarily vague, while the texts are contradictory, alternately asserting that they are unknown in heaven and that there are seven of them there. In numerous references they are also known both as a separate 'tribe' and as a gathering of various types of demons, the most important of these being *etimmu* or ghosts, and *namtaru*, the demon of pestilence.

When we come to ask what they actually did, we find that, sometimes at least, their bark was worse than their bite. They might make a traveller conscious of their presence and then dog his footsteps: not only could they enter houses, whistling, muttering and turning everything upside down, but they could also force their way into the stables and there injure or kill the animals or make them bolt: while if they found a man in a state of sin, having put his god away from him, they could take the god's place. This is the doctrine of possession by evil spirits in the sense in which it was understood in the Middle Ages. No matter how tightly bolted and barred a house might be, they could make their way in and there do their devils' work, causing families to quarrel and setting their members against each other. In fact, every disagreeable circumstance of human existence, great and small alike, was laid at their door. Eventually the sensation of always being encompassed by hordes of invisible enemies, to whose malignity the inhabitant of Babylon ascribed every kind of misfortune of everyday life where we should see merely ill luck, clumsiness or nervousness, must have become hideously depressing. They compassed him on every side, lying in wait for him by day and by night. A man of Babylon who had angered his god through disobedience to his laws was doomed to punishment, and though he might fly from his house, the streets would afford him no protection. 'The man who hath not god as he walketh in the street, the demon covers him as a garment.'

There were others of 'the Seven' who tormented the people of Mesopotamia: the incubi and the succubi, whose embraces no man, struggle as he might, could escape; the she-demon (albeit a daughter of Anu) who prevented children from being born at the due time, or killed the new-born babe: and finally the 'evil eye', under the influence of which nothing could prosper, the rain could be stayed in the sky and the grass prevented from growing, and the herds in the stable and the family in the home alike made barren.

The second main group of evil genies might be described as demons who appeared only intermittently: the *etimmu* or ghosts. They were the spirits of those whose lives had been unhappy: who had been cheated of some expectation, or had died a violent death, or had not enjoyed the happiness they craved. Not surprisingly, they were many in number:—

> 'he whose body is abandoned on the plain;
> he who is not given burial;
> she who dies a virgin;
> she who dies in childbed;
> she whose baby, that she suckled, is dead;
> he who hath fallen from a palm tree:
> he who hath drowned himself . . .'

and countless others besides, including, for example, all who, for any reason, were not granted honourable burial, and had no friend to bring them funerary offerings. They all nursed some unsatisfied claim, and all joined the company of the *utukku* in order to torment the living.

Representations of the Gods

The Assyrians and Babylonians certainly had an anthropomorphic conception of their gods in the Sargonid period: and it can now be taken as certain (though I used not to think so) that, except in a few rare cases, the gods were from the very outset represented in this human form, with no special marks to distinguish them from mankind. It was not until a later period that they were given such special insignia as a crown or other emblem. What happened in Mesopotamia was in fact repeated later in Western Europe. How could the mass of an illiterate population be assisted to recognize the scores of different members of the pantheon? No artist on earth could have given each divinity features sufficiently distinctive to ensure recognition by the mass of the population; and so the Babylonian artist was driven to follow the same practice as the artists of Western Europe with the figures of the saints and apostles on church façades: namely, to give the gods easily distinguishable attributes so as to ensure that the Babylonians should recognize them. Thus early was born religious iconography: and every civilization since then has employed it. The first step was to give the gods a crown: and the normal practice of all religions was followed in that the gods continued to be represented clothed as they were when their likenesses were first conceived, or with but minor variations. This accounts for the fact that, during the late Assyrian period, they are sometimes represented wearing a costume like that worn by the Assyrian kings or that of the gods in the Kassite period, with a tiara which was either cylindrical in shape and crowned with a row of feathers or else ovoid in shape and encircled with several pairs of bulls' horns: these last having been accorded to them as attributes of divinity in the earliest period. But although this might suffice to create a general 'type' of divinity, it was by itself insufficient to make the gods individually recognizable. The solution was found in attaching to each of them some individual and inalienable attribute—weapon, instrument or animal—to serve as his personal mark of identity.

Each god had some legends attached to his name, full of miraculous fights against divine adversaries or frightful beasts:

and it is the animal victim that we find at his side, or beneath his feet—a favourite theme of the artist—while he bears in his hand the weapon he used in the fight, or his special or personal instrument. A single god in whom several aspects of divinity are combined possesses the various attributes of the deities merged in his person. Thus Ishtar as the goddess who makes the corn to grow has a serpent as her companion, to emphasize her character as an earth deity: Ishtar on earth, the lady of battles, is accompanied by a lion, and bears weapons: while Ishtar of the skies, the goddess of love, has a flock of doves.

Attributes and Symbols of the Gods

It may be of interest to give some examples of the various attributes which the inhabitant of Babylon would have seen accompanying, or carried by, his gods during processions, or when he entered their temples (Pl. XXII).

The attributes of Anu and Enlil, who were among the most ancient of the gods, were an egg-shaped tiara. Ea was represented by the symbol of a fabulous monster with the body of a fish and the forequarters of a goat: and he carried a sceptre with a ram's head finial.

The animal belonging to Shamash was a lion, sometimes with wings, and his emblem was the solar disc: while the god himself is often represented with tongues of flame shooting from his shoulders.

The animal of Sin was a mythical dragon, and his emblem the disc of the moon.

Ishtar, besides the animals which we have already mentioned, in her capacity as the lady of battles carried the bow and quiver, and sheaves of weapons sprang from her shoulders.

While the gods of war bore arms, the gods of fertility, like Marduk and, later, his son Nabu, in so far as he inherited the prerogatives of his father, carried branches and a spade. Shala, the lady of the corn ear, was herself represented by an ear of barley. The emblem of Nusku, god of fire, was a curiously wrought lamp in the shape of a shoe.

Adad was depicted standing upon his bull, holding in his hand an axe and the lightning, in the form of a trident with curved prongs: while Ashur was often represented half length, shooting with the bow in the centre of a solar disc surrounded with wings.

The recognition of some of the gods was simplified by their possession of distinguishing characteristics. In the city of Borsippa, near Babylon, Nabu, as we already know, gradually usurped the place of his father Marduk, just as Marduk had earlier ousted his father Ea. As the god of writing and of destiny, Nabu carried the writing tablets and the reed or writing instrument. But in memory of the great god who was his father, Nabu had the same attribute—a fabulous dragon—as Marduk. Among the neighbouring Hittites, a carving of a procession in the open air sanctuary of Yazili-kaya recalls the sacred marriage of the god and the goddess, representing the principles of generation and reproduction: the young god, the son of the elder, takes part in the procession, wearing the same dress as his father, while the son and the great goddess are both mounted on the same animal, a panther, in a striking reminder of the relationship between them.

Carrying this idea a stage further, if the various gods of the pantheon had to be represented in a restricted space, there was no need to reproduce their figures: their emblems and symbols would suffice.

The Numbers and Stars of the Gods

The inhabitants of Mesopotamia furthermore had the curious notion of representing their gods by numbers. The possibilities of calculation inherent in numbers enabled them to extend these calculations to the pantheon itself, and thereby to discover various relationships among its members, imperceptible if the gods were merely considered in isolation.

The way in which these numbers were allotted shows the overlapping of the sexagesimal and the decimal systems of numeration, which were both current in Mesopotamia. Anu's number was 60, the key figure of the sexagesimal system, Ningirsu's 50 and Ea's 40, or alternatively *shanabi* (two-thirds, i.e., two-thirds of 60). Sin's number was 30 (the number of days in a lunar month), Ishtar's was 15, and those of her good genies, as we already know, 10 or 5. Most of these numbers appear to have been quite arbitrarily selected, and except in the case of Sin we do not know the reason for their choice, beyond saying that they must be connected with the degrees of kinship which were believed to exist among the gods: while sometimes the numerical relationships themselves must have been responsible for the nearness of the kinship. Once this point is understood, we can see that the dimensions of the temple, Esagila, may well have concealed some esoteric meaning, not necessarily in the actual numbers but in their implications, so that the measurements contained a whole universe of hidden meanings, which in their turn set in motion celestial powers intelligible only by the initiates in this kind of mathematical language, which for the adepts enshrined the most sacred mysteries, while to the uninitiated they remained merely a set of dimensions.

Both the sun and the moon were gods in their own right, while the other gods were identified with planets or with stars—Ishtar with Venus, Marduk with Jupiter, Ea both with the star Dilgan and also with Piscis Austrinus, Aquarius, Argo and Vela. When, during the first dynasty of Babylon, new ceremonial titles had to be invented for Marduk, a section of the Creation epic suggested that after creating the earth, Marduk imposed order upon the heavens and ordained the courses of the stars. The chapter containing this section is almost entirely lost, but it was made the occasion for ascribing to Marduk, as the saviour of the gods, the sum of contemporary astronomical knowledge: while, by a further twist of thought, it was taken also to represent one more assertion of the supremacy of Marduk over the other gods, since each star was god, hero, or genie and it was Marduk who laid down the laws which they must obey. Jupiter was a particularly appropriate choice for Marduk, for of all the planets its orbit shows the smallest deviation from the ecliptic, and is much the most stable, as befits a ruler. All the stars lay within the realm of Anu and when his authority was at its zenith they formed 'the army of Anu': no mean honour, for they represented the whole company of the gods, including those who were subdued at the time of the great struggle between Marduk and Chaos.

Statues of the Gods

We possess a large number of representations of the gods of the period of the Sargonid dynasty if we count all the cylinder seals upon which they appear: but the number of statues is comparatively very small, and large-scale statues are extremely rare. The probable explanation is that, as we read in the ancient authors, they were made of precious materials, and this fact, coupled with their size, was bound to bring them to the particular attention of the victorious commanders of military expeditions, and consequently doomed them to destruction. There are, however, two which deserve mention. The first is a nude female torso in stone, with a dedication by King Ashur-bel-kala and consequently earlier than the period of the Sargonid dynasty, which probably represents Ishtar of Uruk: it is a heavy and almost formless piece which shows how little feeling the Assyrians had for representing the human body.

The second statue (or rather, one of a pair, the other being less well preserved) is in the British Museum, and is believed to represent the god Nabu. To make sure that it should endure, the sculptor modelled it on the bronze statue of the queen Napir-asu of Susa (now in the Louvre) made some five centuries earlier by the bronze founders of Elam. Like the earlier statue, the figure is wearing a shaped and closely fitting bodice and a ground-length bell-shaped skirt widening at the foot so as to give stability and solidity to the whole composition. The god is standing with his arms raised before him, his hands clasped at about waist height. He is bearded and wears on his head a tiara with crossed horns. The inscription (this statue also dates from the pre-Sargonid period, since its date is about 800 B.C.) carved on the front of the god's garment refers to Sammu-ramat, the female regent in the time of Adad-Nirari III (the original of the legendary Semiramis), and it ends with the solemn exhortation 'Oh man who cometh after, put thy trust in Nabu and in no other god.' This is an unusual but quite reasonable formula, being merely the logical extension of the inscriptions which refer to a number of divinities as 'king of the gods' or 'lord of the gods' without ever venturing to plump finally for any of them.

The theory that the statue represents the god Nabu has not been universally accepted. Against it is the fact that it is only one of a pair, which suggests that the two figures were originally placed at the entrance to a shrine, as was the normal practice with minor deities (cf. the similar statues found at Arslan Tash, and those in the temple courtyard at Khorsabad). Furthermore, the British Museum statue is very plainly dressed and wears very little jewellery, which affords a further parallel with Arslan Tash and Khorsabad, and contrasts with what we know of the statues of the great gods, while the egg-shaped tiara is unornamented. The final argument is that its attitude, with hands clasped at waist height, is quite appropriate to a minor deity or a genie, but not to one of the great gods. This argument is perfectly sound if applied to the bas-reliefs, but when it comes to statuary, the sculptor's prime objects must be stability and solidity. The breaking of a statue of a god, once duly consecrated, would be a disaster, for not only would it make the statue itself in every sense worthless, but it would provoke the wrath of the god himself, so that the statue's attitude might be dictated by the absolute necessity that the work should endure. However, on balance the earlier arguments probably favour the view that the two figures are those of minor deities; the inscriptions which they bear in praise of Nabu do not say that they represent him.

Attempts at Rationalization

The unusual inscription on the British Museum statue is in line with the efforts on the part of the priesthood to reduce the everlasting inconsistency between the assertion that there was but one single king or lord of the gods, and the worship which was often exclusively directed to some other member of the pantheon. We have already mentioned their belief that the real number of the gods was smaller than it appeared, and that this was mainly due to the way in which names had been multiplied. They frequently stressed the importance of the identification of different deities, and asserted that many apparently separate gods were really different aspects of the same one.

We can watch this process at work in certain religious texts:[1] e.g.

'   . . . Irra is Nergal of the city of Kutha,
       Meslamtae is Nergal of the city of Babylon,
       Luhush is Nergal of the city of Kish . . .'

but, inasmuch as elsewhere we read that

'   . . . Nergal is Marduk of the battles,
       Zababa is Marduk of the slaughter,
       Enlil is Marduk of the lordship and of counsel,
       Shamash is Marduk of justice . . .'

we can see that 'identification' consisted in arranging the gods into different groups. One text actually goes so far as to equate the entire pantheon with Ninurta, the other gods being merely parts of his body:—

'. . . Enlil and Ninlil are his eyes
Sin is the pupil of his eyes,
Anu and Antu are his lips,
The Seven divine beings are his teeth,
His ears are Ea and Damkina,
His breast is Nabu . . .'

while the same god was often worshipped in different cities under clearly defined and distinctive aspects:—

'. . . Adad of Bît-karkara is the lord of the rain,
Adad of the temple E-namhe is the lord of the flood,
Adad of Halab is the lord of the wind . . .'

The impression which we gain from these and similar texts is one of a pantheon of considerable fluidity in which a process of gradual assimilation was at work till the various members become little more than different aspects of an all-embracing divinity.

A study of the relationships between gods and men reveals that they were predominantly those of masters and servants, similar to those which subsisted in family life between fathers and children. The conceptions of kindliness or love were entirely absent, at least before the period of the first dynasty of Babylon. God was a master swift to wrath and quick to punish, whose anger could only be assuaged by prayer and, above all, by sacrifices. The only purpose of man's terrestrial life was to worship the gods, a view which finds explicit expression in one of the stories of the Creation:—'Marduk created mankind that he might build temples to rejoice the heart of the gods'. Originally, at all events, there is no sign in Mesopotamian religion of a concept of a god of love and affection, and no trace of any mystical view before the period of the first dynasty of Babylon: and the majority of the religious chants are couched rather in terms of repentance and supplication than of gratitude. Egypt affords a sharp contrast. The Egyptian of the New Empire looked forward with keen pleasure to the daily tasks of his life in the after world: but the inhabitant of Mesopotamia, who was under no illusions about what he might expect to find there, had no wish to quit this life unless his existence had become quite unendurable.

Man as 'Son of his God'

There is no doubt that the first Babylonian Empire marked one of the crucial dates in the history of civilization, and it is precisely now that we can see the beginnings of a new and revolutionary concept. Hitherto belief had centred on one or other of the gods in the pantheon, while, as we know, the kings boasted proudly of being sons of a god. But now this belief began to penetrate every level of society. Every man was 'the son of his god' who would also intercede for him with the other gods: a privilege hitherto claimed as their sole prerogative by the kings, who, ever since the time of Gudea and the third dynasty of Ur, had had themselves represented standing before the great god who governed their fate, led thither by the hand and introduced by the particular god under whose special protection they lived.

A man's personal god was always ready to bring his dependent or 'son' before the presence of the great god and there to plead for him. He would watch over him and keep him from evil influences, alike from the omnipresent demons or from ghosts in search of a victim. But if, by reason of sin, the believer ceased to be 'the son of his god', then the latter would turn his face from him and would leave him desolate, and one of the demons who were eternally prowling around would enter into the place left empty by the god.

The emergence of the idea of god as the protector of mankind was reflected in personal names. The devout man was swift to discard the names which symbolized protection by one of the great gods, in favour of his own 'personal' god. He would choose as his protector one more in scale with his own needs, and he might choose some such name as '[My god] is my refuge', '[my god] hath hearkened to me', '[my god] is my father' or 'man belongs to his god'. It was moreover at this period that the god of whom mankind sought long life or riches, in return for having conscientiously fulfilled his duty towards him, assumed the characteristics, hitherto unknown, of goodness and mercy. His goodness could provide what hitherto had depended solely upon the deserts of the worshipper. This represented a major advance, and in future the devout could address their deities as gods of mercy.

The Beginnings of Mysticism

This was, moreover, the period which saw the beginning of the religious fervour which alone can, as it were, irrigate and fertilize religion. Previously part at least of a believer's duty had been to fear god; but the meaning of the phrase widened till it came to signify an inconceivable and transcendent glory, and whereas previously devotion was equated with the fear of god, that very fear could now be the object of love. In the poem 'The Righteous Man's Suffering', the hero surveys his life in retrospect and sighs, 'And yet my delight was in the fear of god and of my king'. In our period Nebuchadrezzar 'loves the fear of god with all his heart and soul'.

Any doubts that the reader may feel about the spiritual advance which this represents should be dispelled if he considers how little comfort was to be found in the primitive religions of early antiquity. In Egypt, for example, the Pharaoh, himself the son of a god, on death became an Osiris, and alone could ensure that the objects of his benevolence should share in this divine state. But the chosen few who were buried near him were the great and the nobles: the common people had no hope at all of any such bliss after death. This accounts for the discovery in the cemeteries, which could at the king's pleasure be the source of blessings in the next world, of tiny sarcophagi a few inches in length, surreptitiously placed there by the pious, anxious to secure for their dead parents the favours which flowed from burial near the dead king. This need for hope was such that when things settled down again after the first major revolution in recorded history, which brought the Old Empire to a close, although their material conditions were unchanged, the masses were none the less contented since they had satisfied their most keenly felt want, namely, religious right and religious freedom. Thenceforward every man, whatever his earthly condition, could become an Osiris on his death, if he were morally worthy.

The Moral Worth of the Gods

In Mesopotamia, however, religion in its earliest form had conceived of the gods in terms of contemporary mankind, with all its roughness and crudity. By the time that archaic Sumerian religion had been developed in detail, the period of 'nature' worship whose creative power resided in its 'mortal' gods, dying and coming again to birth in the rhythm of the seasons, had passed away: and the gods themselves no longer 'died'. But even so their existence on earth followed the same pattern as human life. When Gilgamesh, king of Uruk, emerges from his palace and passes through the city followed by his retinue of attendants, he meets the goddess Ishtar emerging from the temple, accompanied by her train of priests and priestesses: and they meet as equals. Again, when Ishtar falls in love with Gilgamesh, he—a mortal—rebuffs her—a goddess—with a coarse volley of oaths which we might expect to find exchanged by a pair of Homeric heroes. Smarting for revenge she makes her way to the heaven of Anu, and there asks her father to create something which will rid her of Gilgamesh. This ascent to heaven and the creation of a heavenly bull of unprecedented strength is the only feature of the story which shows the goddess as possessing supernatural powers. During the fight, although Ishtar, after returning to Uruk, stations herself with her followers on the temple terrace in order to savour her revenge to the full, she is cheated of her hopes, and it is Gilgamesh who emerges as the victor; while his companion Enkidu dismembers the bull and hurls a piece at Ishtar's face, threatening to strangle her with a necklace made from its entrails. The suggestion has been made that this passage must represent a later interpolation, expressing a reaction against the practices involved in the cult of Ishtar, such as ritual prostitution, but this is at least doubtful, for the passage remained as part of the epic, and ritual prostitution was still being practised in Mesopotamia when Herodotus was travelling there.

There are other passages in the Creation epic, notably the episode describing the Deluge, in which every kind of failing is attributed to the gods, despite the use of epithets which suggest the contrary. They abuse each other like fish-wives. When the one virtuous man has safely made his escape from the Deluge and offers a sacrifice to the gods, the latter, 'attracted by the savour, gathered like flies over him that sacrificed'. Ishtar, who was opposed to the Deluge, seeks to prevent Enlil, who had decreed it, from participating in the sacrifice, and exclaims, 'May this day be turned into mud! Did I bring forth my people that they might fill the sea like little fishes?' And Enlil, despite being one of the 'great gods', has no better sources of information than any ordinary human being. He does not know that one man has escaped, nor does he know how he has done so. 'Who hath done this?' he asks, and his suspicion falls upon Ea, who is by nature a benefactor of mankind. This is in fact correct, but Ea's warning was given somewhat obliquely, for he approached the hut where the virtuous man dwelt and whispered the vital message through the wattle and daub wall (cf. the later story of the reeds which spoke to king Midas). And we find the great god Ea, the lord of the *apsû*, the seat of all knowledge, lying and stammering like a child who has been found out, 'I said nothing, it was the reeds!' Nor, for all his wisdom, did Ea always give good advice. He warned Adapa, who was also under his protection, and who was summoned to appear for punishment in the heaven of Anu, to be careful not to accept a crumb of food, for if he did so he would surely die. In fact the food which Anu did offer him was the food of life, which would have conferred immortality upon mankind: and it was this well-meaning blunder that laid the burden of death on humanity.

It would take a long time to enumerate the characteristics of primitive man which we can discern in the behaviour of the gods. When Chaos assails them, they are seized with panic, and fly to the heaven of Anu where, crouched on the walls, 'they yelp like dogs'. This is the scene of their appeal to Marduk, and when they have regained their courage they assemble at a banquet, where they get drunk.

All these elements, which one might reasonably expect to find in a primitive period, were however preserved, and the pantheon had scarcely changed even by the end of the Babylonian and Assyrian periods. Gradually, by the attribution of more estimable qualities to the ancient gods, the leaders of the priesthood had built up a concept which could command the worshippers' respect, and in the minds of the more enlightened craven humility might yield to joyful adoration and love: but fundamentally there was no change from the distant epoch in which the original ideas had matured.

Divine Powers. Destiny

Of the powers which the gods were believed to possess, the first and most striking was their limitless power over the whole of mankind, king and peasant alike. They were the source of royalty, whose material expression resided in its insignia, which, as we already know, were believed during an interregnum to return into heaven and there to lie before the throne of Anu. When a new reign had duly begun, then 'royalty descended again from heaven.'

By the time of the Sargonid dynasty, the gods gradually assumed those very qualities which, as we have seen, were conspicuously absent in their primitive state, being described as just, impartial, benevolent and reprovers of evil, which was 'hateful to the great gods'. But despite this the inhabitant of Babylon probably never felt quite sure of his ground with them. Faced with the daily phenomenon of the triumph of evil over good, faith, to remain unshaken, demands a religion of salvation—which that of Mesopotamia was not. In consequence a Babylonian man was bound to live in perpetual fear of some arbitrary divine whim. No explanation is offered for Enlil's resolve to overwhelm mankind with the Deluge.

But the gods possessed a far greater power than this: namely, that of 'fixing destinies'. At the great festival of Marduk held at Babylon at the beginning of each year, after the processions to the temple called the *akîtu* which stood outside the city, the gods assembled in council and 'fixed the destinies' for the coming year, which were written on tablets by Nabu, in his capacity as the scribe of the gods, and thenceforth governed mankind. This had been the case for ever, and their possession was a jealously sought prize. Once, before the creation, they were stolen by the bird Zu, and when Chaos wanted to attack his descendants the gods, the tablets of destiny were in his camp. Marduk could never have been victorious had he not spoken in the gathering of the gods who had entrusted him with avenging them, saying: 'If I am to be your avenger, to slay Tiamat and bestow life upon you, then summon a meeting, magnify and proclaim my position, sit ye down in friendly fashion in the "place of assembly", let me determine destinies by the opening of my mouth even as ye do; whatsoever I bring to pass, let it remain unaltered: that which my mouth uttereth shall never fail or be brought to nought.' The gods duly assembled at a banquet where, under the influence of liquor, they got drunk, their bodies were filled with a sense of well-being, they cried out loudly, their hearts leaped up and they 'fixed the destinies' for Marduk their avenger.

In another context we find a king described as one for whom the gods have fixed a good destiny, which is a variant on being called 'by a good name', but with a wider meaning. Both a good name and a good destiny are a guarantee of a successful future, but whereas the former is left vague, the latter is, or at least should be, more precisely defined. In their annual 'fixing of the destiny' of Babylon, the gods kept a close eye upon the events of the moment, and particularly upon current political issues. The destinies represent yet one more assertion of divine omnipotence and of the supremacy of established order. The destinies of Babylon, as Marduk himself said, bind the company of the gods: for whatever he undertakes cannot be altered, and the words of his lips are immutable. It is at one and the same time a guarantee of order against anarchy, a proof of omnipotence and a limitation on individual free will: and it may even represent an insurance by the priesthood against the whims of royal autocracy. There is nothing improbable about the part played by destiny in a society as tightly organized as that of Mesopotamia, where nothing was left to chance and no loophole left for any unwarranted hope.

We have only to think back to the doctrine of 'the power of the name' to realize how powerfully it reinforced the Mesopotamian view of destinies, since, once they had been fixed and uttered, not only did they thereby acquire a distinct existence of their own, but they were bound to be fulfilled, since their very utterance, or even the mere thought of them, put them well on the way to accomplishment. Destinies played a considerable part in the governance of earthly affairs.

Human sinfulness might occasionally cause the gods to lose patience and avert themselves from mankind, and we have already discussed the widespread belief in the existence of evil genies seeking somewhere to settle and only waiting for an opportunity of this kind to take possession of the vacant place. One explanation of the excessive number of the 'beneficent' features depicted on the religious monuments is not only the desire to strengthen their influence, but also anxiety not to leave spaces into which some evil influence might insinuate itself.

Sin and Confession

In certain respects the Babylonian idea of sin was that common to every religion, but in a number of cases the fundamental differences between Babylonian and modern religion may lead the present day inquirer to feel somewhat baffled. Our knowledge of the subject comes not from comprehensive lists of sins, but from the confessional rituals in which sins were enumerated.

Confession takes very different forms among different peoples.

In Catholic countries it consists of a recital of faults which the penitent is conscious of having committed, together with an assertion of his abhorrence of them and of sincere repentance. In Egypt, where confession was required at the great judgment after death, the believer so to speak assumed a double rôle, and bade his heart not to overwhelm him with guilt before god. An Egyptian would, in fact, make his confession in the negative form, 'I have not done this or that', e.g.,

'I have done nothing which the gods abhor. I have not prejudiced any man against his master, nor have I left any man hungry. I have caused no man to weep. I have never taken life . . . I have never withheld the loaves which were due to the gods . . . I have never done anything lewd in the sanctuary of the god of my own city. I have never given less than the full measure of grain. I have never given less than a full measure of length. I have never given false weight. I have never robbed a child of its milk. I have never dammed running water. I have never hindered the god from receiving his dues.'

In Mesopotamia, by contrast, confession was a laborious affair. Not only did the penitent confess all the sins he knew he had committed, but since it was often possible inadvertently and unconsciously to do something which aroused divine wrath, he also recited all the additional faults he could think of, in case any of his own were thereby included. Confession was usually performed through the agency of a priest, owing to the penitent's inability to give himself absolution.

The large number of examples which we possess, and which, despite frequent repetition, do occasionally introduce some novel feature, enable us to reconstruct a fairly representative list. The priest hearing the confession would ask the penitent 'whether he has offended god or goddess: whether he has lied: whether he has resisted his master: whether he has stirred up enmity among families or friends: whether he has used inaccurate scales, retained what he should have given, or received what was not due to him, or falsified boundary marks: whether he has stolen, or caused others to steal: whether he has broken into another's house, whether he has had intercourse with his neighbour's wife: whether he has committed injustice: whether he has refused to set a prisoner free?'

This is a representative selection of 'conscious' sins, and in the lists we quite often find that the scribes, in copying from different originals, have repeated the same sins several times over.

But besides these 'conscious' sins towards god and man, there was a whole series which might have been committed quite inadvertently and yet could have roused divine wrath. So we find the priest asking the penitent:—

'Whether he has been in the company of a man under a spell: or slept in his bed: or sat upon his seat: or eaten from his plate, or drunk from his glass?'[2]

Or, while he was walking in the streets:—

'Whether he has stepped in the liquid of a libation which had been poured? or trodden in dirty water: or looked upon water for the washing of hands: or touched a woman with unclean hands: or looked upon a girl with unwashed hands: or touched anyone whose body was unclean?'[3]

All these questions referred to ritual impurity, of which the penitent might be entirely unaware, while furthermore, a man under a spell could infect others. Obviously if every action of this character was to be reckoned as a sin, hardly a single citizen of Babylon could have hoped to escape divine vengeance. Equally, since the river itself was a god, spitting or making water in it was an offence of great gravity. It is interesting, however, that to our minds the significance of this entire group of 'sins' is solely a matter of hygiene, and represents practices which would to-day, though for quite other reasons, be frowned upon.

We must realize that the mere inclusion of the particular sin in question in a list of this nature was all that was required, since the 'doctrine of the name' ensured that its utterance brought it into the open and thereby overcame it. Nevertheless by the period of the Sargonid dynasty we find that the rituals employed during the reconciliation between penitent and god express a few words of regret for, and even abhorrence of, sin. Despite all the inflexibility and imperfections of primitive religion, there is some degree of progress which reflects an advance of thought and reveals the difference between the first formulation of these rituals and the form which they had assumed by the period treated in this book.

Doubt

The English Assyriologist, the late S. Langdon, has collected and published, under the title of *Babylonian Wisdom*, a number of texts illustrating how people reacted to the circumstances of daily life.[4] We are already familiar with the doubts which tormented the soul of a man of Babylon in the face of his unmerited misfortune in the poem which used to be called 'The Righteous Man's Sufferings', though a better title would be 'I wish to praise the Lord of Wisdom', which are the opening words of the text.

We can detect the note of pessimism, or at least of indifference, in the dialogue between a master and his slave:—

'Listen, slave, listen, I want to do something.' 'Yes, my master, then do it.'

The slave goes on to emphasize the excellent reasons for his master's decision. The master then declares that he does not now want to do it, whereupon the slave makes a *volte-face* and finds equally good reasons against it. In successive episodes the master wants to go to the palace, to dine, to get embroiled in a revolution, and to take a woman. On each occasion the slave equally approves his master's choice and his reversal of it.

We also possess collections of proverbs, some of which have an ethical flavour:

'Friendship lasts but a day, but posterity lasts for ever.'

'He who is alive to-day dies before to-morrow.'

Others are cynical:

'A royal gift guarantees a favourable prophecy.'

'Does a marsh get the price of its reeds, or a field of its crops?, (i.e., 'you won't get what is due to you').

And finally some practical advice which a modern father might well give his children:

'Don't marry a woman who has had many lovers. If things go wrong, she will leave you: if you quarrel with her, she will flout you. She will bring disaster on any house she gets inside, and ruin any man who marries her.'

The Temples

Originally there were a number of different types of sanctuary, but by the middle of the first millennium B.C. the dividing lines had become blurred, and this in turn gave rise to the form generally used at that date.

The temples of Western Asia fall into three broad groups. An example of the first, which dates from the Sumerian period, can be found in the temple of Ishtar at Ashur. It consists simply of a rectangular chamber containing, at one end, a base on which the image of the god rested.

The second type, which is more distinctively Syrian, consists of a consecrated area either empty or else surrounding a temple which differs from the first type only in having a door in the middle of one of the short sides and the base in the middle of the other, while the sacrificial altar stands in the open, opposite the door. Babylonian temples of the first millennium B.C. are recognizable derivations of these two types.[5]

Let us examine a comparatively unimportant but quite typical temple excavated at Babylon. It was known as the E-mah (the sublime temple) and was dedicated to Nin-mah (the sublime lady), one aspect of Ishtar. Its dimensions were about 160 feet by 110 feet, and its walls were regularly recessed like those of most religious edifices. Like most Mesopotamian buildings it was orientated on a south-west-north-east axis. The entrance was set in one of the shorter sides and, like many doors in Assyrian buildings, it formed a little chamber giving access on the left to a small doorkeepers'

Plan of E-mah,
the temple of Nin-mah

room. The door opened on to a large courtyard which was set slightly asymmetrically to the right, so that there was no direct view from the street right to the far end of the shrine. The courtyard, which led to an antechamber, also contained a well for lustral water. The antechamber led into the shrine itself, which contained the plinth of the statue of the god. All down the right-hand side of the courtyard was a series of long and narrow rooms which were used as living quarters for certain of the priests and as stores for the ritual objects. The same arrangement was found on the left-hand wall with the addition near the wall of a very long chamber, or more properly flanking passage, which also extended behind the wall of the shrine against which the plinth stood. This passage can be explained either as a means of protecting the way into the holy of holies, since the walls, being of unbaked earth, would not in themselves have presented any serious obstacle to intending marauders, and those who did break in would thus have fallen straight into a guarded corridor: or alternatively as a secret means of communication with the sanctuary and the statue of the god, so that the priests could 'rig' the oracles. The expedition which dug at Mari on the Euphrates found a statue of the goddess Ishtar clasping to her breast a hollow vase. This connected with a pipe inside the statue, so that it was possible for someone outside the shrine to make the water gush from the vase as a sign of fertility and divine favour. The sacrificial altar was not in the temple at all but stood some distance in front of the door.

The Temple of Marduk at Babylon

The largest of all the Babylonian temples was that of Marduk. Such was its length (about 470 feet*) that it has only been partially excavated, while the whole complex of buildings covers a rectangular area of over sixty acres. On the west it was bounded by the Euphrates, and on the east by the processional way, at the end of which stood the Ishtar gate. Although excavations in Babylon have been proceeding for many years, the German expedition has only been able partially to uncover it and even this has involved removing about 40,000 cubic yards of rubble.

The temple, which dates back to the first dynasty of Babylon, was sacked by the Hittites when they raided the city and looted the statues of Marduk and Sarpanit. They were later recovered by the Kassite monarch Agum-kak-rime, who embellished them again with precious ornaments, placed a tiara of gold and lapis lazuli on the god's head, and decorated the doors of the shrine with leaves of cedarwood panelled with bronze worked with motifs of dragons, the goat-fish, and the dog, all emblems of Marduk and his father Ea.

The temple during its history underwent a number of restorations to repair the damage resulting from the wars between Babylon and Assyria, whose monarchs, Esarhaddon and Ashurbanipal, after securely establishing their authority, attempted to make good the damage done by their predecessor Sennacherib

* St. Paul's Cathedral is approximately 520 feet long. [Translator's note.]

(689 B.C.). But it was not until the Babylonian dynasty that the temple attained its unrivalled splendour. According to the curious story about Esarhaddon's efforts at restoration, Marduk, in anger against the city, had dictated (*sic!*) to the priests the text of a tablet which forbade any restoration of the temple until after an interval of seventy years. However, at the very moment when Esarhaddon was anxious to put the work in hand, the priests announced that Marduk had reversed the order of the digits (their value, like that of Arabic numerals, varied according to the order in which they were placed), with the result that the seventy years was reduced to eleven, so that Esarhaddon was free to begin. The temple and its tower were so severely damaged during the revolt against Xerxes in 479 B.C., under the Achaemenid dynasty, that Alexander, despite his desire to confer a special mark of favour on Babylon by making it the most important of his capitals, was obliged to abandon his intention of restoring the buildings. He had ten thousand workmen on the job for two months: but even so he was unable to clear more than part of the rubble.

The first feature of Esagila ('the temple of the lofty head') that would strike an observer approaching from the Ishtar gate was the great forecourt. This contained the temple tower together, at one end, with temple outbuildings. The main temple stood in

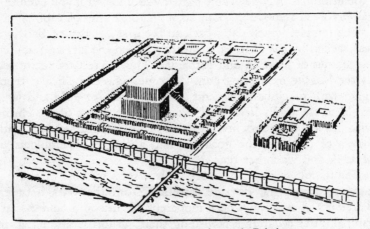

Reconstruction of the temple area in Babylon

(From King: 'History of Babylon', by permission of the author's heirs and Messrs. Chatto & Windus, Ltd.)

the adjacent courtyard, there being several means of access between the two. The open space in front of the temple measured about 110 yards by 90: whereas (for purposes of comparison) those in front of the large and important temples of Belit and Zababa measured only about 105 yards by 45. The actual shrine, known as the E-kur (temple-mountain), like the *ziggurat*, was built on a terrace of asphalted bricks: and there is a theory that these terraces, which invariably form the platform for Babylonian monuments, represent a distant memory of the hills of the region which the Sumerians must have inhabited before they settled in Mesopotamia. This may well be true; but the practice was also dictated by the annual floods of the Tigris and Euphrates; for, though the water might not rise as high as the actual monuments, they introduced a sufficient quantity of moisture into the subsoil to represent a danger to buildings of dry clay, which absorbs water particularly readily. The whole of our knowledge of the interior decoration of the E-kur and the other shrines in Esagila, which were built on the same ground plan as Babylonian sanctuaries, is derived partly from inscriptions left by the monarchs who worshipped there and partly from the description given by Herodotus, who says that he saw there a great statue of the god, a throne with a canopy and a table for offerings, all made of gold and in the aggregate weighing 800 talents, or nearly 24 tons! These figures must, of course, be treated with considerable reserve. Admittedly a surprising quantity of gold was found in the so-called Royal Tombs of Ur in Sumer in the shape of offerings of plate and tomb-furniture; but although some small objects were of solid gold, the majority, which resembled what had already been found in other excavations, consisted of very thin panels of gold repousse work, or even of gold leaf burnished upon the bronze or wooden object of decoration. The temple courtyard at Khorsabad contained a series of wooden pillars each covered with thin sheets of bronze giving a stylized effect of the surface of a palm trunk, the engraved bronze surface in turn being covered with closely fitting and very thin gold leaf, which produced a broad effect of a massive golden pillar. Generally speaking excavation has hitherto yielded nothing of solid gold more substantial than trinkets. We have numerous descriptions of buildings or roofs covered with gold and glittering in the sun. Excavations of such buildings have often brought to light fragments of tiles or bricks covered with a yellow glaze which was a Babylonian speciality and which must literally have glistened in the bright sunshine of the Orient.

The same applies to the so-called precious stones of Mesopotamia. Before the Hellenic period, stones thus described were in fact only what we call semi-precious—lapis lazuli, cornelian and the like. Furthermore the inhabitants possessed formulae for the manufacture of coloured glass and, no doubt through a genuine mistake arising from a lack of technical knowledge of the difference, these formulae are described as if they actually resulted in the manufacture of precious stones. We can form some impressions of the decoration of Esagila from the results of excavation. The exterior, following an ancient Oriental tradition still to be seen in, for example, the mosque of S. Sofia at Istanbul, must have been left plain. Not so the interior, however. Passing through the doors with leaves decorated with bands of chased and gilded bronze (cf. similar doors from Balawat and Susa now in the British Museum and the Louvre respectively) the visitor would have found the walls panelled with marble, above which were paintings in vivid and clear blues, reds and blacks, contrasting with the white ground. Similar examples can be seen in the temple at Mari and the palaces of Til-Barsip and Khorsabad. Possibly too, as on the Ishtar gate in Babylon, there were panels and friezes of enamelled bricks: although this is a type of decoration which requires brilliant light to be seen at its best and seems usually to have been reserved for well-lit exterior surfaces. We know that one large reception chamber in the royal palace at Babylon was decorated with vertical bands of enamelled bricks terminating at top and bottom in large palmettes. The garments of the statues of the gods on their pedestals were richly embroidered with gold; while the hangings, the canopies (especially the 'golden sky' of Esagila), the tables, and the vessels for offerings were made of precious metals or plated with gold. No wonder the fame of the shrine spread far and wide.

The Ziggurat or Temple Tower

The *ziggurat*, which stood near the temple, was called the Etemenanki, which meant 'the temple foundation of heaven and earth'. *Temen* was the word for the foundation stone of a building (borrowed by the Greeks in the form τέμενος (*temenos*) to signify the centre of a group of temples), and the fact that the *ziggurat* was so called is of added significance, for the interdependence of heaven and earth meant that the *ziggurat* of Babylon became the corner-stone of the whole structure. Other temple towers were described as 'links between heaven and earth': and I think that, behind the allusion to the physical fact that the foundations of a *ziggurat* are in the earth and its summit is almost lost in the clouds, lies a profounder conception of the immaterial bond between the two ordered elements in the universe.

A *ziggurat* was a regular feature of every important temple. It stood apart from the main structure, like the campanile of an Italian church. Excavations in Mesopotamia have brought to light two quite different types of *ziggurat*. One predominates in the north of the country. Apart from the terrace which invariably forms its foundation, it consists of a number of super-imposed rectangular platforms of diminishing size, with a gradually sloping path built into the external walls and leading to the top, which was crowned by a shrine. There were generally seven of these platforms or stories, each painted in a colour different from that immediately below or above it. The *ziggurat* at Khorsabad is still standing as high as the fourth storey, and the multi-coloured bricks scattered around it show that, starting from the bottom, the stories were successively painted white, black, red, white, reddish orange, silver and finally gold. Each side of the base measured about 140 feet, and each storey when exposed was about 19 feet high, giving a total height of about 135 feet.

A different type of *ziggurat* is found in the south, that of Ur being taken for our purposes as typical*. The building as we know it appears to have been originally built by King Ur-Nammu, slightly before 2000 B.C., but it underwent a number of restorations, especially under Nabonidus the last king of Babylon. It stood in the *temenos* of Ur together with several other temples and religious monuments, but was associated with the temple of Sin. It was a quadrilateral of about 190 by 145 feet and its corners pointed to the cardinal points of the compass. On one of its long sides there was a nearly vertical staircase at right angles to the terrace, while two further converging staircases

---

* For a restoration of the *ziggurat* of Ur see Sir Leonard Woolley, *Ur excavations,* vol. V, (1939), O.U.P. Plates 84–88. [Translator's note.]

rose from each extremity of the same side and met at the top of the first. This terrace or platform, which was about 50 feet high, was surmounted by two other similar, but smaller, quadrilaterals, joined by a further staircase. The whole construction was some seventy feet high. The walls of each face of every terrace sloped slightly inwards, and were decorated at intervals with projecting panels, the purpose of which was purely ornamental. The whole structure was built of unbaked bricks reinforced with fired bricks bonded with bitumen. The *ziggurat* at Ur did not, in fact, consist of a series of square, almost straight-sided terraces like that of Khorsabad, but took the form of three parallelopipeds one above the other, the top one being crowned with a little shrine surfaced with enamelled bricks of a beautiful deep blue, dating from the restoration by Nabonidus. The bottom storey was coloured black: the next red.

Accounts in ancient literature suggest that the *ziggurat* at Babylon resembled that at Khorsabad. According to Herodotus (I, 181) it measured a stade* in each direction at the base, above which there were seven superimposed terraces, while a road on the outer wall wound upwards from storey to storey. However, at the date of his visit to Babylon the *ziggurat* had been largely destroyed on the orders of King Xerxes (479 B.C.) and so his account must be second-hand, while the lower stories as revealed by excavation suggest that it was built on the 'Ur' plan, but upon a square base. The dimensions are recorded on the tablet known as the 'Esagila tablet': the base being slightly over 293 feet (compared with about 300 as ascertained by excavation). According to the tablet, its height, width and length were all equal, but not those of the individual stories, which were seven in number: Herodotus counted them as eight by including the platform as one. If the tablet is to be believed, the height should have been close on 300 feet.

A number of attempts at reconstructing the tower have been made by archaeologists in their efforts to reconcile the measurements derived from excavation, the information given by the tablet, and Herodotus' account. E. Unger was of the opinion that the Etemenanki must have combined the features of both the northern and the southern types: the two lower stories, as is proved by the remains of the two staircases, belonging to the

* About 200 yards. [Translator's note.]

latter and the four upper stories to the former, the whole edifice being surmounted by a shrine which, or so Herodotus was told, contained a very ornate bed beside which stood a golden table. There was no statue of any kind, and the only person who slept there was one woman of the country selected from among her companions by the god himself. If this account is correct, we have here a chapel dedicated to the 'sacred marriage' of the god.

We also know that there were a number of shrines on each side of the monument at first storey level: and we must keep all these points in mind during any discussion of the use to which the Etemenanki was put.

The fame of this tower became enshrined in Biblical tradition, for it was the original of the tower of Babel. This tradition persisted until it had fallen into such disrepair that it was merely a featureless mound with no traces of any terraces visible, when there was an attempt to identify the tower of Babel with the *ziggurat* of the neighbouring city of Borsippa (Birs Nimrud) which was erected in honour of the god Nabu, son of Marduk: despite the unlikelihood of Babylon's ever having covered so huge an area, since Borsippa lies about ten miles from Babylon. The Borsippa tower has never been properly examined, though it only just escaped an appalling 'exposure' in 1852 at the hands of the Fresnel expedition. Some of the upper surfaces having been vitrified by a serious fire, Colonel Rawlinson and Fresnel agreed that time and money could best be saved by 'exploding a mine to split the tower in two and so expose its core'. Mercifully other preoccupations prevented Fresnel from cutting the Gordian knot in this summary manner.

Besides the great temples which invested Babylon with the character of a religious capital, we should not forget the multitude of shrines and altars which were built in the streets either alongside some building or at street crossings, rather like the *turbés* of the Sultans at Istanbul. It is worth quoting a contemporary inscription.

'There are altogether in Babylon fifty-three temples of the great gods, fifty-five shrines dedicated to Marduk, three hundred shrines belonging to earth divinities, six hundred shrines for celestial divinities, one hundred and eighty altars to the goddess Ishtar, one hundred and eighty to the gods Nergal and Adad, and twelve other altars to various deities'.

And, as if these numbers would be scarcely credible, the tablet emphasizes that 'all these are actually inside the town.'[6]

The Priesthood. The King as High Priest

As might be expected, the head of the priesthood was the king, who was the earthly representative of the god, and the royal titles included those of 'priest of Ashur' and 'supplier' of [the temples] Esagila and Ezida. These titles were not merely honorary. The king both personally offered sacrifices and decided on the performance of certain ceremonies. No doubt he was advised in these tasks by the regular priesthood, but he enjoyed the liberty of action which belonged to his high-priestly office. This tradition was of extreme antiquity, and the title was jealously claimed by each monarch in turn. Since he was clearly unable to perform all the duties which fell to a high priest, he nominated someone to act as his substitute: frequently this might be either one of his sons or one of the senior members of the priesthood (a 'great priest'), and although this substitute derived his powers from the divine favour by which his selection was manifested through the omens, it was the king by whom he was appointed and under whose hands he swore his oath. On the same principle, each important temple was under the authority of a 'great priest'. Not only did the king instal such priests in office but he nominated the holders of less important appointments. This system of nomination led to rivalries in which the king had to make a selection from among those who were jockeying for position. See, for example, the following letter to the king from one of his ministers:—

'As regards the successor to the late chamberlain of the temple, I have said to my royal master that his son and his nephew are both suitable for the post. His son, his nephew and the son of Nabu-ballit, cousin of the chief assistant priest, are coming to be received in audience by the king. My lord will nominate whichever of them he thinks most fit.'[7]

Below the royal high priest and those senior members of the priesthood to whom he had delegated his powers came the generality of the priesthood, collectively known as *shangu* (priests), a name which connoted those who officiated as well as those who administered the affairs of the temples.

The numerous aspects of the priestly function could in essence be reduced to two. The first was to know and to interpret the will of the gods: the second, to bring the believer into peace with god, if that was necessary, and there to keep him.

Diviners. Chanters

The first of these tasks belonged to the diviners; the second, partly to the chanters (*kalû*) who 'soften the heart of the gods' by their hymns and music, and partly to the 'magicians', whose function it was to commend to divine favour the sacrifices offered by the priests specializing in that task and who, by prayer and the due performance of ritual, could deliver the believer from the power of the demons which oppressed him.

The diviners (*bârû*) worshipped all the deities belonging to the pantheon, but claimed to be under the patronage of the gods of divination, and to represent an extremely ancient tradition, since the rites which they practised were believed to have been handed down by Enmeduranki, king of Sippar before the Deluge, whose reign, according to various lists, lasted from 21,000 to 72,000 years. Since Enmeduranki had been endowed with the qualities of physical perfection, his successors must be like him: indeed the texts say that 'the diviner whose father is impure and who himself has any imperfection of limb or countenance, whose eyes are not sound, who has any teeth missing, who has lost a finger, whose countenance has a sickly look or who is pimpled, cannot be the keeper of the decrees of Shamash and Adad' (the gods of divination).

An aspiring *bârû* had to submit to long studies and undergo an initiation ceremony, besides being either shaven completely bald or at least tonsured, in order to comply with the formula of his consecration 'The barber hath done his handiwork upon him'. Since everyday life could not be conducted without the assistance of diviners, and since their services might be called upon at a moment's notice, some were assigned for duty in the palace or the adjacent temple. The letters written by these diviners contain the continually recurring phrase 'the king hath made me seek the meaning' of this thing or that. The diviners attached to the court had to be prepared to interpret anything: and, as officials, they had to take the oath of loyalty. We find an official reminding the king that oaths would be administered on a certain day, including in the order of appearance 'scribes, diviners, the makers of incantations, doctors, the observers of birds, palace officials'. This oath was regarded as something material, a kind of net in which the taker was enclosed. The words of the sacred formula literally meant '[He] will make his way into the midst of the oath'.

The other group consisted of the chanters or *kalû*, who intoned the prayers and chanted them simultaneously with the worshippers, to the accompaniment of appropriate music, consisting of the rhythmical beating of big drums, shaped either like large boxes (*balaggu*) or timbals (*lilissu*), together with harps and citherns. The instruments are not merely reproduced on the monuments, but examples have been recovered virtually intact from the royal tombs of Ur. Almost all the harps were decorated with a little bull or a bull's head, and they must have had a deep tone since their sound was often compared with the bellowing of a bull. Some types of prayer were explicitly described as needing 'to be accompanied by a flute' (*halhallatu*). A large number of religious ceremonies were accompanied throughout by the chanting of the *kalû*, including even some extremely lengthy ones like the reconstruction of a ruined temple.

We possess a list of the chants, all representing various types of lamentation, which were included in the repertoire of the *kalû*. Of these fifty-seven required the accompaniment of a big drum, forty a flute, and forty-seven involved 'the lifting of hands', i.e., had to be uttered with the hands raised in the attitude of prayer.

Exorcists

The *kalû* was in short a singer of incantations, since the aim and object of his chants and his lamentations were purification and protection. The most active participant in these ceremonies was, however, the *âshipu*, the Akkadian equivalent of *mashmash*: the Semitic form of this last being *masmashu*. There are grounds for thinking that there may have been a shade of difference between them, but we do not know what it amounted to. The *âshipu*, whose duty was to utter exorcisms, could, like the *bârû*, claim that he represented a very ancient tradition, and one of the spells which he used ran as follows: 'I am the *âshipu* that was created at Eridu: yea, the *âshipu* that was begotten at Eridu and in Subaru'. The significance of this was that Eridu

was regarded as the most ancient of all Sumerian cities, while
Subaru was the earliest known name of the later Assyria, so that
the *âshipu* is claiming that his roots are deep in the earliest
beginnings of Mesopotamian civilization.

We hear of another subdivision among the priesthood, known
as the *erib-bîti*, namely 'those who have the right to enter into
the sanctuary'. We should however not regard them as being in
any sense a separate class. The name simply refers to those priests
who, as their name implies, had the right of entering the sanctuary and they are included among those already mentioned.

Minor Priests and Temple Staff

The rear is brought up by the temple staff, including the doorkeepers and temple guards, the officials who actually performed
the sacrifice (known as the 'knife carriers'), and the 'throne
bearers'—doubtless those whose duty it was to carry on their
shoulders the litters in which the gods were borne in procession.
These last must have been very numerous, since on some occa
sions a great many statues of the gods were assembled.

A variety of subsidiary activities also took place in the temple:
e.g., by brewers, by makers of confectionery and by pastrycooks
who made the sacred cakes required for certain ceremonies. In
the temples of the late period dedicated to Ishtar, the forecourt
would often be covered with a cloud of the doves which were the
personal birds of the goddess and nested on the top of the temple.
They were religiously looked after and fed by worshippers with
cakes specially made for the purpose in that temple.

Thefts and Brawls in the Sanctuaries

The temple staff included a patrol with the duty of keeping
order, and of preventing or at least quelling brawls and, more
especially, thefts. The latter were extremely common since
the accumulated treasures, in the shape of the ritual furnishings,
vestments and ornaments of the gods, represented a powerful
temptation. There are many references to thefts from temples,
e.g.:

'The golden tablet which is missing from the temple of Ashur
has been seen in the possession of the sculptor X . . . [recom-
mended that] the king should take steps to have him sent for
and questioned.'[8]

'The king, beyond any shadow of doubt, will say "Why has no one given me a report on this?" When the priest X . . . *érib-bîti* [see above] of Shamash left Babylon, he removed the "golden sky" from Esagila.'[9]

The commandant of Khorsabad himself had already drawn attention to himself by his indiscretion in breaking open sealed envelopes. [The report continues].

'Now, he is opening the storeroom which belongs to the god and the king: and as soon as the governor and commandant of Nineveh and Arbela bring the silver to the temple, he removes it.'[10]

The precautions for guarding valuables were continually being elaborated. A goldsmith says 'I have made the crown of Anu . . . I have received twelve minas of gold by way of an offering to Bel, and I have used them for the jewels of the goddess Sarpanit . . . Everything has been deposited in the treasury of the Temple of Ashur, and no one can open it except in the presence of the priest of X . . . Will the king be graciously pleased to send someone duly authorized to open the treasury, so that I can finish the work and send it to the king?'[11]

Sometimes even cases of attempted murder occurred in the temple, as we can see from the following deposition:—

'At the great gate of E-anna X . . . son of Y . . . drew an iron dagger from his belt with the intention of striking Z . . . duly appointed by the king as his chief officer in E-anna. The Court before whom X was brought have placed the dagger under seal. Given at Uruk the 21st day of Kislev, in the 16th year of King Nabonidus of Babylon.'[12]

Services

The attitude of prayer, particularly when offered in public, was with hands uplifted towards the god. The services contained a large element of hymns and prayers in which the congregation joined, and from time to time a pause was indicated during which the congregation uttered a kind of general lamentation. Processions were held not only within the temple precincts, but also throughout the city, the participants including priests, statues of the gods, official representatives (including occasionally the king in person) and worshippers.

An important feature of worship was the sacrificial offering.

This was generally a kid, in which case one part of the animal was burned and the rest belonged to the priests, but it also took the form of the pouring of libations of milk, wine and honey, or of sacrifices of animals, ranging from birds to bulls. A whole army of minor officials was required to perform the various ritual tasks. Prayer demanded the scrupulous performance of traditional observance, and any failure on this score would have destroyed the significance of the ceremonies. The most elaborate were those over which the king presided in his nominal capacity of high priest. Every action—for example, the building of a temple—had to be accompanied by a religious ceremony, and the keynote of every kind of service was purification: understandably enough, in view of the Babylonian terror of even involuntary impurity which might leave a loophole for the tormenting demons. Propitiation ceremonies were also important, in order to combat the malign influences of particular days or months, which might involve the prohibition of even the most ordinary actions of everyday life.

Religious Festivals

Each god had his appointed festivals, but the most important was the celebration of the New Year. This took place in spring in the month of Nisan, and had assumed, with the passing of time, a double character. It had originated in a nature festival, with features which expressed simultaneously nature's grief at the death of all growing things and her joy at their rebirth. On to this had been grafted the glorification of Marduk, celebrating the exploits which had raised him to pre-eminence among the gods. At Babylon the New Year festival lasted for twelve days. In the city Marduk literally 'received' in his temple of Esagila the other gods of the great cities in the shape of their statues, the first to render homage being his son Nabu, who was worshipped in the neighbouring city of Borsippa. It is difficult to be sure of the significance of the different phases of the festival, but at least Marduk's disappearance, if not his actual death, appears to have been mimed. Grief was changed to gaiety on his reappearance, and the entire company of gods was escorted in a great procession to the temple outside the city, known as the *akîtu*, which gave its name to the festival. In the intervening period there had been a performance of some kind of sacred drama representing the events of the Marduk epic: the appeal of the gods to him to be their champion in the struggle against Tiamat or Chaos, his victory, his consecration as head of the pantheon and the exercise of one of his most important prerogatives, namely, the 'fixing of the destinies' of the city of Babylon. The remaining stages of the festival were unrelieved nature worship, consisting of the consummation in the temple of the ἱερὸς γάμος or sacred marriage of the divine couple represented either by two of the statues of the gods or by the high priest and high priestess. This marked the close of the festival, after which the statues were escorted back to their temples in the provinces far or near. Each of the great cities had its own version of the ceremony, with the local deity playing the principal part. Any hitch in its due performance was regarded as an omen of disaster.

Divination and its Justification

The three interrelated fields of divination, magic and medicine were the points at which Mesopotamian religious principles touched life most deeply. The modern world, with the aid of science, can foretell such physical phenomena as the state of the sea, the path of cyclones or the course of an epidemic, and immediately knows what has happened anywhere on earth. Not so, of course, the Babylonians: lacking these advantages they sought enlightenment from the gods about great and trivial happenings alike, in the conviction that the gods revealed their will and their future intentions by a thousand signs which could be properly interpreted, thanks to their disclosure of divination to Enmeduranki, one of the mythical kings before the Deluge. This original revelation, coupled with those vouchsafed each day, elevated divination to the rank of a science and had won for it acceptance as a source of official information. The king regularly consulted the palace diviners before any decision of importance was taken, and the ordinary Babylonian did the same over the events of his daily life. The will of the gods was always ascertained before anything at all was done in Mesopotamia.

The Gods of Divination. The Priests

Two gods in particular, Shamash and Adad, were especially regarded as 'lords of divination'. The former, who was the sun, not only saw everything, but also knew the future. This was also an attribute of Adad, who did not belong to the original Mesopotamian pantheon but was no doubt regarded as possessing the same characteristics in the countries of the west whence he had come. He was the god of the weather, which played an important part in Babylonian magic.

Since divination was in origin divine, it was naturally practised by the priests. Omens were interpreted by the *bârû*, the man who 'saw' or 'inspected'. He carried on the tradition of Enmeduranki and, like his predecessor, must be physically perfect. His training demanded a long period of study, after which he was consecrated; he kept his head shaven and became a member of the priesthood, attached to the temple. Everything was material for divination, for anything could be an omen: and the various methods of interpretation were regulated by closely defined rules. With the aid of a large collection of tablets which had been frequently recopied and added to over the centuries, the *bârû* was never at a loss for an answer. He even kept a record, for example, of any unusual features encountered during sacrifices, for they represented so many clues which, when studied at some later date, might lead to the recognition of some new sign. The 'reading' of omens played a considerable part in the process and frequently made considerable demands upon the scribe's ingenuity. If, for example, an omen had been observed by an inquirer on his right hand, and was judged to be favourable to Assyria, then the same omen must be unfavourable to a country hostile to Assyria: while if the omen had originally been observed on the left, the converse would be true. Thus, four different omens might be derived from the same phenomenon. Briefly, when confronted with an omen, the scribe would examine every conceivable variant upon it, in order to extract a variety of conclusions, provided they were consistent with the original phenomenon. Punning, the importance of which we have already mentioned, played its part in this process. If, for example, the inquirer had seen a bird, the omen would repeat the word, which sounded like one form of a verb meaning 'to save' or 'to be saved'. The terms of the answer were conditioned by the original form of the question.[13]

The inhabitants of Babylon believed that the interpretations of the diviners derived from revelation, and were therefore beyond all question: but their credibility was buttressed by still more evidence. The omens with which certain ancient kings had been helped during crises in their history were still remembered, and if one of these omens were repeated, it was always reassuringly quoted.

Various Types of Divination. Dreams

Taking the types of divination in their comparative order of importance, the simplest was the oracle, uttered either by the god himself or by one of his servants such as a priestess with the gift of prophecy. An obscure oracle was interpreted by a diviner. Interpretation was most frequently required by dreams, which were often the medium through which warnings were conveyed, and collections of them were compiled. It is worth recalling that an inhabitant of Babylon regarded a dream as equivalent to reality, so that to see a god in a dream was the same as seeing him in real life, and whether the state was one of sleeping or waking was immaterial. On the other hand there were no limits to the variety nor to the physical impossibility of the subject matter of a dream, and the business of the scribe was to foresee the least impossible of the circumstances. A modern scholar, faced with a text in which impossible actions are attributed to human beings, should assume them to refer to the interpretation of dreams. A student of the collections of the omens conveyed by various dreams cannot fail to be struck by their reappearance in Greek and Latin texts and even nowadays in modern books purporting to interpret them. This particular type of 'divination' has survived the ages virtually unchanged

Hepatoscopy or Divination by the Liver

This was an important type of divination, but the physical resources required for its performance virtually confined it to the king or to high officials. The Babylonians believed that, when a kid or a sheep was sacrificed, the god revealed his will by the shape, or alterations in the shape, of the various parts of the victim's liver. The method of their interpretation resulted from a tradition enshrined in numerous collections which we possess, though we are handicapped by our ignorance of which part and what alterations are being referred to. This particular method of divination was also widely practised by both the Hittites and the Etruscans; after slaughtering the animal and opening up its body the maker of the sacrifice drew his preliminary conclusions, after which he removed the liver and subjected it to a minute examination. In order to assist them in practising this art, the diviners possessed model livers made of terra-cotta, illustrating the various changes and abnormalities.

Astrology

There were many practitioners of astrology; but it was not astrology as known to the Greeks and the medieval world or as still practised to-day. In order to cast a horoscope at birth, two pieces of knowledge are essential, the first being the zodiac and the second the precession of the equinoxes. The former of these was not known in Mesopotamia before the end of the archaic period, the latter only at the very end of its history (associated with the Babylonian Kidinnu). Babylonian astrology was fundamentally based on meteorology, being founded upon observations of the winds, the colour of the stars, the occultation of the planets and eclipses; and the advice which it conveyed could be interpreted at various levels as referring not only to matters of high policy, but also to the daily life of the private citizen, and especially agriculture. It was in fact more or less the equivalent of the modern weather forecasts.

Omens derived from Births and Chance Meetings

A further type of omen was derived from the births of human beings or of animals and any abnormal circumstances attending them, since these last, being contrary to nature, assumed the meaning of 'signs' (cf. the original derivation of the word 'monster'), and their interpretation was very popular. This was another case in which Latin thought adopted Babylonian practice virtually unaltered.

There were several types of what might be called subsidiary divination, like the study of the flight of birds (which was also employed by the Hittites and Etruscans), of the patterns formed by oil spreading over water or, in the last analysis, of literally every aspect of human environment. We possess collections of numerous tablets of omens drawn from such matters as finding water spilt on the road, or encountering some particular animal or plant; one of the best known opens with the words 'If a town stands upon a hill . . .' Perhaps the best idea of the significance which was attached to accidental meetings is given by the title of the collection known, from its opening words, as 'When an exorcist is on his way to the house of an invalid . . .' Everything which the exorcist met influenced the patient's future.

Divination as practised in this manner might either cheer or distress the inquirer according to the replies he received: but its depressing aspect must have been the perpetual subjection of each individual to every feature of the physical world, which dictated his conduct. As we have already seen, Babylonian man was continually assailed by demons; and now we find him regulating the conduct of his life in obedience to the ubiquitous omens. If he believed that this obedience might earn him a respite, or that the omens were favourable for some undertaking, he stood in grave danger of sharp disillusionment. He must keep in mind hemerology—the science of 'good' and 'bad' days—before embarking on any enterprise, for be it never so good in itself, the character of the day on which he expected to perform it might fundamentally change its nature.

Magic

The practices of Babylonian magic, with which alone we are here concerned, were related to the rituals of exorcism against demons. Not only was it officially recognized, but it was addressed to the gods, it was conducted by priests in the temples, and was an integral part of Babylonian religion, and it is well within the province of any student of Near Eastern archaeology.

We possess the details of many of the Babylonian rituals employed by the priests. Reading them, we realize that they were essentially beneficent in purpose, their aim being to ensure deliverance from demons. It is, however, also possible from the references in these rituals to sorcerers of both sexes to infer that they were fundamentally regarded as a method of defence. Since the sorcerer was the adversary of the priest, we do not know in detail how he attacked his victim. But the practices which were used to counter it give us a very fair idea of the nature of this 'unlawful' magic: and indeed the practices employed by the sorcerer in order to mobilize the forces of evil are the same as the priest employed to invoke the aid of the superior forces which could not fail to triumph.

The Gods of Magic. The Priests and their Technique. Spells

These superior forces were represented by the gods—especially Marduk and Ea—and their attendant good genies. By the date of the religious reforms of the first dynasty of Babylon, Ea, the lord of all knowledge and the benefactor of mankind, had gradually surrendered almost all his active powers to his son Marduk, though he still remained the final recourse in case of difficulty and was often appealed to by his son for help.

We are by now familiar with the power over a person or an object conferred by 'the power of the name': by knowing it, by uttering its name in the appropriate tone of voice, by writing it or by physically representing it. Magic derived its essential nature from the application of these principles by the exorcist priest known as the *masmashu* or *âshipu* (priests who pronounced the incantation or *shibtu*). No virtue was intrinsically inherent in the *âshipu*: he derived his powers from his consecration and from his being the representative of the gods of magic, with whom he was identified during the exercise of his sacred office. At the moment of its performance he would cry out 'The *âshipu* who was created in Eridu [the holy city of Ea]—I am he.' He uttered the words of the special ritual for averting demons, clothed in robes of red (the prophylactic colour against evil spirits) or wearing a kind of fish-like skin to emphasize his relationship with Ea, the lord of the waters of the abyss. The words which he uttered were not left to improvisation, for since they had once been revealed by the gods, they were immutable without losing their power. In the name of the gods of heaven and earth the priest called on his adversary by name (this very exposure robbed him of his power), and conjured him to cease to torment the believer and so to depart, and, calling the whole company of the gods to the aid of the sufferer, he exorcized the demon. This ritual was reinforced with a number of symbolical actions such as the burning of substances which the evil spirits were supposed to resemble,[14] and the untying of the knots in which the sorcerer was symbolically imagined to have entangled his victim: finally a spell was cast to undo the effects of the spell originally cast by the sorcerer upon his victim. This spell was similar in form to those practised in medieval Europe, and consisted in the making of small images to be tortured and destroyed—in a word, sympathetic magic.

During these ceremonies the *âshipu* traced circles with a magician's wand round himself and anyone else he desired to protect, with the words: 'In my hand I hold the magic circle of Ea, in my hand I hold the cedar wood, the sacred weapon of Ea, in my hand I hold the branch of the palm tree of the great rite.'[15]

This was not the limit of the magician's powers. It was he who consecrated the statues of the gods and the objects used in worship and so brought them to life by 'washing and the opening of their mouths' as was done in Egypt. This ceremony consisted in touching them with an appropriate instrument and the recitation of formulae. By this means the statues came to life, and not only the statues but even the objects connected with the cults, like the musical instruments—the *lilissu* or the sacred timbals—which provided the accompaniment.[16]

The *âshipu* sometimes even lent his help to the gods. Thus, when the moon god Sin was attacked and oppressed by demons (which caused a lunar eclipse), he joined in prayer and incantation with the other gods to bring him safe deliverance.

All these ceremonies were performed to the accompaniment of chants (which were words of which the natural power was reinforced by the tone in which they were uttered and the number of those participating): of dances which mimed the actions the *âshipu* intended to take in order to hasten their accomplishment: and of music. This is the proper interpretation of the chants of war and of love and the dances of war and the chase, designed to leave their quarry defenceless.

There is even reason to think that, if the *âshipu* performed the whole cycle of the ritual correctly, they could lay even the gods under some measure of constraint. The operations of sympathetic magic, like watering plants in order to induce rain, or the union of divine statues, or of priest and priestess, to encourage fertility on earth, caused a reaction in heaven on account of the links between them. A further example can be found in a curse, which was bound to be fulfilled if its words were more than empty breath. In one case at least—in the Gilgamesh epic—we find a god giving effect to a curse against his will. When Enkidu cursed the temple prostitute, Shamash, the sun-god, appeared to Enkidu and reproached him for his attitude towards one who had done him many kindnesses. Yet although Shamash reproached Enkidu for it, he was compelled to change the hapless temple prostitute into a bitch.

The Possibilities inherent in Babylonian Magic

Even a cursory examination of the practice of Babylonian magic shows both that it was serious in its intentions and that it was genuinely moral in purpose. It had eschewed all the material ends which later systems have claimed to attain: it offered no short cuts to wealth or honour, and it gave no promises of eternal youth: the didactic semi-religious poems had pronounced once and for all upon the vanity of such a quest. The man of Babylon who coveted such things must seek the aid of the sorcerer, for the *âshipu* would have none of him. This concept is reinforced by certain amulets which we possess. Some of these are symbols of the gods, intended to reconcile man with god and place him under divine protection, while others represent evil spirits which, when clearly seen and exposed for what they are, are rendered harmless: and others again reproduce hunting scenes, and particularly herds of animals (a very common theme on cylinder seals) which must have been designed to ensure the success of the enterprises of their owners. It is fairly clear that Babylonian magic, like Babylonian divination, defied the laws of change and remained virtually unaltered over many centuries.

Babylonian Medicine. The Sacerdotal Phase

Babylonian medicine, like magic, rested upon anxiety to discover the cause of the evil, and involved the techniques of magic and divination combined. In its earliest and most primitive phase it lay entirely within the province of the priests. The invalid was a man either 'possessed' in the medieval sense of the term or afflicted by a demon which was regarded as the cause of his malady. Since by definition every invalid was a sinner, a case in which the complaint defied diagnosis, and thus prevented the recognition of the demon which caused it, necessitated the discovery of the sin which, once successfully achieved, would be equivalent to unmasking the demon concerned. With this in mind the *âshipu* would read over the list of sins which the patient might have consciously or unconsciously committed: once the sin in question had been identified the *âshipu* would have overcome the demon which had taken advantage of the sin to 'occupy' the patient, and was thereby enabled to pronounce the proper exorcism.

On the other hand in a case where the symptoms were sufficiently well known for the demon to be immediately identified, there gradually grew up, parallel with the incantations, the acceptance of a method of healing which could counter the assaults of the demons and was designed to force them to leave the patient. This led to the employment in antiquity of medicine made of nauseous and putrid substances: sometimes even of excrement. Frequently a rudimentary prognosis developed from the way in which certain symptoms were regarded as 'omens' of later developments: later on, when they were better understood, they became elements in a genuine form of prognosis.[17]

If treatment along these lines proved unsuccessful, it was considered advisable to temper the threats of exorcism with certain promises in order to induce the demon to depart. The priest might for example take a sucking pig and, after making an elaborate comparison of the pig's head, body and legs with the equivalent parts of the patient, offer it as a habitation for the demon. This simply represented an attempt to induce the demon to make an exchange, but there were other cases in which a mere reed was actually used instead of a pig, and here we can see an undeveloped and unconscious groping after what is now called 'transfer of sensibility'. An alternative method was to read out to the demon a list of the gifts he would receive, the point being, of course, that this would make them materialize, on the same principle as the lists of offerings on Egyptian tombs which passersby were begged to read (p. 187). Thus the she-demon Lamashtu, who killed pregnant women and young children, was bribed to go away with offers of the provisions she would need on her journey to the nether regions, with ornaments, with an ass to cross the desert and with a boat for the passage of the waters beneath the earth.[18] (Pl. XXIV.)

A bronze plaque in the De Clerq collection shows the whole scene; we see the patient lying in bed, surrounded by exorcists wearing their robes, and with good genies busy repelling the

assaults of the notorious seven devils, while Lamashtu is in retreat with her promised load of gifts.[19]

The Emergence of the Critical Spirit

Gradually credulity began to give place to the critical spirit,
and the art of healing, perhaps unconsciously, began to employ
materials either of proved therapeutic value or superficially
related—e.g., in shape or colour—to the patient's condition. It
was the era of the 'wise woman': when, for example, jaundice
would be treated with doses of yellow medicine, just as medieval
Europe would order stag's horn or powdered crayfish shell (the
so-called 'crayfish eyes') for the sake of their phosphates or
calcium carbonate content. It was the time, too, when the
magical prescriptions began to insist upon the importance of the
precise moment of gathering plants of medicinal value—a piece
of knowledge still carefully observed by modern herbalists, well
aware that the relative strength of their various ingredients varies
not merely from month to month but from hour to hour.

Pre-Hippocratic Medicine

The first millennium saw a fundamental change. Exorcism
dwindled until it was of secondary importance and different
techniques of healing, albeit for the most part crude, were applied
to each complaint, while prognosis took account of the 'critical
days' concept of the Hippocratic school. By the period of the
Sargonid dynasty, a patient in Mesopotamia could be treated
on a system of pre-Hippocratic medicine administered by the
asû (from the Sumerian *a-zu*, one who divines knowledge from
water). The *asû*, or doctors, formed a corporate body from whose
members the chief physicians to the king were drawn, and the
correspondence which they carried on with the king's household
shows that they remained quite unmoved by the grumbling of
their royal patients.

Death. The Nobles and the Common People. Funerals.
The After World

At about the middle of the first millennium B.C. there was
nothing very striking about the tomb of the ordinary inhabitant
of Babylonia or Assyria. Besides the plain stone tomb, long thin

sarcophagi were coming into use, with an oval aperture on the upper surface through which the corpse was inserted and the lid then closed. Eventually sarcophagi of this form were universally adopted, and whole cemeteries of them exist dating from the Parthian period. Then however, just as earlier, the burial places of the poor had no distinctive feature.

But the death of a king was an event of major importance, which affected everyone without exception, for it was an extremely bad omen for the future of the country. He spanned the gulf between earth and heaven, and his death therefore naturally disturbed the established order of things, while the omens associated the king's decease with the withering of vegetation and the failure of the floods: with the suspension, in a word, of everything which made the earth fruitful.

Conversely, a coronation was marked by a general quickening of life, with rich harvests and good growing weather. Both Hammurabi in the preface to his Code and Ashurbanipal in his Annals speak of the opening years of their reigns as a kind of Golden Age, thanks to the trust reposed in them by the gods. Consequently, therefore, when the king died, mourning was officially observed throughout the land. A letter from Ashur says 'The day that we heard of the king's death, the people of Assyria wept.'

We possess a text of Ashurbanipal which shows him making a grant of funeral honours to one of his courtiers and attempting, in the manner normal to the ancient world, to protect his tomb by the usual curses on those who tried to violate a grave. It runs as follows:—

'The day when in my palace the general Nabu-shar-uṣur shall meet his destiny with untarnished honour, he shall be buried in the place where he wished, that he may rest in the place of his choice. See that he be not removed from his resting place, and let no man raise his hand in violence against the place. He was a good and a brave man, and if any man disturb him as he rests in his grave, the king his master will be sore displeased and will show him no mercy.'[20]

All this, however, was no spontaneous expression of grief for a dear friend: we have just entered the age of formal mourning, and this was an expression of official regret for a public misfortune. The alleged relationship between the death of the monarch and the withering of the vegetation is accounted for by the way that he was equated with the dead Tammuz: and the expressions of sorrow closely resembled those used at the death of the god. It was this thought which probably accounted for the ceremonial associated with a royal funeral. The dead Tammuz was exposed to his worshippers for two or three days, and we have a letter addressed to king Esarhaddon assuring him of obedience to his orders, that the body of his royal predecessor should be exposed for three days, and thereafter for one further day in the city of Arbela. This exposure took place either inside the palace or just outside one of the city gates, and we have a letter explaining that the great gate of the city had been opened and the population permitted to pass through it to mourn before the dead king. Sometimes the period of mourning was of considerable duration. Thus, when the king's mother died, at the beginning of Nisan (the first month in the year), the prince and the army went into mourning for three days. In Siwan (the third month) official mourning began again. When, as we have said, the Assyrians went out of the city gate, 'the commandant paraded his officers before the governor, wearing red robes and golden bracelets. Kinsa, the "weeper", accompanied by his sons [i.e., by his band of followers] wept before them.' This is clear evidence for the participation of 'official weepers' under a leader.

The Funeral Ceremony

And so to the funeral. Lapped in aromatic fragrances, anointed with pure oil and clad in his royal robes, the king was laid in his sarcophagus, a huge rectangular stone chest with a lid and great rings inset so that it could be moved by passing cords or rods through them. For the last time the body was exposed to the sunlight: the lid was fixed firmly in place with bronze bolts, a label was affixed uttering a curse against anyone who might attempt to open it and the burial took place, usually inside the palace, after which sacrifices were offered on behalf of the dead monarch. The excavations at Ashur brought to light the sarcophagi of a number of Assyrian sovereigns concentrated in one area of the palace. The treasure which was buried with a king represented a perpetual threat to a royal tomb, and none has in fact been discovered complete with its contents. The sarcophagus of Shamshi-Adad V, now in the Berlin museum, is in the form of a rectangular chest, slightly wider at the top than the bottom and raised from the ground on two transverse stone ridges. Besides the ring-shaped tenons, the lid carries at each end a bronze staple which gives point to the phrase 'I will seal the opening of the sarcophagus with solid bronze.' No doubt originally seals were fixed round the staples and indeed round the entire sarcophagus.

The Royal Substitute

We considered some aspects of the 'substitute' in the section on medicine, and we find a further instance of their employment in the royal substitutes, whose functions were not merely to perform his duties but also to undergo on his behalf the afflictions which the gods had in store for him. The simplest instance was the royal cloak, which, as symbol of the king's power, could replace him in certain ceremonies. No doubt the Assyrians saw no more virtue in it than what it possessed as a sign of the royal authority: we on the other hand would incline to see it in an impalpable but unmistakable embodiment of its royal owner. Sometimes the king's place might be taken by a statue dressed in the royal robes, but, when the omens were very unfavourable, a living substitute was selected, either from among the minor palace officials or, more usually, from among the courtiers, who regarded the duty of playing the king's part, despite the attendant risks, as an honour. Although the substitute (*puhu*) lived in the palace, the king, as it were from behind the scenes, continued actually to govern. This kind of situation tended to arise if, for example, there was an omen prophesying disaster at some future date, e.g.:—

'If during an eclipse the planet Jupiter can be seen, it means safety for the king: but instead of him someone, great or humble, shall die.'

The king's safety was conditional upon the fulfilment of the second part of this omen, which would otherwise have recoiled upon him. So long as no death occurred among the greater or lesser courtiers, the substitute took the risk on the king's behalf, until the duly expected death occurred, when he reverted to his former status.

Should the omen threaten continuing danger to the king, then the gods would be satisfied by nothing save his death, and in that case the priests would ordain that the substitute should 'go to meet his destiny': i.e., should be put to death. This actually happened in the reign of Esarhaddon to Damqi the son of the commissioner of Akkad. He had offered himself as royal substitute and was chosen by a prophetess who said to him 'Thou shalt assume the kingship' and presented him with the royal weapons in the presence of a large gathering. From that moment onwards Damqi was the ostensible ruler of both Assyria and Babylonia: but the omens grew worse and worse and finally, in order to save the king, he was put to death and buried with royal honours. A tomb was built for him and for his concubine, who also was of the palace and who had to die together with her husband. Their two bodies were duly exposed and mourned and a holocaust was offered, so that all the evil omens were duly exorcized. The letter giving a full account of the affair ends with the words, 'The ceremonies of expiation are completed, and the heart of my lord the king may be at peace.'[21]

The Condition of the Dead

After death everyone, king and commoner alike, entered the *arallu*, or underworld. Its seven encircling walls and guarded gates rightly earned it the name of 'the land of no return', and we have seen the price that Ishtar had to pay to enter it. There are two traditions about the condition of the dead during their sojourn there. The first, and more usual, visualized the dead as 'like winged birds', which is reminiscent of the Egyptian view of the dead as resembling human-headed birds. The second tradition is derived from the dream of Enkidu (in the Gilgamesh epic). When he went down to the underworld he was easily able to recognize the kings, the high priests and those who had held great offices: while a king of Assyria who is recorded in a text as having visited the nether regions in a dream (which was, from the Assyrian point of view, equivalent to doing so in actuality) saw there all its inhabitants endowed with the characteristics ascribed to them on earth. Perhaps a third tradition is worth mentioning: when Enkidu after his death gained permission from Nergal to reascend to earth and there speak with his friend Gilgamesh, the god opened the earth like a trapdoor through which the spirit of Enkidu passed towards his friend like a cloud or a vapour.

In this region, illumined by no ray of light, wholly shrouded in dust, airless and lacking food and drink, the only sustenance of the spirits of the dead was the funerary offerings. If no man remembered them, then they returned to earth to plague the living, subsisting as best they might on such miserable scraps of food as they could find in the gutters. The privilege of having their families near them and, the height of bliss, of drinking fresh water, was reserved to the very few who had won special glory in war. This was a very ancient idea, and had to be interpolated into one of the earliest versions of the Gilgamesh epic—cf. the hero's anxiety to 'make a name' for himself.

There are no explicit references to the idea of a judgment after death, though some texts suggest one. None the less, it seems that, though the gods of the underworld had power to deliver judgments, these mainly affected the living—that is, they could shorten their days on earth and afflict them with illness. The uncertainty of this doctrine results from a variety of simultaneous traditions in the religious centres of Mesopotamia.

And now we have traced to its final conclusions the life of an inhabitant of that country in about 600 B.C.

CONCLUSION

PERHAPS the main impression, at least on the material plane, that we carry away from this long survey is that the life of an inhabitant of Babylonia in about 600 B.C. must have closely resembled that of any inhabitant of the Orient up to about fifty years ago, before the appearance of the internal-combustion engine had shattered the even and monotonous tenor of his existence. In the densely populated quarters of Baghdad we can no doubt see the physical appearance of the streets of Babylon with its open-air markets, offering the same wares, the little stalls of the craftsmen, its very houses built on the same plan as that revealed by the excavations at Ur dating from about 1800 B.C. in the 'time of Abraham'.

The reign of Nebuchadrezzar must have witnessed the same kind of festivities as can be seen to-day, and the same dances, with two rows of dancers advancing and retreating to the accompaniment of the women wailing and clapping their hands in the rhythm of the dance, and must have heard the sound of the self-same instruments.

The Babylonian temples may have perished, but St. Sophia at Istanbul suggests the massive severity of their exteriors, unrelieved by external decoration. Gone, too, are the *ziggurats*: and yet we can see their fellow to-day in the round tower at Samarra and its external spiral staircase.

Watching the behaviour of the crowds during the sacred drama with which the Shiites celebrate the descendants of Ali we can see in imagination the festival of Marduk at Babylon, and the rise and fall of the mourners' voices to-day must re-echo the lamentations that were heard at late-Assyrian funerals. But in the spiritual life there is a deep—an unbridgeable—gulf; that life, though lived beneath a radiant sky, which must, one would think, have made existence a joy, and which by keeping alive the practices of a nature religion gave fresh vigour and glory to the vital forces, was yet, despite all this, stifled beneath the dogmas of what was surely one of the harshest religions ever practised by man. Gods who were violent and swift to wrath, relentless in the demands which they exacted from mankind, entangling every action of daily life in a web of pitiless obligations: an imagination which peopled the world with demons and monsters ravening after their prey; nature hostile and at every point full of warnings, at every moment offering an opportunity for some unsuspected sin of omission or commission; an after life even more wretched than earthly existence, where all must lament being cut off from the light of earth and half engulfed in the dust of the Orient, the horror of which has to be experienced before it can be believed—this is the impression of unrelieved misery left by the pitiless religion to which the inhabitants of Babylon were prisoner.

Prisoners indeed, king no less than peasant: for no matter how much the common people might envy their monarch, he no less than they was a hostage at the mercy of his priests, the slave of the complexities of a crushing ritual.

Hard as must have been the life of an Egyptian, it could not subdue his natural good humour, his gaiety and his jokes over his daily work. But the man of Mesopotamia was a stranger to laughter: never, it seems, did he learn to relax. His efforts created a brilliant civilization, no less powerful than that of Egypt and of greater renown in Western Europe, which lies so deep in its debt, than the culture which flourished on the banks of the Nile. But spiritually the two were poles apart. The unrivalled fame of Babylon towered over the ancient world, and deservedly so: but how few among us would have chosen it as our home!

APPENDIX A

Explanation of Problem 3 (p. 224)

This is set out in Thureau-Dangin, *Textes Mathematiques Babyloniens*, No. 147.

[*Note.*—The signs for 'minutes' and 'seconds' are here used to indicate fractions in successive powers of 60.

Thus $1' \ 30'' = \dfrac{1}{60} + \dfrac{30}{60 \times 60}$]

$$\frac{x}{7} + 25'' = \frac{1}{11}\left(\frac{x}{7} + 25''\right) + 50'$$

or

$$\frac{x}{7} - \frac{x}{7 \times 11} = \frac{25''}{11} + 50'' - 25'$$

or

$$\frac{(11 - 1)x}{7} = (11 + 1) \times 25'$$

or

$$\frac{10x}{7} = 5'$$

∴

$$x = \frac{7 \times 5'}{10} = 3' \ 30'' \text{ of a mina} = 3\tfrac{1}{2} \text{ shekels.}$$

This actual example is a case where the operation itself is unjustifiable. The result is correct, but the answer was probably known before the steps to reach it were composed.

APPENDIX B

Methods of Calculating Astronomical Distances

(From Thureau-Dangin, in *Revue d'Assyriologie et d'Archéologie orientale*, XXVII (1930), No. 2.)

THE distance between the stars which [the text in question] places on the same parallel (the Tropic of Cancer) are expressed in three systems of measurements, in the following relationship:

1 *talent* or 60 *minas* = 12 *danna* (in Akkadian, *bêru*), or 360° (*ges*) 'on the ground' (*ina qaqqari*) = 648,000 *danna* 'in the sky' (*ina šame*).

In the first system the measurements are in terms of time: the weight of water escaping from a clepsydra measures the time between the passages of two stars at the meridian (1 talent of water = 1 sidereal day). In the second system the measurements are in terms of the size of the arc. In the third system the measurements are in terms of length. The *danna* and the *ges ina qaqqari* are respectively $\frac{1}{12}$ and $\frac{1}{360}$ of an imaginary circle supposed to lie 'on the ground'. The *danna* and the *ges ina šame* are measurements of distance intended to express real distances 'in the sky'. The Tropic of Cancer would measure 648,000 *danna*, or 6,928,416,000 metres (about 4,300,000 miles). Assuming the length of the equator to be in the proportion of 10 : 9 to that of the Tropic of Cancer, it would measure about $\frac{648,000 \times 10}{9}$ *danna*, or about 720,000 *danna*.

In the second system the measurements of arc derive originally from measurements of time. The distance between two stars lying on the same parallel can be expressed alternatively in 360th parts of the sidereal day or in 360th parts of the circle. The Babylonians appear for a long time not to have distinguished between the *ges* as a measurement of an arc ($\frac{1}{360}$ of the circle) and the *ges* as a measurement of time ($\frac{1}{360}$ of the day). Evidence for this can be seen in the fact that they only appear to have divided the ecliptic, like the parallels, into 360° at a late date.

REFERENCES

CHAPTER I

[1] G. Contenau, *Manuel*, IV, pp. 1,764 ff.

[2] G. Contenau, *Les Civilisations anciennes du Proche-Orient* (Collection 'Que Sais-je?', Paris, 1945).

[3] G. Contenau, *Manuel*, IV, pp. 1,795 ff.

[4] G. Contenau, *Manuel*, IV, pp. 1,939 ff.

[5] G. Perrot and Ch. Chipiez, *Histoire de l'Art dans l'Antiquité*, II, p. 146.

[6] Herodotus, I, 193.

[7] G. A. Olivier, *Voyage dans l'Empire ottoman* (Paris, year IX), II, p. 419.

[8] E. W. Moore, *Neo-Babylonian Business and Administrative Documents* (Ann Arbor, 1935), No. 150.

[9] G. Contenau, *Manuel*, I, p. 70.

[10] E. W. Moore, No. 121.

[11-14] E. W. Moore, Nos. 46, 61, 68, 186.

[15] E. W. Moore, No. 152.

[16] Herodotus, III, 106.

[17] Herodotus, VII, 40.

[18] E. Pottier, *Musée du Louvre. Catalogue des Antiquités assyriennes*, No. 165.

[19] G. Contenau, *Manuel*, I, Fig. 18.

[20-21] E. W. Moore, Nos. 147, 132.

[22] G. Contenau, *La Médecine en Assyrie et en Babylonie*, p. 195.

[23] F. Hoefer, *Chaldée, Assyrie, Médie, Babylonie, Mesopotamie*, etc. (Paris, 1852), p. 161, No. 1.

[24] G. Contenau, *La Magie chez les Assyriens et les Babyloniens*, Pl. III, p. 128.

[25] A. Layard, *Discoveries in the Ruins of Nineveh and Babylon* (London, 1853), p. 339. Vigouroux, *Dictionnaire de la Bible* (Paris, V. 2, 1916), Fig. 316.

[26] A. Parrot, *Mâri* (Paris, 1936), p. 168.

[27] E. Botta, *Le Monument de Ninive*, I, Pl. LXV. Vigouroux, *Dictionnaire* II. 2 (1926), Fig. 650.

[28] G. Contenau, *Trente Tablettes cappadociennes* (Paris, 1919).

[29] G. Contenau, *Les Tablettes de Kerkouk et les Origines de la Civilisation assyrienne* (Paris, 1926).

[30] A. T. Clay, *Business Documents of Murashu Sons* (Philadelphia, 1898. The Babylonian Expedition of the University of Pennsylvania, IX).

[31] Ch. Fossey, 'Rapports de valeur entre l'argent et divers metaux sous la dynastie chaldéenne (625–538)', *Revue des Etudes sémitiques et Babyloniaca* (Paris, 1937), pp. 42 ff.

[32] Waldo H. Dubberstein, 'Comparative Prices in later Babylonia (625–400)' *American Journal of Semitic Languages*, LVI (1939), pp. 20–43.

[33] G. Contenau, *Manuel*, IV, pp. 1,887 ff.

CHAPTER II

[1] Botta, *Le Monument de Ninive*. V. Place, *Ninive et l'Assyrie*. Perrot and Chipiez, *Histoire de l'Art*, Vol. II.

² F. Thureau-Dangin (and others), *Til-Barsib.*

³ R. Labat, *Le Caractère religieux de la Royauté assyro-babylonienne* (Paris, 1939).

⁴ G. Contenau, *Manuel*, IV, Fig. 1,244.

⁵ L. and J. Heuzey, *Histoire du Costume dans l'Antiquité classique*: Egypte, Mesopotamie, etc. (Paris, 1935).

⁶ G. Contenau, *Arts et Styles de l'Asie antérieure* (d'*Alexandre le Grand à l'Islam*) (Paris, 1948), Pl. XLVI.

⁷ V. Place, *Ninive et l'Assyrie*, Pl. LVII. Vigouroux, *Dictionnaire*, IV, 1 (1912), Fig. 97. Gadd, *Stones of Assyria*, Pl. 40.

⁸ G. Contenau, *Manuel*, IV, pp. 2,224-35, Figs. 1,253-60. See also, for examples recently excavated at Nimrud, Prof. M. E. L. Mallowan in *Illustrated London News* for 1950-3, and *Iraq*, XII-XV.

⁹ M. Rutten, 'Scénes de Musique et de Danse', *Revue des Arts asiatiques* (1935), pp. 218-24.

¹⁰ G. Contenau, *Manuel*, IV, Fig. 1,045, p. 1,931.

¹¹ G. Contenau, 'Un bas-relief assyrien du Musée du Louvre, *Journal asiatique* (1917), pp. 181-9.

¹² L. W. King, *Bronze Reliefs from the Gates of Shalmaneser* (London, 1915).

¹³ A. Layard, *Monuments of Nineveh*, II, Pl. XXIV and I, Pl. XXX. Vigouroux, *Dictionnaire*, II. 1 (1926), Figs. 37 and 429.

¹⁴ A. Layard, *Monuments*, II, Pl. LXXI. Vigouroux, *Dictionnaire*, IV. 2 (1912), Fig. 411.

Chapter III

¹ E. Lefébure, *Sphinx*, I (1896), pp. 199-202; also *Mélusine*, VIII (1897), col. 217 ff.

² Luckenbill, *Ancient Records* (Chicago, 1926), II, p. 65.

³ F. Thureau-Dangin, 'L'Exaltation d'Ishtar', *Revue d'Assyriologie*, XI (1914), pp. 141 ff.

⁴ Délégation en Perse, *Mémoires de la Mission de Susiane*, XXVII (1935), Nos. 233-4.

⁵ P. Perdrizet, *Revue des Etudes grecques*, XVII (1904), pp. 351-60.

⁶ S. Langdon, *Sumerian Liturgies and Psalms* (Philadelphia, 1919), pp. 332 ff.

⁷ Ch. Fossey, *Manuel d'Assyriologie*, I.

⁸ E. Drioton, *La Cryptographie égyptienne* (Nancy, 1934).

⁹ C. J. Gadd and R. Campbell Thompson, 'A Middle Babylonian Chemical Text', *Iraq*, III (1936), pp. 87-96.

¹⁰ R. Labat, *Le poème babylonien de la Création* (Paris, 1935). Also *Babylonian Legends of the Creation* (British Museum, London, 1931).

¹¹ Vigouroux, *Dictionnaire*, supplement.

¹² G. Contenau, *Le Déluge babylonien* (Paris, 1941). Also *The Babylonian Story of the Deluge* (British Museum, London, 1929)

¹³⁻¹⁸ R. Pfeiffer, *State Letters of Assyria* (New Haven, 1935), Nos. 159, 205, 211, 212, 151, 153.

¹⁹⁻²² F. Thureau-Dangin, *Textes mathématiques babyloniens*, Nos. 140, 243, 147, 239.

²³ R. Pfeiffer, No. 303.

²⁴ B. Meissner, *Babylonien und Assyrien*, II, pp. 411-13.

²⁵ F. Thureau-Dangin, *Revue d'Assyriologie*, X, p. 215.

²⁶ Ch. Fossey, *Revue des Etudes sémitiques et Babyloniaca* (1935), pp. 11 ff.

²⁷ G. Contenau, *Manuel*, IV, Fig. 1,045.

CHAPTER IV

[1] British Museum, *Cuneiform Texts*, XXIV, Pl. L.
[2] Ch. Fossey, *La Magie assyrienne* (Paris, 1902), pp. 53 ff.
[3] R. Campbell-Thompson, *The Devils and Evil Spirits of Babylonia* (London, 1903-4), II, pp. 137 ff.
[4] S. Langdon, *Babylonian Wisdom* (London, 1923).
[5] M. Rutten, *Babylone* (Paris, 1948), Fig. 5, p. 72.
[6] M. Rutten, p. 46.
[7-11] R. Pfeiffer, Nos. 242, 245, 247, 353, 252.
[12] E. W. Moore, No. 117.
[13] Ch. Fossey, *Textes assyriens et babyloniens relatifs à la divination* (Paris, 1903), pp. 4-5.
[14-15] G. Contenau, *La Magie chez les Assyriens et les Babyloniens* (Paris, 1947), pp. 163, 168.
[16] G. Furlani, *La Religione Babilonese e Assira* (Bologna, 1928-9), II, pp. 173 ff.
[17] Ch. Virolleaud, 'Pronostics sur l'issue de diverses maladies', *Babyloniaca*, I (1907), pp. 96-9.
[18] F. Thureau-Dangin, 'Rituel et Amulettes contre Labartu', *Revue d'Assyriologie*, XVIII (1921), pp. 168 ff.
[19] G. Contenau, *Magie*, Pl. VIII.
[20] J. Kohler, *Assyrische Rechtsurkunden* (Leipzig, 1913), No. 16.
[21] R. Labat, *Le caractère religieux de la Royauté assyro-babylonienne* (Paris, 1939), p. 360.

BIBLIOGRAPHY

(See also References and Sources of Illustrations)

General works

G. Contenau, *Manuel d'Archéologie orientale*, Paris, 4 vols., 1927, 1931, 1947.
L. Delaporte, *Mesopotamia*, London, Kegan Paul, 1925.
G. Furlani, *La Civilta Babilonese e Assira*, Rome, 1929.
Seton Lloyd, *Twin Rivers*, O.U.P., 1947.
B. Meissner, *Babylonien und Assyrien*, Heidelberg, 2 vols., 1920–4.

CHAPTER I
Geography. Inhabitants. Languages.

O. Gurney, *The Hittites*, London, Pelican Press, 1952.
G. M. Lees, F.R.S. and N. R. Falcon, 'The Geographical History of the Mesopotamian Plains', *The Geographical Journal*, CXVIII, I, 1952.
E. Pittard, *Les Races et l'Histoire*, Paris, 1924.
Les Langues du Monde, Paris, 1924.

History

Cambridge Ancient History, Vol. III, 1925.
G. Contenau, *Histoire de l'Orient ancien* (en collaboration avec J. Capart). *L'Asie occidentale ancienne*, pp. 146–336, Paris, 1936.
L. Delaporte, *Les Peuples de l'Orient méditerranéen*, Paris, 1938. (Collection 'Clio').
C. J. Gadd, *History and Monuments of Ur*, Chatto & Windus, 1929.
L. W. King, *History of Babylon*, London, Chatto & Windus, 1919.
A. Moret, *Histoire de l'Orient*, t. I et II de *L'Histoire générale* (direction G. Glotz), Paris, 1936.
A. T. Olmstead, *History of Assyria*, Charles Scribner's Sons, New York, London, 1923.
S. Smith, *Babylonian Historical Texts*, Methuen, 1924.
Sir Leonard Woolley, *Ur of the Chaldees*, London, Pelican Books, 1938.

Chronology

Les Premières Civilisations. Vol. I of *Peuples et Civilisations* (Halphen et Sagnac), Paris, new edit., 1950.
E. Cavaignac, 'Les Listes de Khorsabad', *Revue d'Assyriologie*, XL (1945–6).
A. Poebel, 'Assyrian King List from Khorsabad', *Journal of Near Eastern Studies*, I, (1942), pp. 247–306, 460–92, II (1943), pp. 56–90.

The Structure of Society

E.-M. Cassin, *L'Adoption à Nuzi*, Paris, 1938.
E. Cuq, *Etudes sur le Droit babylonien*, Paris, 1929.
G. R. Driver and J. C. Miles, *The Assyrian Laws*, O.U.P., 1935.
G. R. Driver and J. C. Miles, *The Babylonian Laws* (Vol. I), O.U.P., 1952.

R. Pfeiffer and E. A. Speiser, 'One hundred selected Nuzi texts', *Annual of the American Schools of Oriental Research*, Vol. XVI, 1935-6.
V. Scheil, *La Loi de Hammurabi* (*Mémoires de la Délégation française en Perse*, t. IV), Paris, 1904.
V. Scheil, *Recueil de Lois assyriennes*, Paris, 1921.
F. R. Steele, 'The Lipit-Ishtar Law Code, *American Journal of Archaeology*, LI (1947), p. 658 s.
J. Klima, 'Au sujet de nouveaux textes juridiques d'époque préhammurabienne', *Archiv Orientalni*, XVI (1949), p. 334 *seq.*

Houses

G. Perrot et Ch. Chipiez, *Histoire de l'Art dans l'Antiquité*, t. II, Paris, 1884, Faber & Faber, 1936.
Sir Leonard Woolley, *Abraham*, Paris, 1936.

Lighting and Heating

A. Séguin, *Etudes sur le Pétrole dans l'Asie occidentale ancienne*, IIᵉ Congrès mondial du Pétrole, Paris, juin 1937. (Comptes rendus des travaux.)

Cities

O. E. Ravn, *Herodotus' Description of Babylon*, Copenhagen, 1942.
M. Rutten, *Babylone*, Paris, 1948. (Collection 'Que sais-je?').
E. Unger, *Babylon*, Berlin, 1931.

The Countryside. Navigation

R. Clay (Maxwell Hyslop), *Tenure of Land in Babylonia and Assyria*, 1938, Institute of Archaeology, Occasional Papers, No. 1.
Max Ringelmann, *Essai sur l'Histoire du Génie rural*, t. II, Paris, 1907.
G. Contenau, 'Drogues de Canaan, d'Amurru et Jardins botaniques', *Mélanges syriens offerts à M. R. Dussaud*, t. I, pp. 11–14, Paris, 1939.
J. Laesspe, 'Reflections on Modern and Ancient Waterworks', *Journal of Cuneiform Studies*, VII, 1.
E. W. Moore, *Neo-Babylonian Business and Administrative Documents*, Ann Arbor, 1935.
A. Salonen, *Die Wasserfahrzeuge in Babylonien nach sumerischakkadischen Quellen*, Helsinki, 1939.

Livestock. Horses

E. Douglas Van Buren, 'The Fauna of Ancient Mesopotamia as represented in Art', *Analecta Orientalia*, XVIII, Rome, 1939.
H. A. Potratz, *Das Pferd in der Frühzeit*, Rostock, 1939.

Dress

H. Frankfort, *Cylinder Seals*, London, Macmillan, 1939.
L. et J. Heuzey, *Histoire du Costume dans l'Antiquité classique*, L'Orient (*Egypte, Mésopotamie, Syrie, Palestine*), Paris, 1935.
R. de Vaux, 'Sur le Voile des Femmes dans l'Orient ancien', *Revue Biblique*, XLIV, 1935, pp. 397–412.

Business. The Cost of Living

G. Contenau, *Trente Tablettes Cappadociennes*, Paris, 1919.
G. Contenau, *Les Tablettes de Kerkouk et les Origines de la Civilisation assyrienne*, Paris, 1926.

W. H. Dubberstein, 'Comparative Prices in later Babylonia (625–400 B.C.)', *American Journal of Semitic Languages*, 1939, pp. 20–43.

Ch. Fossey, 'Rapports de valeur entre l'argent et divers métaux sous la dynastie chaldéenne (625–538)', *Revue des Etudes sémitiques et Babyloniaca*, 1937, p. 42 *seq*.

CHAPTER II

Royal Palaces. Khorsabad

E. Botta et E. Flandin, *Le Monument de Ninive*, Paris, 5 vols., 1849–1850.

G. Loud, *Khorsabad*, I, *Excavations in the Palace and at a City Gate*, Chicago, 1936.

G. Loud and Ch. B. Altman, *Khorsabad*, II, *The Citadel and the Town*, Chicago, 1938.

V. Place, *Ninive et l'Assyrie*, Paris, 3 vols., 1867.

Encyclopédie photographique de l'Art, Paris. (Editions 'Tel'). *L'Art de la Mésopotamie ancienne*, *Le Musée du Louvre*, légendes explicatives par M. Rutten, t. I, 1939, pp. 161–320; t. II, 1936, pp. 1–160.

Excavations

Assyrian Sculptures in the British Museum, Reign of Ashurnasirpal, London, 1914.

Assyrian Sculptures in the British Museum, from Shalmaneser to Sennacherib, London, 1937.

Bronze Reliefs from the Gates of Shalmaneser, King of Assyria, 860–825 B.C., London, 1915.

M. Brion, *Les Fouilles, Résurrection des Villes mortes*. I. *Mésopotamie*, etc., Paris, 2e edit., 1948.

C. J. Gadd, *The Stones of Assyria*, Chatto & Windus, 1936.

Seton Lloyd, *Foundations in the Dust*, O.U.P., 1947.

Seton Lloyd, *Ruined Cities of Iraq*, 3rd ed., O.U.P., 1945.

M. E. L. Mallowan, *Excavations at Nimrud*, for the British School of Archaeology in Iraq, supported by various other organisations; see *Illustrated London News* (1950), July 22, 29, (1951) July 28, August 4, (1952) August 9, 16, 23, (1953) August 8, 15, 22. *Iraq*, XII, 2, (1950); XIII, 1, (1951); XIV, 1, (1952); XV, 1, (1953).

F. Wetzel, *Assur und Babylon, Kunst und Kultur des Alten Orient*, No. 17, Berlin, 1949.

A. Parrot, *Archéologie mésopotamienne*. I. *Les Etapes*, Paris, 1946.

Palaces in the Provinces

F. Thureau-Dangin et collaborateurs, *Arslan-Tash*, 2 vols., Paris, 1931.
Til-Barsib, 2 vols., Paris, 1936.

The Concept of Monarchy

R. Labat, *Le Caractère religieux de la Royauté assyro-babylonienne*, Paris, 1939.

The King's Day

H. T. Hall, *La Sculpture babylonienne et assyrienne au British Museum*, Paris, 1928.

P. Handcock, *Mesopotamian Archaeology*, London, 1912.

War

D. D. Luckenbill, *Ancient Records*, Vol. II, Chicago, 1926.

F. Thureau-Dangin, *Une Relation de la Huitième Campagne de Sargon*, Paris, 1912.

CHAPTER III

General works

G. Contenau, 'De la valeur du nom chez les Babyloniens et de quelques-unes de ses conséquences', *Revue de l'histoire des Religions*, LXXXI, 3, 1920, pp. 316–332.

G. Contenau, 'Notes d'Iconographie religieuse assyrienne', *Revue d'Assyriologie*, XXXVII, 1940–1.

Ch. F. Jean, *Sumer-Accad*, Paris, 1925, pp. 7–36 (on names).

G. Dossin, 'Le Vêtement de Marduk', *Museon*, LX, 1–2, Louvain, 1947, pp. 1–5. 'Brg'yh, roi de KTK', *Museon*, LVII, Louvain, 1944, pp. 147–155.

M. Th. Böhl, 'Die fünfzig Namen des Marduk', *Archiv für Orientforschung*, XI, 1936–7, pp. 191–218.

Writing

G. Contenau, 'Les Débuts de l'Ecriture cunéiforme et les Monuments figurés, *Revue des Etudes sémitiques et Babyloniaca*, 1940, pp. 56–67.

G. R. Driver, *Semitic Writing*, Schweich Lectures for 1944, O.U.P., 1948.

Ch. Fossey, *Manuel d'Assyriologie*, Paris, t. I. 1901; t. II, 1926.

M. Rutten, 'Notes de Paléographic cunéiforme', *Revue des Etudes sémitiques et Babyloniaca*, 1940, pp. 1–53.

Literature

E. Dhorme, *La Littérature babylonienne et assyrienne*, Paris, 1937. *Choix de Textes religieux assyrobabyloniens*, Paris, 1907.

Ch.-F. Jean, *La Littérature des Babyloniens et des Assyriens*, Paris, 1924.

Religious Literature

R. Labat, *Le Poème babylonien de la Création*, Paris, 1935.

G. Contenau, *Le Déluge babylonien. La Descente d'Ishtar aux Enfers*, Paris, 1941.

F. Thureau-Dangin, 'L'Exaltation d'Ishtar', *Revue d'Assyriologie*, XI, 1914, p. 141 *seq*.

Epic Literature

G. Contenau, *L'Epopée de Gilgamesh, Poème babylonien*, Paris, 1939.

A. Schott, *Das Gilgamesh Epos*, Leipzig, 1934.

R. Campbell-Thompson, *The Epic of Gilgamish*, Oxford, 1930.

S. Langdon, 'The Legend of Etana and the Eagle', etc.: *Babyloniaca*, XII, 1931, p. 1 *seq*.

Ethical Literature

F. Martin, 'Le Juste souffrant babylonien', *Journal Asiatique*, juillet-août, 1910. (Cf. E. Dhorme, *Littérature babylonienne*).

S. Langdon, *Babylonian Wisdom*, London, 1923.

Royal Correspondence

R. Pfeiffer, *State Letters of Assyria*, New Haven, 1935.

L. Watermann, *Royal Correspondence of the Assyrian Empire*, Ann Arbor, 4 vols., 1930–6.

G. Dossin, 'Archives épistolaires du Palais de Mâri', *Syria*, XIX, 1938, p. 105 *seq.*—*Correspondence de Samsi-Addu*, Paris, 1950.

J. R. Kupper, *Correspondence de Kibri-Dagan*, Paris, 1950.

Mathematics

O. Neugebauer and A. Sachs, *Mathematical cuneiform Texts*, New Haven, 1945.

A. Rey, *La Science orientale avant les Grecs*, Paris, 1930.

F. Thureau-Dangin, *Esquisse d'une histoire du système sexagésimal*, Paris, 1932.
—*Textes mathématiques babyloniens*, Leyden, 1938.

Astronomy

A. T. Olmstead, 'Babylonian Astronomy, Historical Sketch', *American Journal of Semitic Languages*, LV, 1938, pp. 113–29.

F. Thureau-Dangin et F. X. Kugler, 'Distances entre étoiles fixes, d'après une tablette de l'époque des Séleucides', *Revue d'Assyriologie*, X, 1913, p. 215 *seq.*; XI, 1914, p. 1 *seq.*

Botany. Chemistry

R. Campbell-Thompson, *Assyrian Herbal*, London, 1924.—*On the Chemistry of the Ancient Assyrians*, London, 1925.

Artistic Conventions

R.-C. Flavigny, *Le Dessin de l'Asie occidentale ancienne et les Conventions qui le régissent*, Paris, 1941.

M. Rutten, 'Le Paysage dans l'Art de la Mesopotamie ancienne', *Syria*, 1941, p. 137 *seq.*

CHAPTER IV

General Works

E. Dhorme, *Les Religions de Babylonie et d'Assyrie*, Paris, 1945. (Collection 'Mana'.)

Ivan Engnell, *Studies in Divine Kingship in the Ancient Near East*, Uppsala, 1945.

A. Frankfort, *Kingship and the Gods*, University of Chicago Press, 1948.

G. Furlani, *La Religione Babilonese e Assira*, Bologna, 2 vols., 1928–29.

C. J. Gadd, *Ideas of Divine Rule in the Ancient East*, Schweich Lectures, 1945, O.U.P., 1948.

S. H. Hooke, *Babylonian and Assyrian Religion* (Part II, Mesopotamia), London, Hutchinson, 1953.

Ch.-F. Jean, *Le Milieu biblique. III. Les Idées religieuses et morales*, Paris, 1936.

S. Langdon, *The Mythology of all Races*, Vol. V, *Semitic*, Boston, 1931.

J. B. Pritchard, *Ancient Near Eastern Texts relating to the Old Testament*, Princeton University Press, 1950.

Nature Religion

G. Contenau, 'La Religion de Sumer', *Histoire des Religions*, t. I, Paris (Quillet), 1948.

The Gods

S. Langdon, *Tammuz and Ishtar*, Oxford, 1914.

J. Plessis, *Etude sur les textes concernant Ishtar-Astarté*, Paris, 1921.

A. Moortgat, *Tammuz*, Berlin, 1949.

Iconography

G. Contenau, 'Notes d'Iconographie religieuse assyrienne', *Revue d'Assyriologie*, XXXVII, 1943, pp. 154–70.

L. Legrain, 'Les Dieux de Sumer', *Revue d'Assyriologie*, XXXII, 1935, p. 117 *seq.*

H. Vincent, 'La Représentation divine orientale archaique', *Mélanges syriens*, I, p. 373 *seq.*

Attributes of the Gods

E. Douglas Van Buren, *The Flowing Vase and the God with Streams*, Berlin, 1933.—'The Rod and the Ring', *Archiv Orientalni*, XVII (1949), II, pp. 434–50.

H. Danthine, *Le Palmier-Dattier et les Arbres sacrés*, 2 vols., Paris, 1937.

N. Perrot, *Les représentations de l'arbre sacré sur les monuments de Mésopotamie et d'Elam*, Paris, 1937.

Destiny

M. David, *Les Dieux et le Destin en Babylonie*, Paris, 1949.

Sin

Ch.-F. Jean, *Le Péché chez les Babyloniens et les Assyriens*, Plaisance et Paris, 1925.

Temples. Ziggurats

G. Contenau, 'La Tour de Babel', in *Le Déluge babylonien*.

H. Lenzen, *Die Entwicklung der Zikurrat von ihren Anfängen bis zur Zeit der III Dynastie von Ur*, Leipzig, 1942.

M. Rutten, *Babylone*.

V. Scheil et M. Dieulafoy, *Esagil ou le temple de Bêl-Marduk à Babylone*, Paris, 1913.

Th. A. Busink, *De Toren van Babel*, Batavia, 1938.

A. Parrot, *Ziggurats et Tour de Babel*, Paris, 1950.

Sir Leonard Woolley, *Ur Excavations*, Vol. V, *The Ziggurat and its Surroundings*, London, O.U.P., 1939.

The Priesthood

E. Dhorme, 'Quelques prêtres assyriens d'après leur correspondance', *Revue d'Histoire des Religions*, CXII (1916), p. 125 *seq.*; CXVI (1937), p. 5 *seq.*

M. Rutten, *Contrats de l'époque séleucide conservés au Musée du Louvre*, Paris, 1935.—'La Cour du dieu Mardouk': *Revue d'Histoire des Religions*, Paris, 1939.

Rituals

F. Thureau-Dangin, *Rituels accadiens*, Paris, 1921.

F. Thureau-Dangin, 'Rituel pour l'expédition en char', *Revue d'Assyriologie*, XXI (1924), p. 127 *seq.*

F. Thureau-Dangin, 'Rituel et Amulettes contre Labartu', *Ibid*, XVIII (1921), p. 168 *seq.*—'Le Voyage de Lamashtu aux Enfers', *Ibid*, XXXI (1934), p. 120.

R. Labat, *Hémérologies et Ménologies d'Assur*, Paris, 1939.

Festivals

S. A. Pallis, *The Babylonian Akitu Festival*, Copenhagen, 1926.

M. Rutten, *Babylone*.

E. Unger, *Babylon*.

H. Zimmern, *Zum babylonischen Neujahrsfest*, Leipzig, 1906.

Divination

G. Contenau, *La Divination chez les Assyriens et les Babyloniens*, Paris, 1940 (with bibliography).

G. Furlani, 'Sur la Palmomantique chez les Babyloniens et les Assyriens', *Archiv Orientalni*, XVII, 1949, I, pp. 255–69.

Magic

G. Contenau, *La Magie chez les Assyriens et les Babyloniens*, Paris, 1947 (with bibliography).

Medicine

G. Contenau, *La Médecine en Assyrie et en Babylonie*, Paris, 1938 (with bibliography).

Death

R. Labat, *La Royauté assyro-babylonienne*.

E. Ebeling, *Tod und Leben nach den Vorstellungen der Babylonier*, Berlin, I, 1931.

A. Kleveta, 'Le Jugement infernal dans les Croyances babyloniennes', *Archiv Orientalni*, XVII (1949), I, pp. 374–83.

SELECT INDEX

(to be used with Table of Contents)

IN THE NORTON LIBRARY